MW01265399

ULTIMATE PATIENT SATISFACTION

Designing, Implementing, or Rejuvenating an Effective Patient Satisfaction and TQM Program

JOHN F. O'MALLEY

 Healthcare Financial Management Association

McGraw-Hill

New York   San Francisco   Washington, D.C.   Auckland   Bogotá
Caracas   Lisbon   London   Madrid   Mexico City   Milan
Montreal   New Delhi   San Juan   Singapore
Sydney   Tokyo   Toronto

Library of Congress Cataloging-in-Publication Data

O'Malley, John F.
   Ultimate patient satisfaction : designing, implementing, or
rejuvenating an effective patient satisfaction and TQM program /
John F. O'Malley.
     p.   cm.
   Includes bibliographical references and index.
   ISBN 0-7863-1219-X (alk. paper)
   1. Patient satisfaction.   2. Customer relations.   I. Title.
   [DNLM: 1. Patient Satisfaction.   W 85 054u 1997]
   R727.3.043   1997
   610.69'6—dc21
   DNLM/DLC
   for Library of Congress   97-26913
                                                CIP

McGraw-Hill

A Division of The McGraw·Hill Companies

Copyright © 1997 by The Healthcare Financial Management
Association. All rights reserved. Printed in the United States of
America. Except as permitted under the United States Copyright Act
of 1976, no part of this publication may be reproduced or distributed
in any form or by any means, or stored in a database or retrieval system, without the prior written permission of the publisher.

1 2 3 4 5 6 7 8 9 0 BKM / BKM 9 0 9 8 7

ISBN 0-7863-1219-X

Printed and bound by Book-Mart Press, Inc.

This publication is designed to provide accurate and authoritative information in regard to the subject matter covered. It is sold with the
understanding that neither the author nor the publisher is engaged in
rendering legal, accounting, or other professional service. If legal advice or other expert assistance is required, the services of a competent
professional person should be sought.

—From a Declaration of Principles jointly adopted by a Committee of the
American Bar Association and a Committee of Publishers.

McGraw-Hill books are available at special quantity discounts to use as
premiums and sales promotions, or for use in corporate training programs. For more information, please write to the Director of Sales,
McGraw-Hill, 11 West 19th Street, New York, NY 10011. Or contact
your local bookstore.

ULTIMATE PATIENT SATISFACTION

Dedications
This book is dedicated to patients everywhere,
and to those doctors, nurses, and support personnel
who put caring above care, especially:
Jane M. Peters, R.N., B.A.N.
North Memorial Medical Center
Robbinsdale, MN.
The professional paradigm for emulating and achieving
Ultimate Patient Satisfaction
and
Patrick Francis O'Malley, my father and inspiration.
A man of great wisdom,
a man I did not know nor love enough
and
National Patient Recognition Day
February 3rd

PREFACE

Reflecting on my mistakes over the years, and now as a healthcare consultant, I started realizing that the marketplace is inundated with generic books on customer service and satisfaction. Few, if any, are providing today's healthcare providers the critical insight and information necessary for formulating their own effective patient satisfaction program, or better yet, to augment, and more important, to rejuvenate their current efforts. The need for such a book became quite evident to me. I envisioned a different kind of book though, a reference that empowered the reader to move their organization beyond common sense patient satisfaction, a special book that would help you in propelling your organization into creating a proactive mind-set and a proactive environment that excelled at delivering the highest level of patient satisfaction with consistency. You will discover that this book, *Ultimate Patient Satisfaction*, is just such a book, and if you will, just what the doctor ordered. I wrote this book with you in mind, the healthcare professional, in a proactive, unending quest to deliver the highest level of patient satisfaction. To that end, I wanted to start filling that me-too service void by providing a wealth of enabling tips, tools, and techniques you can start using today for gaining a competitive ledge in patient satisfaction. That is no typo, I believe in creating competitive ledges, not edges, besides, sharp edges become dull too fast. The competitive ledge enables you to keep that competitive edge and more. Now scabbard that concept for a while, you will learn more about competitive ledges later.

Even at the risk of upsetting some readers, I wanted this book to be an in-your-face, gut-wrenching, politically-incorrect, hands-on (around the throat?) approach for helping all healthcare professionals and providers interested in achieving the highest level of patient satisfaction within their organization. Remember, when you stop truly caring about your patients, regardless of how well you cared for them, and how great their outcome, you are compromising your profession, and in doing so, no longer a professional. To my way of thinking, a healthcare professional cares just as much with their heart, if not more, than with their hands. Patients before policies and paperwork, I say, start freeing nurses to do what they do best, caring for the sick.

The primary purpose of this book is to start you thinking differently about your employees and patients. I want this book to function as your daily Total Quality Management (TQM) inspiration, your mentor, and action-guide for helping stir your creative juices, and also helping all serious healthcare providers get serious about achieving Ultimate Patient Satisfaction. You will find the mind-sets, concepts, and ideas present herein will help you in turning employees, into satisfied employees, and dissatisfied patients into satisfied patients, and satisfied patients into very satisfied patients, and by doing so, achieving total customer satisfaction (TCS). You will also discover that this book is a journey of kinds, fueled with ready to use approaches, training materials, employee programs, and management tools that will rocket your creativity light years ahead of the competition in delivering your service and in the end, obtaining Ultimate Patient Satisfaction. However, all said and done, deep down inside, I know this book was really written, with the intention of benefiting, present, and future patients everywhere, so that their journeys through the maze of healthcare systems and providers' offices, hospitals, and outpatient centers will be more dignified, more caring, and a less stressful ordeal.

Sincerely, John F. O'Malley

C O N T E N T S

Chapter 16

Turning Testimonials into Referrals   205

Chapter 17

Surveying Those Who Know Best   214

Chapter 21

Dealing With Upset Patients   266

Chapter 22

Patient Crisis Management   290

Chapter 23

Ultimate Patient Satisfaction   301

Appendix

INTRODUCTION

The Future of Healthcare . . . More or Less

The differentiating differences . . .

What is all the fuss about? Simply this. Our industry is caught up in a relentless, if not violent, change of menu. Everywhere you look, every time you turn around, everyone is trying to eat your lunch. The meek may inherit the earth, but they will not survive long as healthcare providers. In an increasingly financially focused and burdened environment, where the demand for overall medical services is declining and where the provider supply is grossly exceeding the realistic demand, healthcare reform (employer-driven change) is sending providers scrambling (a less threatening way to say merging, acquiring, and reengineering) to differentiate themselves from the hordes of me-too caregivers in oversaturated markets. Patients and covered lives are being sold as a commodity between insurance companies and managed care organizations in their quest to achieve strategic mass and value, or better yet, to please Wall Street investors.

The realities of supply and demand economics are changing the healthcare industry, and in the process, will be forcing you and your organization to do more, with less. Employers, via their managed care and federal agency henchmen, are aggressively driving reimbursement down, way down, below Medicare, to the point where, day by day, Medicaid rates are starting to look mighty attractive. How many of us ever dreamed of a Medicaid Health Maintenance Organization (HMO)? Do you remember when a Medicare patient, because of their lower than fee-for-service reimbursement rate, was a patient to shun, and done so by many hospitals, physicians, and healthcare providers in lieu of commercial payment opportunities? I am saddened to say, I can.

Furthermore, in this confusing, unforgiving, and fast-changing industry, healthcare providers are also being told to standardize medical care and improve outcomes. Responding (reacting) to the increasing pressures brought on by managed care's expanding market penetrations and growing competitive environments, you will quickly discover that doing more for less is fast becoming fundamental to your existence. Though a simple prophecy, many providers will find it difficult to march to the new beat of healthcare's drums because they still hold on to the past. Though not openly, there are still too many physicians and healthcare executives resisting the change before them. To be a successful healthcare provider, you and your organization will have to focus on giving *more*, doing well, and receiving *less*. Hence, the key basic premise for successful growth strategies and creating a strategic plan must consider and account for the "More-for-Less" factor. If you are going to survive and thrive as you move into the 21st century, you better get into high gear and start operating more efficiently and cost effectively in a "More-for-Less" organizational environment. And to better position your organization for longevity, you will need to take into account and plan for the following 12 key "More-for-Less" realities:

1. More service value—less reimbursement;
2. More efficiency—less costly;
3. More responsive—less hassle;
4. More streamlined—less complex;
5. More computerization—less paper;
6. More networking—less independence;
7. More satisfaction—less complaints;
8. More for them—less for you mind-set;
9. More open communications—less code-of-silence;
10. More patient empowerment—less provider power;
11. More standardization—less your way; and
12. More positive outcomes—less medical malpractice.

ALL THE KING'S PROVIDERS

As our provider world turns and unravels under the chaotic pressures created by healthcare reform, by managed services, and by care standardization, you can expect the grand old healthcare oak to bend, sway, and give way to change, losing a few limbs in the process. So start getting ready. As pointed out, you will be providing more added-value to your services in return for less reimbursement, becoming more efficient in running your business while being less costly in the process; becoming more responsive to your customers' needs, thus eliminating the hassle of doing business with you; making your operational demeanor more streamlined to better serve your customers and less complex to access and use; employing more computers and enabling digital technologies throughout your delivery system and using less paper; affiliating with more people, organizations, and networks in becoming a continuum-of-care team player and being less independent in nature; ensuring more customer satisfaction in every service encounter, word spoken, and deed performed, thus generating fewer complaints from those we serve, realizing that there will be more of them to serve and fewer of us to do the serving; you will have to be more open about testing, treatment, and outcomes and less secretive in your doings, silencing forever the professional code-of-silence creed that destroyed the medical profession; patients will have more power to pick and choose and you will have less power to control and direct; there will be more standardization of healthcare based on science and less practice-as-you-wish medicine; and finally, you will be pushed to deliver more positive medical outcomes and less medical malpractice will be tolerated, if any. The handwriting is on the wall and has been for sometime; unfortunately, many healthcare providers have yet to visit the wall, let alone know where the wall can be found.

> Humpty Healthcare sat on a wall,
> Humpty Healthcare had a great fall,
> All the king's providers and all the king's physicians,
> Couldn't put Humpty Healthcare together again.

In summary, the end result is that healthcare entities will be receiving fewer reimbursement dollars for their efforts while at the same time being required to provide benchmark services, quality, and medical outcomes. However, by approaching each of the 12 elements with an open mind you will discover that the door to prosperity will swing open to reward those who proactively and ethically knock the loudest. But be on your toes, the gang-of-12 will also usher healthcare providers into another era of strategic importance, the era of Ultimate Patient Satisfaction.

This era will reign supreme, dominating the delivery of health-care services and forcing providers to understand and aggressively embrace patient satisfaction's strategic importance. As third-party payor's unrelenting pressures establish the lowest realistic reimbursement for a given service, pricing will no longer be a major competitive issue. And as standardized optimum quality is established for a given medical procedure, quality will cease to be a competitive strong point. If you cannot consistently deliver acceptable quality, you will become extinct, fossilizing in the silt of change with all the other inflexible healthcare providers. As you can see, eventually, we will be reaching a point where the rules for engagement across our industry will hard press any healthcare providers, for-profit or not-for-profit, to turn price and quality into a major competitive advantage without compromising patient care. Each provider will find it increasingly more difficult to differentiate themselves from their competition based solely on price and quality. In such a me-too delivery environment, patient satisfaction will reign supreme as the only truly differentiating denominator separating one healthcare provider from another. Placing your patients before profits is guaranteed to generate a healthier return on assets in the long run. Care-ism before capitalism!

Up until most recently, many healthcare providers considered patient satisfaction as a by-product of their business or job, quite often being delivered by a financially focused but disinterested management team; from the patient's perspective, in a dignity-compromising manner and unsuitable environment. Patient satisfaction was usually someone else's responsibility, further down the management tree. However, healthcare visionaries are quickly putting the pieces together and learning that Ultimate Patient Satisfaction (UPS, pronounced up's) is critical to their ability to effectively differentiate themselves from the competition in a me-too delivery system, to their long-term success, and more important, it is everyone's primary goal and responsibility in the organization, regardless of title and position.

The UPS concept and approach to achieving the highest level of patient satisfaction is based on energizing and rejuvenating an organization by encouraging and empowering its employees to proactively seek out patient encounters and to create upscale interactions in their every word and deed. In any organization, whether it be a healthcare network, a medical complex, a freestanding hospital, an independent, or an upstart medical practice, it is up to every person, from upper management on down, to ensure the highest level of customer service and patient satisfaction is consistently upheld throughout the system, including physicians. Only when such a commitment is championed and sustained will the highest level of patient satisfaction, Ultimate Patient Satisfaction, be forthcoming and gain significant strategic value. In other words, you need to be focusing on gaining upmanship in satisfying your patients before someone else does.

In order to gain the upper hand as a healthcare provider, you need to upstage the competition in delivering your products and services. Research has shown that the upshot of great service is excellent customer satisfaction, which in return, creates an upswing in revenues. However, one does not have to swim upstream and get uptight about providing great patient satisfaction. By focusing on delivering your products and services better than anyone else, in and of itself, cause an upsurge in patient satisfaction. This upward momentum will energize both you and your employees to the upper bounds of patient satisfaction, Ultimate Patient Satisfaction.

We all know that caring for patients has its ups and downs, but whenever providing for the upkeep of patient service becomes an uphill battle, the reason almost always lies with upper management. It is up to upper management to uphold the principles of customer service in an upbeat manner while instilling in employees that patient satisfaction is of the utmost importance to their and the company's overall success.

Upgrading your service and patient satisfaction often forces you to turn your company upside-down in the process. You must force change by uprooting bad habits, policies, and procedures. This organizational uprising will surely cause an uproar and even upset some uppity people. However, upending obstacles that impede your organization's ability to deliver the highest level of patient satisfaction is everyone's uppermost priority. Do not forget that your company's bottom line is directly proportional to how up your employees are to delivering the highest level of customer satisfaction possible. The key to staying up-to-date regarding patient satisfaction is to remember, "Never be satisfied with your patients' satisfaction." After all, excelling at patient satisfaction is the upstanding thing to do from anyone's perspective, especially the patient's, and is also very uplifting to the ones providing the service as well. After it is all said and done, the upside is that patient satisfaction pays big dividends. It is that simple.

Healthcare providers basically have and serve four major external customer groups: patients, payors, plans, and physicians (five, if you count the *paper-holders* for the Wall Street driven for-profit corporations). However, let us not forget, all are subservient to the patient. The power of the patient has been grossly overlooked and underestimated by providers and payors alike. Stop and consider that if patients (the people) were totally satisfied with the existing healthcare system (access, cost, and outcome) they, as a voting group, would not permit managed care, politicians, and others to change the system. The people, in time, spurred on by horror stories and consumer advocate groups, would revolt, as is happening in California at this writing. We the people allowed our healthcare delivery to be changed, reformed, and taken apart, in hopes of a better system. However, we are all creatures of habit, some more than others, and we all resist change. The greater and quicker the change imposed on us, the more vehemently our resistance to that change will be. However, it is only when the pain endured from resisting change becomes greater than the pain imposed by changing, do we accept change. The greater the pain, the quicker the change. When we hurt, we will rapidly move out of our comfort zone, toward change. In healthcare, pain is the capsulized version of "You are not going to be reimbursed."

Without an effective and competitive patient satisfaction program in place, no healthcare provider, no matter how large or small, will survive into the 21st century. Healthcare providers need to move beyond the me-too, ineffective, pseudo-patient satisfaction mind-sets, programs, and care-less-managers and employees that permeate our organizations. You have to start benchmarking your patient satisfaction efforts, However, while healthcare is a numbers game, patient satisfaction is no game, but serious business. Ultimate Patient Satisfaction is serious business and a downhill battle, starting at the top of the organization. And, so serious is patient satisfaction that no one person can be held accountable. It is a team effort or wasted effort.

PATIENT SATISFACTION ORIENTATION

Ultimate Patient Satisfaction's underlying mind-set, premise, and philosophies are all anchored in proactively searching for, identifying, and resolving dissatisfying and satisfactory patient encounters, and elevating the same to the ultimate level of patient satisfaction. You will

FIGURE I-1

Patient Satisfaction Orientation

Patient	Dissatisfaction	Satisfaction
Service	Present	Past
Action	Proactive	Reactive
Position	Demonstrative	Corrective
Response	Real-time	Post-encounter
Focus	Patient	Provider
Delivery	Anticipating	Completed
Caring	Emotional	Empathetic
Survey	Face-face	Remote
Team	Acting	Discussing
Opportunity	Present	Future

discover that Figure I-1, Patient Satisfaction Orientation Table, shows the strategic importance of proactively searching for, identifying, and resolving dissatisfied patients' concerns, issues, and problems first. Dissatisfied patients before the satisfied is the secret behind achieving Ultimate Patient Satisfaction. The chapters that follow will be useful in helping you create the necessary personal, coworkers, and organization mind-sets to guarantee success.

In helping you to get in the right mind-set, or perhaps jar the mind, consider the following bits of information about patient satisfaction:

- Patient satisfaction is subjective, not objective, from both patients and your perspectives.
- Patient satisfaction is difficult to measure, satisfaction is an attitude, a complex emotion at best.
- Patient satisfaction is influenced by a host of factors, many not related to your service.
- Patient satisfaction is quickly and easily changing, especially long-term satisfaction.
- Patient satisfaction is not a solo event, but a team encounter.

"Proactiveness is the willingness, the ability, and the spirit to thrive outside one's comfort zone in times of uncertainty"

John F. O'Malley

1

Prioritizing Your Customers

All your customers look good when you don't have a plan . . .

Customers. Where did they originate from? Going back in time, way back, if you made something of perceived value or provided a skilled service, your earliest customers were more than likely your family members, taking or trading with other family members for various products and services. As the word spread of the family member's skills in making a product or providing a service, people outside the immediate family, relatives and neighbors, started acquiring those goods and services. The family member's customer base started to grow outwards from the service point of conception. As the word gradually spread to adjoining clans, villages, and beyond, there grew a greater demand for the products and services, forcing other family members to become involved in providing the product and servicing the increasing number of customers. The family business was born. As the news of this great product disseminated further afield, the demand increased further, until people were traveling great distances to purchase those products and services. Other families started emulating the originator of the product and service that everyone wanted. A cottage industry was created. Enterprising entrepreneurs eagerly started buying the products and services and sold them to those with less immediate access; the middleman crept into society. Did not healthcare start at home? Has not healthcare delivery traveled the same past, give or take a few detours?

YOUR CUSTOMERS

But no matter how you look at it, when it comes to customers, healthcare is truly a unique industry. I can not think of another business segment where the customer is confronted with such a quagmire of decision makers, such an endless gauntlet of gatekeepers to run, such a lack of standardization. An industry inundated with an overabundance and overwhelming hodgepodge of ill-defined, confusing, and misleading rules and regulations governing reimbursement, utilization, and access to healthcare services. And the least informed is the end user, the patient, our number one customer. Most healthcare providers have overlapping customers. You have some customers directing or controlling access to your services for other customers. It is a complex system at best. There is an ancient Chinese proverb I made up that states, the more complex the system, the simpler the fraud. As you know, for most of us, our customers are to be found within a general pool that can be divided into six fundamental groups: patients, physicians, payors, plans, providers, and people.

Patients

Patients are the end user, the person who experiences the healthcare delivery system firsthand, the person who is actually undergoing the examination, the diagnostic testing, the procedure, the treatment, the surgery, the hospital stay, the rehabilitation, and also, I am sorry to admit, the often unnecessary physical and mental pain associated with medical intervention. There are four types of patients, each with different needs:

1. Potential—never have;
2. Existing—currently are;
3. Dormant—have been; and
4. Repeat—will be again.

Physicians

Physicians are the very essence and stewards of medical intervention, our designated guardians of our physical and mental well-being, the dedicated general practitioner and specialist champions of the sick, and sometimes the givers and takers of life itself. The once steerers, but now gatekeepers who are often being forced to compromise patient care to ensure a healthy corporate profit.

Payors

Payors are usually the employer that is providing healthcare coverage for its employees and their dependents. Also the individual fortunate enough to have the means to pay on their own for healthcare. And do not forget those who pay all or a portion of their healthcare benefits as a monthly premium, a deductible, and a copayment. Let's not forget the insurance companies who pay, but with someone else's money.

Plans

Plans are the managed-care plans in all their diversity and delivery networks. Battling each other for referral control and hence, control of healthcare itself, and marketplace dominance. The middlemen of healthcare. The gatekeeper's paradise on earth.

Providers

Providers are the numerous medical and non-medical independents and networks of healthcare providers within your service area with which you work closely to ensure each patient receives the continuum of care and treatment necessary to achieve maximum medical improvement, the internal and external healthcare referral highways.

People

People are the entourage of family members, friends, and fellow workers who transport, accompany, wait, support, and visit the patient throughout the medical intervention encounter. This unsung core of caring ambassadors and walking advertisements who forms perceptions and opinions regarding your ability to deliver a humanistic style of healthcare. It is estimated that a hospital having 20,000 inpatients during a given year will experience over 100,000 visits to their facility. Do you have a written plan to ensure a patient's entourage's satisfaction? If not, why not?

There is yet another group of people or customers we often forget to include in our patient satisfaction planning: our coworkers. These are the people who knowingly or unknowingly form our delivery teams. Your coworkers throughout the organization, with whom you work on a daily basis, knowingly or unknowingly, who support you directly or indirectly in delivering a total service package to your customers, whoever they are, need to be treated as favored customers also if you expect to deliver Ultimate Patient Satisfaction with consistency. This seventh group could be rightly called personnel.

DIFFERENTIATING YOUR SERVICES

The Competitive Ledge™ is a marketing position obtained that best enables an entity to respond to its customer needs within an extended window of opportunity, outside the immediate- or short-term response capabilities of the competition. The Competitive Ledge™ amplifies the strategic ability of an entity to allocate and maneuver its people, resources, and services to exploit business opportunities unimpeded by the competition. Gaining and keeping The Competitive Ledge™ requires you to take a quantum leap in revolutionizing your industry and delivering your services and to lead where others hesitate to venture. Obtaining and maintaining Ultimate Patient Satisfaction is gaining a competitive ledge.

REENGINEERING TO DIFFERENTIATE

The purpose of reengineering is to do more than improve, enhance and modify; it causes you to rethink the status quo past that which is holding your organization back and possibly keeping you from achieving Ultimate Patient Satisfaction. Reengineering forces a change in thinking that helps you better determine what functions, processes, tasks, products, and services need to be strengthened, abandoned, or created to best position you for the future. Delivering what your customers (patients) want is an integral part of gaining Ultimate Patient Satisfaction. You also need to be focusing on differentiating the way you deliver your services from the competition by delivering your services better than the competition. Start thinking retail, not healthcare, to differentiate yourself from me-too providers.

VALUE-ADDED HEALTHCARE PROVIDER

In today's competitive arena, you need to be driving toward establishing your organization as a value-added provider by developing the following six strategic healthcare areas:

1. Pricing—attractive;
2. Quality—uncompromising;
3. Service—exceeding expectations;
4. Outcomes—benchmark setting;
5. Networks—strategic alliances; and
6. Technology—enabling and telemedicine.

2

The Power of Patient Satisfaction

We the patients, we the people, and we the nation's conscious . . .

It should be quite evident to any healthcare provider, worth their re-imbursement, that all their customers are very important. However, as a consultant, I am often asked why I strongly believe that the patient is the most important customer, even more so than the referral source or the payor. In response, I firmly state my position, which is that I believe the patient end user is your most important customer of all for the following three intertwined reasons to which no other customer can lay claim:

1. The patient is healthcare's reason for being and the focal point for delivery.
2. The patient's attitude and compliance are critical in achieving maximum medical improvement.
3. The patient can directly and indirectly cause the demise of any healthcare provider.

SUBSERVIENT TO THE PATIENT

On further reflection, the previous three reasons also lead me to believe that every person working in the healthcare industry, including you and me, is subservient to the patient in one manner or another. Without the patient, there is no logical reason for healthcare providers to exist. Yet we are often caught taking our patients for granted, thinking of them as only a policy number, a claim, a room number, or just a nuisance in our busy everyday quest for maximum reimbursement. In the past, taking a patient for a ride was standard and accepted practice, especially when increasing one's own reimbursement. Remember when it was common practice for a patient to be admitted to a hospital on a Monday for routine surgery that Friday? Whose idea was it to change the focus from inpatient to outpatient services? Surely not a hospital administrator. And how many physicians are still taking their patients for an expensive ride because they are refusing to order a less expensive home health service, only because doing so would dry up their office revenue stream? Maybe what America needs is a patient air bag that inflates upon medical and financial malpractice impact to protect the unwary and uninformed patient, our only reason for being.

And while we are on the subject of what I believe, I also believe that the patient is so important that delivering a me-too patient satisfaction level is not good enough to stay competitive in today's healthcare environment. Nor can or should patient satisfaction be left to marketing alone. Patient satisfaction is everyone's primary focus and responsibility, from top to bottom, especially starting with the board of directors and senior management as their number one job. Remember. If you take care of your top line, your bottom line will take care of itself. And among your customers, the patient is your top line. Along those lines every hospital, physician, and independent healthcare provider and related business needs to move their employees (customer service specialists) beyond the mind-set for delivering status quo patient satisfaction by leading them toward achieving Ultimate Patient Satisfaction.

DEVIL'S ADVOCATE

However, before you read on about patient satisfaction, the key component of Total Customer Satisfaction (TCS), it is important for me to play the devil's advocate. There is a growing number of company executives, both in and outside the healthcare industry, who are constantly questioning and debating the true impact great customer satisfaction has on their profitability. The two questions business executives are most often asking are: Does the level of a company's customers' satisfaction really translate into a healthier, more prosperous company? and if so, How? Many inquisitive healthcare executive minds want to know the answers, especially those who are spending significant time and money trying to increase their customers' level of satisfaction. It makes common sense, if customer (patient) satisfaction does not affect one's bottom line, why spend your time and money trying to achieve it? To answer those questions from a healthcare provider's perspective, many assumptions and facts need analyzing. Let me present the facts and a few assumptions and you can decide for yourself.

Thanks to managed-care's cost reduction aggression, most providers by now are realizing that healthcare is a business, and not a humanitarian freebie. Even a not-for-profit healthcare entity needs to generate a profit, whoops, excuse me, excess revenue. That's right, $25 million in excess revenue, but mind you, not profit. To my way of thinking customer satisfaction is all about business, the business of acquiring, retaining, and developing referral sources and their resulting referrals, the patients, all of which has a direct impact on any healthcare provider's revenue generating and profitability. Word-of-mouth advertising is not dead, especially in healthcare. For those of you interested in learning more about generating referrals, I present the concepts behind acquiring, retaining, and developing healthcare referrals and referral sources in great detail in my book, *Managed Care Referral*, Irwin Professional Publishing, 1996.

To a proctologist, bottoms up (patients) and bottom line are directly related, if not somewhat symbolic of one another. As a proctologist, you cannot be out of compliance with accepted good business practices and expect to keep your bottom line healthy, no matter how many bottoms you scope. You need to be running your healthcare entity as a business, or you're going to go out of business, no matter how great your bottom outcomes. Hence, focusing all your resources on achieving patient satisfaction to the point of neglecting other key business aspects such as employee satisfaction, profitability, clinical outcomes, and information systems will only lead to an acute disaster.

However, delivering benchmark patient satisfaction makes good business sense for all healthcare providers, large or small, but you still have to deal with the daily conscience balancing act between the care delivered and the cost of delivery. Good business practices are the heart of any healthcare entity, going hand-in-hand with good medical practices and producing the best outcome.

BOTTOM-LINE HEALTHCARE

I am a strong believer that customer satisfaction is very important in any business undertaking, but especially more so in caring for people needing medical intervention. To further expand on my belief, and I hope yours, that patient satisfaction is directly tied to your bottom line, consider the following three fundamental, but compelling reasons for your mental scrutiny.

First, I am a firm believer in self-prophecy, you are what you think. Therefore patients who think and retain a positive mental attitude and optimistic outlook while under medical supervision and intervention unconsciously self-administer a powerful psychological antibiotic. This psychological antibiotic can often quicken the healing process and affect the medical outcome for the better. Logic only dictates that the more satisfied your patients are with their level of care, those who are providing that care, and the delivery environment, the less anxiety and negative feelings creep into their psychological pharmaceutical formulary. Just as humor and laughter have been proven to have medical value in keeping people healthy and getting them well faster, patient satisfaction has the same effect. Ultimate Patient Satisfaction offers your patients mental stepping stones toward creating, retaining, and reinforcing a positive mental attitude. Though it may be difficult to scientifically quantify, patient satisfaction is a critical part of the total patient care process and case management. Ultimate Patient Satisfaction is truly a wonder drug and as such, I am confident future research will substantiate my feelings on the subject. In the meantime, Ultimate Patient Satisfaction should be freely available without a prescription, over-the-counter if you will, by all reputable healthcare providers and their customer service representatives (employees).

Secondly, most people seeking medical intervention rely on third-party advice, word-of-mouth advertising from their family members and friends. According to a 2006 adult telephone survey by

Kaiser Family Foundation and the Agency for Health Care Policy, when choosing a doctor or health plan, which few people are qualified to do anyway, Americans are more likely to rely on the advice of family and friends than the recommendations of employers or independent rankings. Nearly 60% of those surveyed said they did not think their employers were a good source of information, noting that an employer's main concern was saving money on health benefits. The same study indicated that only 15% of those surveyed were influenced by ratings by local news outlets. When they have a choice, people are creatures of habit and choose familiarity over the unknown healthcare provider. A point worth remembering is that for most people the initial referral decision starts with a woman, in the home, then moves to the doctor's office or hospital emergency room. In the end, and for the previously stated reasons, I believe Ultimate Patient Satisfaction has a direct and traceable effect on a healthcare provider's profitability.

Thirdly, seeking medical care is a great deal more personal than buying a service or retail product such as a dress, a car, or a house. While both medical and retail decisions can impact your quality of life, a faulty medical decision could end your life. You may kill for a dress, but I am sure you would not want to be found dead in it. I also believe we must also pursue the obtainment and maintenance of Ultimate Patient Satisfaction for the following three overpowering reasons:

1. We owe it to our patients and their family members.
2. We owe it to our employees.
3. We owe it to ourselves.

Would you find it difficult not to agree with this reasoning? It makes logical, if not strategic, sense to me, so let me share my reasoning further. As a healthcare provider, do not your patients deserve to be cared for in the most patient-friendly environment possible? Do you want your employees working with the right attitude, the right tools, and the right information to enhance their personal on-the-job satisfaction and productivity? And what about your own high standards; do you want to provide the best products and services to your customers and patients? If you answered "no" to any of the three questions, quietly close this book, throw it in the trash, and go about your business. But let me forewarn you, be prepared to lose weight as the competition eats your lunch, day in and day out. The chances are good that I will be seeing you on the street corner selling roses or holding a sign reading, Healthcare for food. However, those of you who responded with a downright honest and resounding yes, read on; a way of life will unfold before your eyes, a life worth living.

DOMINANT COMPETITIVE ADVANTAGE

As a die-hard marketing and sales person, deep down inside, I know that achieving Ultimate Patient Satisfaction will give me a dominant competitive advantage to prosper in today's demanding healthcare environment. To me, that is just like an immune shot. By now you have guessed that Ultimate Patient Satisfaction is a powerful marketing tool and an even greater corporate asset. Without UPS, you will still and always be a me-too provider. With it, however, you will elevate yourself to a most enviable position. A position that best enables you to grow and prosper by keeping your current customer base and attracting new business, encouraging your patients to freely engage in positive word-of-mouth image building on your behalf, lessening your chances of a patient-initiated medical malpractice lawsuit, differentiating your services from those of the competition, enhancing your negotiating value with managed-care plans and employers, maximizing patient cooperation and compliance, and gaining the highest possible level of patient care and medical outcomes.

A spin-off of the aforementioned benefits is that your organization will experience major improvements in overall employee and customer satisfaction. As you can sense by now, the organizational synergy gained by achieving and maintaining Ultimate Patient Satisfaction is significant and critical for any healthcare entity or person endeavoring to sustain a viable future in healthcare, to increase overall revenues and profits, and to create a benchmark working and delivery environment. Once achieved, Ultimate Patient Satisfaction acts as a powerful magnet, drawing patients, physicians, plans, payors, and the right people to your door. Using this book as your guiding force, you can achieve Ultimate Patient Satisfaction by harnessing your burning commitment and sterling efforts to serve and care for your most important customer, the patient.

THE POWER WITHIN

So where does the power of patient satisfaction come into play? Simply put, you and other healthcare providers are subservient to the patient. The livelihoods of physicians, managed care plans, and payors are all dependent on keeping the patient satisfied. There are no exceptions. If, over time, you lack the commitment or resources to consistently satisfy your patients, in time, your referral sources, payors, and plans will start questioning the rationale for continuing a provider (business) relationship with you. You must understand the underlying reality of being subservient to the patient. Whether you are doing business with physicians, managed care plans, or payors (employers), they cannot, nor will they sustain a business relationship with a provider that causes them undue grief, lost revenue, and weakens their competitive position. As an example, assume an employer is being inundated by a significant number of stressed out, complaining, and unhappy employees and their family members, all of which is stemming from the quality and level of service provided by you and your staff. Is your staff's behavior and actions a direct reflection of you and your inaction? You better believe so. Even if you do not know, let alone condone, what your staff is doing, you are still responsible and will be held accountable by others. In World War II we hanged many a defeated country's generals for the actions of their soldiers. Ignorance of their soldiers' deeds was no excuse for the generals being exonerated. Now do not panic or worry, to my knowledge no healthcare provider has ever been hanged for providing poor service, though the concept may have some judicial merit. To the employer, considerable time is being spent, no wasted, on resolving employee concerns and problems related to you. The employees' morale and productivity are being adversely affected and blamed on you. Step into the employer's shoes for a moment. What would you do if you were the employer? No Nobel prize-winning economist is needed to calculate or figure out what the employer's next step will be. You guessed it. The employer contacts their insurance agent, who contacts the managed care plan's provider contractor, who notifies you, in so many words, that you are off the panel. You are outside looking in because you did not look out for your patients. You are history, healthcare toast as we say. Please pass the I-Told-You-So jelly. That is the power of patient satisfaction.

As touched on earlier in the book, but worth expanding on, is the point that if Americans were completely satisfied with the current healthcare system from the standpoint of easy and impartial access, quality of care, level of service, medical outcomes, and affordability no sane politician would have ever attempted to change the status quo and risk the wrath of irate voters. Not even Hillary Clinton would undertake such a bold and suicidal move. However, we all know that the vast majority of Americans are sick and tired over the way our country's healthcare system has faltered in its stewardship and its fiduciary responsibilities to the people it serves. We the people, we the patients, and we the upsets have let anyone, and everyone, take a stab or shot at doctoring up our ill healthcare delivery system and industry. Is there a saving light at the end of the healthcare tunnel? I think so, but do not get your hopes up too far. I am afraid it is just another wandering endoscope probing in the darkness for signs of change, or is it dollars? But all hope is not lost; there are many healthcare providers, physicians, and networks out there regaining stewardship and significantly improving for the benefit of their patients. As costs are becoming more competitive, many payors are already shifting their emphasis to quality and patient satisfaction as the key and differentiating factors in provider contracting. I strongly believe that patient satisfaction will become the major differentiating factor of the two. Can you think of a healthcare provider that is a contender for the Nobel Prize in Patient Satisfaction? Did your organization come to mind?

PROVIDER TO PATIENT TABOOS

After reading this far, I hope you also realize that the power of patient satisfaction is real, and that it will continue to grow in significance as more healthcare, medical, and provider information finds its way on to the Internet, into consumer groups, and into patients' hands. If you do not want to experience the direct or indirect wrath of dissatisfied patients, via their health plans, payors, and word-of-mouth advertising consider creating and enforcing an Ultimate Patient Satisfaction program with substance. You will find that a good way to get started is by reviewing the 15 primary ways your organization and its employees (customer service representatives) can upset and lose a patient. I guarantee that if you commit any of the following taboos, let alone with any consistency, your days as a healthcare provider are numbered. Remember, never tolerate any person or action that is:

1. Disregarding or being indifferent to your patient's physical and mental discomfort;
2. Prolonging your patient's waiting, especially without a timely explanation for the delay;

3. Being apathetic to your patient's problems and concerns;
4. Compromising your patient's dignity pre, during, and post examinations and procedures;
5. Breaching your patient's confidentiality;
6. Being insensitive when requesting patient payment;
7. Being rude in collecting patient insurance information and medical history;
8. Failing to effectively respond to your patient's communications needs and cultural differences;
9. Showing disrespect toward your patient's family members and guests;
10. Exposing your patients to an unsanitary and unsafe environment;
11. Treating your adult patients as children;
12. Misleading your patients about their medical condition or costs;
13. Engaging in a practice or treatment that is not in the patient's best interest;
14. Contributing to lowering employee morale; and
15. Committing healthcare fraud.

COSTLY BEHAVIOR

A few words to close out this chapter regarding the financial benefit healthcare providers receive from delivering Ultimate Patient Satisfaction. A survey of more than 1300 supermarket employees by McGraw-Hill and London House would suggest that service orientation appears to parallel other work-related behavior. Employees who are excellent service providers are less likely to abuse company time or steal from employers. In contrast, poor service providers were 52% more likely to follow unsafe practices on the job and 63% more likely to damage company merchandise or take things without permission. So remember that *behavior*, not experience, drives productivity and reduces costs. What does this have to do with healthcare? You are not comparing apples to oranges, you may say, but I see a direct correlation between an employee who is delivering Ultimate Patient Satisfaction and the same employee being more trustworthy, more productive, and more of a team player. Don't you?

FIGURE 2–1

Patient Satisfaction versus Dissatisfaction

Satisfied Patients	Dissatisfied Patients
Cooperate more, in compliance more	Less cooperative, out of compliance more
Cost less money to treat	Cost more money to treat
Less likely to sue provider	Most likely to sue provider
Maximize system's resources	Drains system's resources
More willing to learn, educating easier	Less willing to learn, educating difficult
Minimize staff's stress	Generate more stress for staff
Complimentary of care and service	Complains of care and service
Ambassador of good will to family and friends	Ambassador of bad will to family and friends
Present favorable impression to employer	Present unfavorable impression to employer
Give approval to managed care organization	Complain to managed care organization
Get better faster	Take longer to get better

DISSATIFIED PATIENTS

Another point you want to consider is the power of dissatisfied patients. You will find your dissatisfied patients are more costly to care for than satisfied patients. By reviewing Figure 2–1, Patient Satisfaction versus Dissatisfaction Table, you will gain a better understanding why dissatisfied patients have the power for causing devastating havoc throughout your organization and beyond. Typically, medical malpractice lawsuits are settled in the neighborhood of $250,000 and $450,000. As an exercise in cost analysis, consider having a team or a department estimate the possible costs involved with a dissatisfied customer going through the system. The estimate may very well be the catalyst for accelerating the quest for Ultimate Patient Satisfaction.

Remember, you can have some of your patients dissatisfied some of the time, but when most of your patients are dissatisfied most of the time, you will quickly learn that your patients have the power most of the time to make you disappear, perhaps sooner than you think.

3

CHAPTER

Patient in a Box

Demands, demands, and more demands, woe is the patient . . .

Being a patient is very demanding. There is more to delivering healthcare than doctors, drugs, and documentation. When we are sick, the getting well or medical intervention healing (MIH) process is not a one-dimensional event, but a complex multifaceted set of circumstances. Medical intervention healing is a process consisting of five distinct yet closely interrelated and influential outcome components, any of which can directly or indirectly affect the patient's medical outcome for better or worse. I define those five MIH components as the physical, psychological, spiritual, financial, and self-prophecy of getting well. Any patient satisfaction program needs to consider and address all five components. To me this represents the patient's box. Can you envision a box with no sides? Give it a try and read on.

THE BOX

Once medical intervention is triggered into action, all too often, the patient is forced into a box without a top or a bottom and no tangible sides. Though the patient's box is invisible to the caregivers, the delivery system, and support people, the box is there. So real in fact that it actually confines your patient, psychologically that is, within the anxieties and pressures associated with receiving patient care. The number of sides a patient's box has is directly related to the severity of his or her illness or injury and the extent and cost of medical intervention. Its size is measured not in inches and feet but in the nature and magnitude of psychological demands placed on the patient by those who compose the box. And depending on your patient's satisfaction level, this invisible box will be supportive or destructive in nature. Here is another ancient Chinese proverb I made up: Great medical outcomes are found in insignificant patient boxes.

As an example, for an acute care patient the box might look similar to that depicted in Figure 3–1. As you can see, in effect, the box consists of 12 sides, one for each of the many people boxing the patient in with demands, questions, and requests. In a highly stressful medical intervention situation, many patients will start finding the psychological ramifications of patient care, especially over time, just as confining as physical restraints. This psychological boxing in or confining environment is held together by the rules, regulations, financial pressures, and related demands each patient is bombarded with within a healthcare delivery system. Nevertheless, each patient must physically and emotionally confront this seemingly endless barrage while receiving care. Some patients are better equipped than others to engage the medical bureaucracy. Some patients even receive encouraging support from one side of the box against another side.

THE BOXING PROCESS

Typically, excluding an emergency, the patient's box starts taking shape in the home with an immediate family member (usually female) or significant other recommending and insisting on medical intervention. The patient's close friends, relatives, and neighbors follow suit encouraging medical care, even recommending a good physician. Medical coverage and managed care plan guidelines, authorization requirements, and restrictions are reviewed and evaluated by the potential patient, family members, employers, and insurance carriers. Patients are often forced to endure confusion, inferior service, and unnecessary pain as healthcare givers and healthcare keepers are jockeying for increased profits and reduced costs, respectively. Once the decision to seek medical treatment is made and permission is received, a visit to the doctor is arranged, though for most men this

FIGURE 3–1

The Patient Box

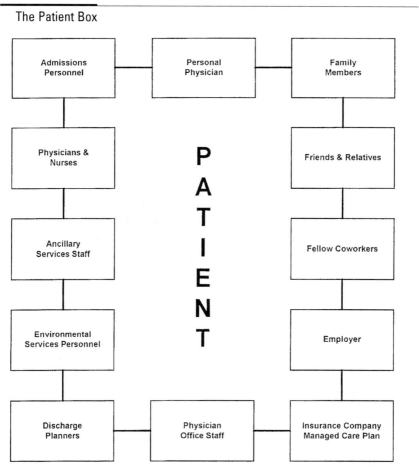

could mean several years in the planning. Since this usually means taking time off from work, now the patient's employer is more involved and needs to determine the impact the employee's medical needs and treatment will have on operations (the bottom line). Family members verify medical coverage again to be on the safe side, the reimbursement side. At the doctor's office, staff members commence probing for insurance coverage, then move onto the doctor stuff, the make-your-eyes-cross probing, the examination, testing, diagnosis, and finally determining the level of medical intervention required.

Patients are often the last to know their medical condition, a fact many people dislike and complain about to deaf ears. It is finally determined that surgery is the best medical option and arrangements are made at a reputable hospital (or more likely an outpatient surgery center). On hospital admission day, the patient is quizzed about the method of payment and insurance coverage (the really vital signs) and is engulfed in a confusing avalanche of dos and don'ts. During the stay, the patient is visited by and cared for by an army (the old days), or more appropriate today, a squad of cross-trained personnel. New physicians, different nurses, environmental services, and maintenance personnel coming and going, popping in and popping out at will, and they are all dressed alike to confuse the patient even more. The caregivers and support people migrate through the patient's room, often without even a comforting smile, understandable English, or friendly acknowledgment that another human being, let alone their patient, exists in the room. Family members and visitors cluttering the patients room, making demands, and asking the staff annoying questions. Success. The patient made it through surgery with all ten toes and no money. But now faces the challenging, if not intimidating, discharge process, more often than not, without any direct communications with his or her personal physician. Home again. Your family home care entourage and support group are gathering in force. More questions to answer. And the confusing, outrageous, and error-riddled bills (never in your favor) keep pouring in. The daily anxiety associated with improving one's health, getting back to work, and living a normal life weighs heavy on the patient. And you thought the patient was sick in the hospital; check them out now. The cost of getting well will make anyone sick in America. What an adventure healthcare is for the trusting patient and the family to experience. You bet your life on it, and often do, unbeknownst to you. But what about those patients who have to contend with culture, race, and language barriers and negative biases, do they not find the whole healthcare process of accessing medical intervention and receiving appropriate care more than intimidating, but terrifying at best?

Hopefully, you found the patient in the box scenario helpful in better understanding what your patient is experiencing while in your charge, the constant confusion, endless interrogation, pushing and pulling, the tug of wills, and the conflicting interests. As healthcare providers, we must all try harder to care before caring. I like to think, no believe, that if we all remembered that man was created in God's image, our caring for humanity may take on new meaning and significance.

You will quickly discover that by delivering your services at a level that produces Ultimate Patient Satisfaction, your patients will find their invisible box a less terrifying, less confining, and less stressful psychological experience. However, sometimes in the process of lessening the patient's psychological trauma from being placed in a box, you may have to box a few ears along the way. The best way I know for keeping your patients out of boxes is with honest and open communication. Or simply put, remember to put your patients before paperwork, policy, and personnel. So do not forget, boxes are for jacks. Nobody else need apply, especially your patients.

As proctologists would say, there is just one more thought that needs pondering before leaving this chapter behind. Stop and think a minute, unless you are speed reading. If Americans perceived going to a doctor or a hospital as a great way to have fun, why has Disney not opened Medicalland? Medicalland, where for three E-tickets you get to ride through Snake Pit Oddities, Medical Mishaps Menagerie, or Doctors of the Caribbean.

CHAPTER

Terrorism in the Hospital

Patient or prisoner, you decide . . .

To achieve Ultimate Patient Satisfaction we need to travel many roads and turn over just as many rocks, searching for root causes and possible solutions. This is such a journey in the decade of service-oriented hospitals and healthcare providers. The hot buzzwords in the industry are patient satisfaction, guest relations, patient advocates, customer relations, and internal marketing or so I have been told. Upon one's stepping back and taking a closer look, are we inadvertently shooting ourselves in the foot by undermining all the good customer satisfaction programs are expected to accomplish? Are we not creatures of habit? *Terrorism in the Hospital*, patient or prisoner, suggests that maybe we are the true casualties of caring as a result of our own self-serving intentions, bad habits, and hurried efforts. Patient or prisoner, you judge for yourself.

PRISONERS

During the past 20+ years working in the healthcare industry, my interest in military history, slowly but surely got the better of me. I began to change the way I saw the treatment of patients in a typical hospital inpatient setting. As a point of reference, each of the 11 to

16 basic principles of warfare has for all practical purposes a corresponding marketing tenet; just the name is different. Over time, I came to realize a stunning, if not chilling, correlation between being a patient in a hospital and a prisoner of war. The customary and usual procedures for admitting, processing, and caring for patients in hospitals conjured up the most frightening analogy, being a prisoner of war (POW) in your own hometown (Figure 4–1). How could this be true of such a caring and concerned profession? Did I read too much Clausewitz and Sun Tzu for my own good? I do not think so. Terrorism in the hospital is alive and habitually doing well, maybe more than most healthcare providers realize, let alone want to admit. Maybe POW is really the acronym for Prisoner On Ward?

ATROCITIES

As a result of live, on-location media coverage and probing investigative reporting, most people have heard or read about the various atrocities inflicted upon captured soldiers during the Vietnam, Kuwait, and Bosnian wars. We have come to loathe the treatment hostages endured while being held by various Middle East terrorist groups. The basis for

FIGURE 4–1

Patient or Prisoner

Capture	Release
Medical Intervention	Maximum medical improvement
Identification . . .	Posttraumatic stress disorder
Interrogation . . .	
Isolation . . .	
Internment . . .	
Insecurity . . .	
Indignities . . .	
Indigestion . . .	
Infliction . . .	
Intrusion . . .	
Interrogation . . .	
Inescapable . . .	

this profound analogy, *Terrorism in the Hospital*, patient or prisoner, is the uncanny similarity between the experiences shared by a patient upon being admitted to a hospital and the treatment a prisoner or hostage might suffer during captivity. Nonsense you say! What possible connection could there exist between how prisoners of war and hostages are treated based on the way physicians and hospital employees interface and care for their patients? You believe that healthcare providers are caring people, here to help, to comfort and to heal patients, not to treat patients like prisoners of war. That is what I thought and believed too until the overwhelming assault on my consciousness and an irreversible invasion of my beliefs occurred. No, I am not talking about planned atrocities to our patients; on the contrary, most patients still leave hospitals better off than on their arrival. However, there are some unfavorable and disturbing statistics challenging that statement. According to Public Citizen, a national consumer watch group, of the 33 million people seeking care in a hospital setting, more than 335,000 receive treatment-related injuries.

It is estimated that 80,000 to 100,000 hospitalized Americans are killed each year by causes unrelated to their initial medical condition at admittance. And weekly, more than 1000 patients are killed in American hospitals due to physician and staff negligence. Uncanny as it seems, we lose more patients each year than all the military personnel killed in the decade-long Vietnam war. By keeping an open mind while reading on about the suggested correlation between patients and prisoners you will better visualize and understand the patient environment offered unintentionally at most hospitals today. You can make your own determination regarding if there is any truth or substance to this soul-searching analogy for yourself.

CAPTURE

To start with, there is a war raging across the land, where medical battles are being fought daily against the rampages and destruction brought on by sickness and disease. The battlefields are physician offices, hospitals, and other healthcare facilities. The front line warriors are the many physicians, nurses, other healthcare professionals, and support staff. And there are casualties among the inflicted and dying seeking help, comfort, and healing. And yes, we do take prisoners; we call them patients. Upon capturing the enemy, the following battlefield scenario might unfold!

Interrogation

Prisoners are initially searched and undergo an *interrogation* to gather as much basic information as possible, such as who they are, their rank, unit, and mission. In healthcare, the capture usually takes place in some doctor's office (or an emergency department) where the patient surrenders to the physician and is interrogated as to their name, means of payment, and medical condition. Prisoners are often stripsearched in the quest for more information, not unlike the patient's body being interrogated via probing hands, cold instruments, and body fluid-collecting procedures. Next prisoners are held until they can be moved to the rear for further interrogation and internment. A patient is typically treated (held) by the physician (an emergency department) until arrangements can be made to admit the patient to the hospital for further processing and care.

Internment

All prisoners are *interned* for the duration of the war and even longer in some circumstances. The internment camp usually holds many prisoners and as is the case, not a fun place to be. A patient is admitted to a hospital, their place of internment for the duration of their illness or until discharged. Once interned, prisoners are subjected to renewed and redundant interrogation by highly-trained professionals. The interrogation process is more intense, structured, and formal as the interrogators relentlessly make every effort in securing secret information in the possession of the prisoner and deemed highly helpful to their war effort. Information extracted from prisoners is checked and rechecked to substantiate its authenticity before being passed on to military intelligence for further processing. A prisoner may even be asked (forced) to sign documents important to the interrogators. Does the process sound familiar to you? In the hospital, our professional interrogators are called admitting clerks. Their job is not complete until they secure the most valuable piece of patient information to help us fight our reimbursement battles, the patient's medical coverage and policy number. Heaven help the patient who has difficulty producing that highly prized bit of information. The interrogation process will go on until that medical coverage and policy number are divulged. This vital information is verified and passed on along with numerous signed documents to the accounting office for further processing.

Rest assured that most admitting clerks can hold their own against the best-trained military interrogators. Surely you can remember the old war stories about the days when hospitals interned patients for 15 to 30 plus days. We make money when people are sick, not well. It appears to me our incentive is backwards. Could it be that capitated healthcare plans are the miracle drugs the general accounting office has been searching for to improve the general health of the general population?

Isolation

To reduce individual prisoner resistance and increase their cooperation during internment, captors must quickly establish control over their captives. Control is established first by *isolating* prisoners from all their familiar surroundings, support systems, and the outside world. Prisoners are plunged into a totally unfamiliar living (existing) environment that is more often than not totally alien to them. Enlisted personnel are isolated from their officers to destroy unity and support. Do we not employ the same tactic when patients are isolated from family members for extended periods of time, or when the hospital staff speaks a foreign language, both literally and technically, or the moment a patient's personal and daily customs are violated and community support systems are cut off? It's only natural that anxieties, fears, and confusion take over, psychologically forcing the prisoner and patient's subconscious dependency on their keepers. The prisoner soon learns that their well-being and future lie in the hands of their captors and for the patient, the hospital's internment team, all strangers to both. Generals never use their best troops to guard prisoners. They are used for more important services. Whenever possible are not hospitals, because of reengineering and cost reduction pressures, arguably using staff with the lowest technical skill level permissible to deliver their services?

Identity

Next in the ongoing process of gaining control over prisoners is to remove their self-*identity*, a psychological form of isolation effective in controlling others. Throughout history, captors have known there is no better way to dehumanize a prisoner than to take away their self-esteem and identity. Most, if not all, of the prisoner's personal possessions are taken away, their clothing is exchanged for a more simplistic generic garment and they are given and referred to as a number or by degrading names. Over time, the prisoner's identity is stripped away, one layer after another. Without their personal identity, the prisoner becomes less aggressive and more submissive in nature. When a patient steps through the hospital's glass doors of internment, they are entering a foreign domain, a place filled with the hustle and bustle of strangers, dimly lit hallways, and unsolvable mazes. A patient quickly becomes isolated from their normal lifestyle and living cycle and is thrust outside their comfort zone. Fear soon creeps in from isolation. The fear of the unknown and of losing their identity and personal control starts the psychological assault that eventually undermines the patient's self-confidence. How often is an inpatient referred to as a room number by the nursing staff? Room 307 needs a bath, but we need to clean up our act.

Intimidation

The prisoner or hostage becomes *intimidated* by their captor's dominance, the unfamiliar and stressful environment and the numerous and restrictive rules. They start feeling inadequate in dealing with the intimidating situation and lose their will to resist, relinquishing more personal and daily control to their captors, complete obedience shortly follows. When a patient is admitted to a hospital, they gradually find themselves being intimidated by the sterile environment, the abundance of preoccupied staff, unfamiliar smells and sounds, unfriendly signage, elevator doors that never open, lonely intimidating hallways that seem to go on unremittingly, the strange equipment with all the bells and whistles going off at once, and the endless procession of sick people wandering the corridors. The patient starts to feel intimidated and helpless in this assimilating and confusing world and wonders "Who are these strangers who have accepted and placed my life in their hands?" The more intelligent and educated the patient is, the less intimidated they become by the system, only to find ways to beat the system, not unlike the pilot-prisoners staying at the Hanoi Hilton.

Interrogation

Prisoners are repeatedly *interrogated* to ensure their story is airtight and the collected information is correct; any deviations could bring swift and unpleasant consequences to the prisoner. Our patient finds the going no different. Day in and day out, the patient interrogation process goes on. Every department verifies the previously collected patient information, medical history, and payment plan. The tireless parade of interrogators drills the patient for yet more bits of information. Another nurse, a different doctor, and now a technologist, the parade goes on. When will this interrogation stop, the patient wonders?

Insecurity

The abrupt changes experienced by prisoners of war breed a high degree of *insecurity* into them. Building insecurity is yet another indispensable and well-known factor in gaining control over individuals. It is well known that personal clothing, jewelry, and private possessions afford a certain level of security and confidence to prisoners, so they must go. This insecurity, or loss of control, over their own well-being will start generating a high level of anxiety, leaving prisoners to wonder who is looking out for them. Prisoners are forced to trust their captors, who in reality, usually have no deep personal regard for a prisoner's well-being. Upon being admitted to a hospital, we strip the patient of nearly all their outer attire and personal things. We will even take their false teeth if the occasion arises. Most patients experiencing such major and rapid changes in their lives and surroundings find the whole process overwhelming, if not scary. After visiting hours are over and family members go home, a patient is prone to feel lonely and insecure and to start to question who really cares about them now. "Is my call-light broken? With so many patients in the hospital and fewer nurses, can I possibly mean much to the hurried staff? After all, I heard the nurse refer to me by my room number to another person, 'See what 122 wants now.' Did they already forget my name?" Surely, insecurity is festering in the mind of the seemingly deserted patient.

Indigestion

Food for prisoners and hostages is expected to be bad. *Indigestion* is very common among prisoners, mainly because they are fed foods that they are not accustomed to eating. Prisoners are fed only enough to sustain life, to keep them alive until their release. This approach to feeding prisoners also keeps them in a state of weakness, a tactic used to minimize forceful resistance to their captor's demands. You might expect airplane food, that is if you ever receive more than a bag of high-fat peanuts, to be of questionable quality, quantity, and digestibility. However, hospital food is prepared to be nutritious and healthy for patients. Right? What's the number one thing that happens to patients in a hospital? They quickly start losing weight. Talk about a bad case of indigestion, experts suggest at least 30% of patients in hospitals are malnourished. Furthermore and just as shocking, an estimated 50,000 preventable deaths each year occur in hospitals because of malnutrition. Many patients strongly believe that if it were not for the digestible food visitors smuggled past the nurses' stations (easy to do as most nurses are buried in paperwork and seldom raise an eye above the countertop to see who is there) they would have surely succumbed to starvation. To make matters even more indigestible, hot food arrives cold and cold food may not arrive at all. And often the food tray is left out of reach. But the root cause is that most physicians and many dieticians are not knowledgeable enough about the effect various pharmaceuticals have on food digestion and the body's ability to absorb nutrients, especially since every person is affected differently.

Intrusion

As a prisoner of war you have no privacy; your captors *intrude* on your isolation at their whim. Patients fare no better it seems. Their room is constantly being invaded by an army of doctors (seldom theirs), nurses, phlebotomists, dietary personnel, housekeeping, and other support people. Your much needed rest and sleep are frequently intruded upon, as you are awakened to see if you are sleeping well. Prisoners can expect to be crowded together but a semi-private room affords a patient little freedom from intrusions and privacy is out of the question, especially once their cell (room) mate's family and friends start marching in and parading out all hours of the day and night. We make a habit of collecting patients' bodily fluids and taking their vital life signs intrusively around the clock. The patient is frequently asked to go, when they already went. How much can one give for their country and freedom?

Indignities

Because they are treated as an innate object or just a number, prisoners are subjected to all kinds of intended *indignities* while interned. There is no privacy, you can be stripsearched and explored top to bottom (no pun intended), required to relieve yourself in plain view of others, and worse yet, be ignored by your fellow human beings. "You can see what?" the unnerved patient shyly quivered. We start by putting patients in drafty, see-through gowns that we ourselves would not be caught dead in. Patients are required to wear plastic ID wristbands so strangers can make sure they have the right body on which to execute their assigned search and destroy missions. I barely know you and you want me to bare it all. I am your patient, handle me with care and dignity.

Inflict

Torture is often an integral part of captivity and every prisoner's worse nightmare. Prisoners know that there is always the possibility that they will be mistreated, even tortured, by their captors out of revenge, frustration, or just for sadistic fun. However, most prisoners endure the *inflicted* physical pain and do not break under torture. On the contrary, it is when the prisoner is returned to their cell or holding area and starts thinking about the hideous acts and painful torture awaiting them; that is when the vast majority of prisoners crack. The mental stress and agony the prisoner's mind conjures up and inflicts on its owner far outweighs any physical pain the captor can dream up to put them through. The uncertainty of the unknown is more unbearable than the foreseeable torture itself. Every voice, each footstep and distant noise that reaches the prisoner's ears produces nerve-wrenching anguish, anxiety, and fear inside them. The mental torture never stops during the endless hours of waiting for someone to return and take them away. I know you would never intentionally torture a patient, let alone think about inflicting pain. Besides, it is against the law, right? We also ensure our patients have ample time to spend pondering the perceived tortures that await them that afternoon or the following day. After being admitted to the hospital a perfect opportunity is offered patients to sit alone and worry what is next. He or she is taken in short order to their room to wait, minutes turning into mental hours. This initial isolation will likely result in patients unnecessarily inflicting self-imposed mental anguish on themselves, such as the strange and curious sounds down the hallway, the groaning and moaning of the sick and the faint, or even the staff on occasion mumbling outside their door (talking about them?). All must be endured until finally someone shows up to ensure internment is finalized. Oh yes, our indirect tortures are cleverly and well camouflaged behind medical necessities, various protocols, and strange sounding technical names.

We are great at redefining and disguising our tortures as exploratory surgery, biopsy, specimen collection (mining in veins), intravenous placement, and the good old standby, lower gastrointestinal (GI) series. The snap of the rubber glove will make most men flinch. In the name of medicine (or reimbursement) we are always inflicting pain on our patients by probing, sticking, and opening their bodies. And we are not done or satisfied until a tube of some kind or another has been forcefully inserted into every accessible and unoccupied body orifice. To the patient's untrained eye however, we are always trying to place a large, square whatchamacallit into one or more of their small round openings, or at least that is how it feels. For the patient, their room quickly becomes a holding cell and our invasive fetish for collecting, snipping, and testing their daily torture to endure. And do not forget the MRI unit, a million-dollar claustrophobic tester every hospital has but does not need, which is quickly passed off as a high-tech diagnostic imager.

Indifference

Gaining control over prisoners and hostages also requires showing them little, if any, personal attention. This *indifference* causes many prisoners to further lose their self-esteem and identity. Hence, their captor assumes a friendly status in the mind of the prisoner whenever attention is finally given, regardless of the type and amount shown. We all want to be liked, loved, and shown attention. Unfortunately, this contagious indifference has crept into the hospital's everyday operations. Indifference starts in admitting with the indignant branding (ID wristbands) ritual, the noncommunicative doctors (usually theirs), and the chart-oriented nurses too busy to do what they do best, care for the patient's physical and mental needs. Indifference permeates the hallways and corridors where passing hospital staff, too preoccupied with last night's bowling scores, neglects to say hello to patients and visitors. Forget it, a staff smile is out of the question as insensitive employees are busy pushing by patients and visitors to get on the elevator, cold dietary personnel placing the patient's food tray out of their reach, and no one remembers the patient's name without reading the chart at the end of the bed. Am I just another warm body in this cold, indifferent hospital, the patient frustratingly wonders?

Interrogation

Finally, the war is over, the prisoners are released and sent home, but not before one last *interrogation* to make sure everything is in order. It is discharge time at the hospital, the patient is going home, but not before being interrogated again. This time we want to know how patients rated their hospital stays; was everything to their liking and was the nursing staff nice? In the end, we are likely to hold a post-discharge interrogation in a couple of weeks to see how the patient really feels about us and their stay at the hospital. Once home, the patient may receive interrogating calls from their managed care plan, their employer, or an outside survey company representative reviewing their stay at your hospital, but seldom from their doctor.

Inappropriateness

The prisoner of war upon returning home is debriefed by military intelligence to gather information on how they were treated while being interned. Should it be determined that prisoners were treated inhumanely or *inappropriately*, criminal war crime charges may be pursued against the captors. Not unlike the prisoner, the patient will also be debriefed. The interrogation starts at home by family members and friends, the managed care plan may also call, and hopefully, the patient will hear from their physician, proactively showing post-hospital stay interest. Underneath the caring and empathy, each is searching for any sign of nonprofessionalism or inappropriate care. In the event such actions have been determined to have occurred, a malpractice lawsuit is sure to ensue.

Inescapable

Once removed from the indignities and hardships of being a prisoner of war, many soldiers experience Posttraumatic Stress Disorder (PSD) reliving the events of captivity over and over again. Recurring nightmares prepare for their nightly disabling assault, waiting for darkness to strike a torturous sleep. When will it end? Many patients after returning home after a short hospital stay will experience their own PSD as well. In short order, their mailboxes turn into cornucopias spewing forth an endless stream of medical, hospital, and physician bills. Postcare Shock Disorder sets in. Patients start worrying how they are going to get the money to pay their medical bills. Insurance will pay some, but not all. Will I have to sell the house, use up my life savings, and work three jobs the rest of my life? Unnoticeable at first, but chronic anxiety, hyper alertness, and insomnia take over their lives and are the telltale signs of PSD. Due to staggering healthcare costs, many patients after successful medical intervention are worse off than before. Their health is better now, but their lives are not better off. We exchange the burden of illness for a sickening financial burden. How many of us are comfortable taking what so many cannot afford to give? Without healthcare insurance our industry would crumble into dust; only the wealthy could afford medical care. Doctors would once again be bartering for their services.

The prisoner of war comparison is too close a fit for my comfort and I am sure that of the patient. You can arrive at your own conclusions. I only ask that you, regardless of your healthcare profession and provider entity, have the time to reevaluate your patient satisfaction efforts and truly become more sensitive to your patients' physical and mental needs and feelings. You are a creature of habit and as such resist change, even changing for the better. The biggest obstacle you and your organization have to overcome to start delivering consistent Ultimate Patient Satisfaction is change. And just by chance you do not recognize all the facets of terrorism in the hospital, remember, never be satisfied with your patient's satisfaction. *In conclusion*, it is also important that you realize that each of the terrorism elements presented here starts with the letter "I." So answer this simple question, Am I unknowingly this "I," and the terrorist within? Hopefully not.

5
CHAPTER

Physicians, the Beginning of the End

"First, do no harm."— Hippocrates, the "Father of Modern Medicine"

The patient-physician relationship is the fundamental instrument in delivering quality medical care and Ultimate Patient Satisfaction. Most medical intervention is under the direct or indirect control or supervision of a physician, whether a medical, osteopathic, or chiropractic doctor. After making that statement, I respectfully submit that many other people are on occasion actively practicing medicine, such as nurses, case managers, corporate executives, and even do-gooders on the Internet. That is another book for another day.

Because physicians are the beginning of the end in the patient satisfaction ritual, if you contract with, work with, or are depending on physicians to deliver all or a part of your services, whether via a solo practice, in a group practice, or under a management contract, you need to fully understand the impact doctors have on your ability for achieving Ultimate Patient Satisfaction. Please remember, we are not about slam-dunking doctors, a Michael Jordan I am not, but are only examining one of the most key and critical elements, which out of fear is mostly overlooked or neglected by healthcare providers in the quest for the highest level of patient satisfaction, Ultimate Patient

Satisfaction. What you are about to read is not a positive endorsement for our healthcare and medical industry's stewardship, but must be told, politically correct or not, to be corrected.

HAZARDOUS TO YOUR HEALTH

Based on the Harvard Medical Practice Study released in 1990, and the growing preponderance of supportive research unknown to the general public and medical community(?), experts estimate that every *seven* minutes, on average, a person dies from medical malpractice in an American hospital. Hey, forget about patient satisfaction, this shocking and appalling fact alone should close hospitals left and right across the land. According to Harvey Rosenfield, the author of, *Silent Violence, Silent Death, The Hidden Epidemic of Medical Malpractice,* Essential Books, 1986, an estimated 80,000 to 150,000 patients die in hospitals every year as a direct result of neglect, incompetent or even criminal physicians, and hundreds of thousands more are injured. However, this appears to be only the tip of the iceberg and a chilling thought in and of itself, because the numbers do not account for the patients killed and injured in outpatient clinics, surgery centers, imaging centers, psychiatric facilities, nursing homes, and physicians' offices. According to Chicago U.S. District Court records, August 27, 1987, under oath, M.D.s admitted they had almost no knowledge of 60% of the body, its musculoskeletal system. Why would such a seemingly important fact like that be hidden from the public?

Talk about patient satisfaction, this sounds more like patient dissatisfaction at its highest level. More than likely, you have heard the joke, "The surgery was a success, but the patient died," well, maybe it is not a joke. Medical malpractice has a direct and negative impact on your organization's ability to achieve and maintain not only patient satisfaction but employee satisfaction, the secret to Ultimate Patient Satisfaction.

A basic, yet stellar premise of Ultimate Patient Satisfaction is to minimize, if not completely eliminate, medical malpractice within your healthcare and medical delivery system. You and your organization's fiduciary responsibility is to protect the patient at all costs. Part of this responsibility and accountability is ensuring everything humanly possible is quickly and effectively being done for extricating all egregious acts of medical malpractice from the delivery of healthcare. This means aggressively abandoning the medical practitioners' self-serving code of silence, or in reality, a conspiracy of silence against the patient. When was the last time, if ever, you saw mentioned in a healthcare organization's mission statement something to the effect, ". . . and to eliminate the perpetrators, origins, and root problems associated with medical malpractice . . . " Search your soul, and you will not let the medical malpractice epidemic live on. This is one medical practice or plague that needs to die by the hands of doctors themselves. Where is the "Dr. Kevorkian" of medical malpractice when you really need him?

AVOIDING A MEDICAL MALPRACTICE LAWSUIT

I am glad to say that not every doctor is a malpractice case in drag. The vast majority of physicians are caring practitioners, but things do happen to the best of us. However, there are many things doctors can do to lessen their exposure to a patient-initiated lawsuit. Legal experts estimate, and it is by now common knowledge, that anywhere from 70% to 80% of all medical malpractice lawsuits are a direct result of *poor* doctor-to-patient communications. The physician was sued, not because of the outcome per se, but because the doctor did not display an open, friendly, and caring attitude toward the patient and the family members. This interpersonal flaw had the doctor marching down the courthouse hall. What really pushes a patient into suing is the fact the doctor is perceived to have an attitude problem, though money has been known to tip the scales on occasion. Considering it from another viewpoint will also be helpful. The number one reason for married couples to divorce in America is also poor communication. Married couples stop effectively communicating with each other. This leads the couple to find superficial or hidden-agenda problems, which in turn drives numerous wedges of discontent between them. Once the splitting reaches a certain point, there is no turning back. Divorce is imminent. Then it makes sense to reason that when a patient sues the physician, the patient is actually divorcing the doctor. The patient in action is saying, "We are finished, I will seek another doctor to be my healthcare partner." So, if you want to greatly lessen your chances of a medical malpractice lawsuit, you need to start aggressively demonstrating a personal interest in each patient's physical and mental well-being. This is especially true for physicians who must painstakingly excel at doctor-to-patient and doctor-to-family member encounters and communications. Remember the patient box described in Chapter 3? As healthcare providers, we do not always have the luxury of caring for the type and caliber of people we prefer, though I believe we just need to prefer to care regardless of the patient.

TAKE YOUR MEDICINE LIKE A MAN

Patients put a high value on honesty and forthrightness, and research seems to suggest the same. Patients and family members want doctors and healthcare providers to admit their mistakes, not cover them up or evoke the code of silence. Quickly admitting you made a mistake can have a significant effect on whether the patient feels deceived, humiliated, or neglected. Any delay risks the patient's perception that you are attempting to cover up by hiding the seriousness and facts.

Consider using the following 13-step approach for coughing up the truth, whether you are dealing with a serious, or not so serious, mistake:

1. Hesitate only long enough to notify the appropriate risk manager(s) that an error was made and the patient or family must be told.
2. Assume the attitude that you are breaking bad news.
3. Tell the patient or family member that you have bad news to relate.
4. Clearly state that you or someone else made a mistake.
5. Communicate using honest, simple, and precise language.
6. Explain what happened by telling as much as you know to that point in time.
7. Explain the seriousness of the mistake and the effect on the patient.
8. Inform the patient and family what is being done, or needs to be done, to correct the problem or situation.
9. Express that there will be no charge for the services necessary in responding to the mistake or situation.
10. Apologize to the patient or family.
11. Ensure that you have honestly answered all questions and addressed all concerns the patient and family have about the mistake and related consequences.

12. Expect the patient and family to become upset and possibly express anger, be prepared to respond appropriately.
13. When a serious or life-taking mistake occurs, ensure the facility's risk manager is prepared to appropriately step in and deal with the situation.

ENHANCING PHYSICIANS' BEHAVIOR

The first priority in the initial doctor-patient encounter must be to quickly establish a friendly, caring rapport and trust with the patient and their family members. This goes for your office staff as well. They in essence grease the skids of patient satisfaction, set the tone of your encounter with the patient. This is your fundamental relationship, the springboard of things to come, and on which overall patient satisfaction is built. To that end, all must be committed. What can a physician do to lessen the chances of a medical malpractice lawsuit? Well, I have compiled a list of 25 behavior action items that can make a significant difference in reducing a doctor's attorney fees. And what is even better, not one of the 25 behavior actions will cost you one dime of reimbursement. So start making a professional and personal commitment to the following:

1. Creating a caring, friendly, and open professional relationship with *each* patient.
2. Ensuring that your staff creates and maintains caring, friendly, and professional relationships with each of *your* patients.
3. Respecting each patient's social standing, worth, and *dignity*.
4. Respecting each patient's sex and *privacy*.
5. Accounting for and respecting each patient's ethnicity, religious, and cultural *differences*.
6. Listening *patiently* to each patient, do not interrupt.
7. Being *polite* to each patient.
8. Maintaining a *professional* demeanor with each patient in all that you say and do.
9. Respecting each *patient's* family members and guests.
10. Respecting each patient's time by *being* on time yourself.
11. Keeping each patient's expectations *realistic* and preparing them for any adverse side effects or consequences.

12. Involving the patient in all *decisions* regarding their treatment and care.

13. Maintaining professional attire, grooming, and personal and medical *hygiene* at all times.

14. Documenting every stage of the patient's examination, diagnosis, treatment, and care in a *comprehensive*, clear, readable, and appropriate format.

15. Adopting patient-friendly billing policies and *sensitive* collection procedures.

16. Avoiding cases where the patient's personality *conflicts* with yours.

17. Abstaining from cases where the patient or their family members are difficult to work with, or *unhappy* with your proposed treatment plan and current efforts.

18. Determining your *limitations*, avoiding obvious high-risk situations and *not* accepting cases that you are not properly trained, experienced, or equipped to take on.

19. Being *honest* about accidents, adverse results, and exclusions regarding the patient's diagnosis, treatment, and care; never attempting to cover up your mistakes or knowingly mislead a patient or their family members.

20. Referring and accepting patients to and from ethical doctors and *quality* healthcare facilities only.

21. Treating each patient as *you* would want to be treated as a patient.

22. Learning and using *body* language to effectively communicate with your patients.

23. Refraining from exaggerating, misleading, or promising specific outcomes or a level of quality in your *advertising* and promotional endeavors.

24. *Guaranteeing* medical outcomes when predetermining such end results are nearly impossible to do or predict.

25. Remembering that doctors make the *worst* patients, bar none.

The previous principles not only hold true for doctors but will also hold true for all people in your organization. I cannot count the number of healthcare providers that permit (encourage) their staff to assume any personal attire, any personal grooming style, and any personal attitude, all in the name of employee morale. Usually, however, it turns out to be counterproductive to building patient acceptance, confidence, and trust. Patients cannot tell one caregiver from another without a program. The doctors look like business men and women just off the street and always in a perceived rush, and the dietary staff wear scrubs and look like nurses. But I will make you a guarantee anyway. If you and your staff adopt, and religiously adhere to, the 25 principles as outlined previously, you, your associates, and your organization will be less likely to be confronted with a patient-originating medical malpractice lawsuit than those that do business as normal. Hopefully, you realized that the previous principles for avoiding a medical malpractice lawsuit are closely and strategically aligned with actions required for achieving Ultimate Patient Satisfaction.

One more, but important point, oxytocin needs to be mentioned. I can imagine a baby gnawing on the mother's tender nipple, one at a time, slurping back and forth between the two, the little gumming, gnawing mouth sucks. Surely this cannot be a most pleasurable experience to the nursing mother in and of itself. Unless of course, the mother received some kind of positive reinforcement in the process. Oxytocin to the rescue! When a mother is suckling her newborn baby, oxytocin is released en mass into the mother's bloodstream, causing other chemical reactions to occur, releasing a flood of pleasure-producing compounds. You just had a suckling-baby high. That high kept the mother from saying, bye. That is bye to the gnawing baby. Because the oxytocin high acted as a powerful bonding agent between the mother and her new baby. The baby was kept and everyone was satisfied, mom, baby, and dad. The human race has been on the run ever since for a higher high. How can the oxytocin connection help you? Well, if you want to build great rapport and do it quickly, make reassuring body contact with your patients. Instead of standing at the foot of the bed talking with your patient, start positioning yourself at the side of the patient's bed. And when talking with your patient, take hold of their hand or place your hand on their shoulder and gently pat or stroke the point of contact. Oxytocin will be released into the patient's bloodstream and perform its magical bonding act on your behalf. Your patients will not only sense your caring, they will also start feeling good about it. Give it a try, I guarantee you will also feel and sense the difference in your patients' attitudes. Additional supportive information to be reflected on for keeping physicians out of hot water is research conducted by the Agency for Health Care Policy and Research that showed physicians asking patients for their opinion, eliciting questions, using humor, and employing explaining conversation were significantly less likely to be sued by their patients.

PHYSICIAN PERFORMANCE SURVEY

Over the years, I also found that most hospitals and healthcare providers seldom engage in conducting patient satisfaction surveys specifically dealing with doctors and their bedside manners. Instead, most surveys were focused on the non-physician providers. Yet you will find that doctors' interactions with patients and your employees, especially the patient's, attending specialists, and those in training, greatly affects your organization's ability to deliver a high level of patient satisfaction. Doctors are often one of the underlying causes of poor nursing morale that goes unchecked for fear of offending the insensitive doctor, but what about offending the nurses and patients? Are we so afraid of what we will learn, or confirm what we know, but ignore? Are a doctor's bedside manners and interpersonal skills not key to patient satisfaction? However, such a survey tends to be avoided because it could turn up concerning behavior and information we would rather not confront a doctor about, especially a high referral source. Sound familiar? Let us not start upsetting the medical staff is the most common response why such surveys are to be avoided like the plague.

What Did the Doctor Say?

As a good example, in fact more of a testimonial supportive point, to my knowledge the American Medical Association (AMA) has never made a national survey to determine the extent and the financial impact of medical malpractice (estimated to be $60 billion annually). And if they did, my research has failed to locate such a document. Because physician-patient encounters are such a critical part of your organization's overall patient satisfaction, especially in an inpatient environment, you need to take the position that information regarding patient-physician encounters, communications, and bedside manners is important and paramount to gaining high patient satisfaction levels. Consider the following far too common example; there are many physicians practicing in America who do not have a working understanding of our national culture, nor adequate command of the spoken English language, yet the doctor is expected to effectively communicate with the patient. On occasions, strongly accented, foreign-sounding English has interfered with effective physician-patient communications, often to the point where the doctor is totally not understandable. Like you, I have also overheard a physician giving orders to a nurse, bearing silent witness to the nurse's puzzled expression when asking another nurse to interpret what the doctor said. Surely this type of language barrier has to pose a communication problem for many patients, as well as the physician and supporting staff. Why just being a Yankee in the south can cause communication problems, especially if you are the Yankee. You may find the article, "Language Barriers in Medicine in the United States," *JAMA*, March 1, 1995, Vol 273, No. 9, of great interest and insight.

Physicians' egos, as well as our own, are the prime enemy of successful healthcare research and marketing. Try not to let people's egos keep you from the job at hand. If you now realize the major impact physician-patient encounters have on patients' satisfaction and you are contemplating conducting a physician survey, I think you will find the following seven-step guideline helpful in undertaking such a task. Remember, you are using the survey to facilitate improvement in patient satisfaction, and not for the purpose of criticizing physicians. The seven-step approach I highly recommend is as follows:

1. Determining the objectives of the survey.
2. Informing your medical staff that such an undertaking is necessary for the following reasons and secure their support.
3. Ensuring that one or more of the medical staff is extended the opportunity and encouraged to participate in the survey's design, execution, data analysis, and summary presentation.
4. Reviewing the conclusions with the chief of staff and senior physicians, and seeking their advice on all points of concern.
5. Providing the medical staff with a generic report, having the chief of staff review and address specific physician concerns with appropriate doctors or parties.

6. Creating an action plan for changing any undesirable medical staff behavior.

7. Keep the chief of staff and medical staff well informed about the progress being made or the lack thereof.

We all know that surgical and floor nurses know the good physicians from the mediocre physicians, from the bad physicians. Yet seldom do we appropriately respond to their observations and testimonials, good or bad. Someday this valuable resource will be polled and the results will be used by hospitals and the medical staff as a key factor in the process of credentialing a physician for hospital privileges. Why is this critical part to determining medical outcomes, the physician-patient encounter and communications, not part of the Joint Commission on Accreditation of Healthcare Organizations accreditation process? If patient satisfaction is to be part of the accreditation process, it only stands to reason that the physician-patient element should also be part of the evaluation.

As pointed out in Chapter 15, "Creating a Survey," the questions and response rating methodologies are especially critical and should not be attempted by an inexperienced person. However, what follows is a list of some typical questions you might want to ask a patient regarding their personal physician's conduct and interpersonal skills during the patient's hospital stay. Though I am making reference to a hospital stay, the same questions presented here can easily be modified to cover most physician-patient encounters regardless of your needs and facility.

INPATIENT PATIENT SATISFACTION

PHYSICIAN ENCOUNTER SURVEY

During your hospital stay would you *(1)* strongly agree, *(2)* somewhat agree, *(3)* agree, *(4)* disagree, or *(5)* strongly disagree with each of the following statements regarding your personal physician. Please circle your level of agreement.

My physician visited me daily during my hospital stay.	1 - 2 - 3 - 4 - 5
My physician always greeted me with a smile.	1 - 2 - 3 - 4 - 5
My physician did not appear rushed.	1 - 2 - 3 - 4 - 5

My physician spent adequate time with me   1 - 2 - 3 - 4 - 5
during each visit.

My physician was genuinely warm and caring   1 - 2 - 3 - 4 - 5
toward me.

My physician was genuinely concerned about   1 - 2 - 3 - 4 - 5
my feelings.

My physician kept me well informed about my   1 - 2 - 3 - 4 - 5
treatment plan.

My physician kept me well informed about   1 - 2 - 3 - 4 - 5
my progress or lack thereof.

My physician showed genuine concern about   1 - 2 - 3 - 4 - 5
my outcome.

My physician kept me well informed about   1 - 2 - 3 - 4 - 5
my medications.

My physician was genuinely sensitive to my   1 - 2 - 3 - 4 - 5
special needs.

My physician was very responsive to my   1 - 2 - 3 - 4 - 5
family members' questions.

My physician answered all my questions to my   1 - 2 - 3 - 4 - 5
satisfaction.

My physician discussed my discharge plan with   1 - 2 - 3 - 4 - 5
me prior to my being discharged.

My physician appeared to work well with the   1 - 2 - 3 - 4 - 5
hospital staff.

My physician washed his or her hands before   1 - 2 - 3 - 4 - 5
examining or touching me.

My physician communicated effectively.   1 - 2 - 3 - 4 - 5

My physician had my pain level under control   1 - 2 - 3 - 4 - 5
to my satisfaction.

My physician reduced any anxiety that I had   1 - 2 - 3 - 4 - 5
prior to and during my hospital stay.

My physician made sure I was being treated well   1 - 2 - 3 - 4 - 5
during my hospital stay.

With a little revamping, the same line of questioning can be used to determine the patient's satisfaction regarding encounters with other doctors, such as any of the attending specialists and staff physicians. You also probably noticed that because of the generic nature of the questions, the physician focus can readily be changed to learn more about nurse-patient encounters by modifying the questions, specifically, changing the word "physician" to "nurse." Again, the presented questions are to assist you in designing your own survey questionnaire.

GETTING IT OFF MY CHEST

As I pointed out in earlier chapters, employee satisfaction is key to delivering Ultimate Patient Satisfaction consistently. However, there are many healthcare providers, including physician practices that sacrifice maximum employee morale and job satisfaction because of the demoralizing behavior of one or more physicians. Many healthcare executives accept rude, socially unacceptable, and in some instances, totally disruptive behavior and tantrums from physicians because of the almighty dollar. Employees are afraid to report incidents or questionable actions and to stand up for their rights and those of the patient for fear of persecution or losing their job. Well, let me tell you, things need to change. All too often, physicians do not see themselves as a self-centered, disruptive force in the delivery of medicine, especially in their own practice. Some doctors act like visiting bullies at the nursing stations, taking their frustrations and inadequacies out on the nearest nurse, fearing no retribution. The system has allowed, if not encouraged, such actions by the lack of concern or backbone shown by those best in a position to force change, such as the chief of the medical staff, the administrator, the president, the chief executive officer, and the chairman of the board. I know physicians who would surely find it extremely difficult working for themselves, that is, having to work for a boss like themselves. I also realize that many doctors endure a lot of peer pressure, the kind of pressure surrounding referral source politics, disgruntled patients, and a seemingly ever-changing practice environment. Everything is not coming up roses for medical doctors, especially after the profession is still staggering from losing medical clinical control, declining reimbursement, and the standardization of care. As the pressure builds, many physicians are left with only one place to vent, on the backs of their staff or someone else's employees, like hospital nurses. However, pressurized as it may be, the practice of medicine is no excuse for doctors to explode at will and to be rude and obnoxious to supporting staff. Remember, physicians cannot go on thinking their patients and your staff are inferior intellectually, socially, or financially. Our parents' and grandparents' society elevated doctors to their lofty position in life (with the AMA's help), and ours can easily pull them down, especially with the growing encouragement and support from consumer groups. Has not the physician pedestal been more than a tad unstable in recent years? By the way, I have many physician friends, good friends at that, who truly care about the people and community they serve, I only wish there were more.

PRACTICE SUICIDE

It is not enough that most physicians are doing everything possible to practice quality medicine and keep their patients satisfied. Caught up in the business of practicing good medicine (why are doctors always practicing medicine?) many doctors pay little attention to their office operations on a daily basis. This phenomenon I call, practice-suicide. Key administrative functions, patient processing, billing, collections, payroll, employee supervision, and business issues are managed by the physician's office or business manager. The overwhelming majority of office managers do an outstanding job, especially those who have the appropriate formal education, business background, and interpersonal skills to manage a challenging business while at the same time leading and coaching the office staff. However, there are still many physician offices being run using archaic management technologies and business methodologies that are keeping the doctor's patients from experiencing Ultimate Patient

Satisfaction. And there still exists a large number of doctors permitting, knowingly or not, their practices (business) to be run and dominated by an office manager employing fear, closed communications, and tightly controlled activities, no matter how insignificant. I refer to these dysfunctional practice managers as "iron matriarchs of office management." Not to be disrespectful, but because more often than not the office manager is a female, though I must confess, I also know many male office managers who would feel quite comfortable and at home in a suit of armor. My experience has shown that usually, the iron matriarchs of office management put on a good facade, but in reality, most are poor managers lacking the necessary skills for running a practice like a business. There is a tendency to be inefficient at billing and collections, to have terrible interpersonal skills, and to be totally dysfunctional when it comes to building office morale, let alone patient satisfaction. They also tend to have been around awhile, demonstrating exceptional interoffice survival skills. However, these iron matriarchs of office management are actually very good at destroying the physician-patient relationship by weakening employee morale. This in part is achieved by attracting marginal employees and losing good performers. We are all creatures of habit, and as such, can endure under inefficient management oppression for the sake of a needed job. Hence, many employees are often suffering while the doctor is busily caring for patients. Watch out, for on occasion the iron matriarchs of office management syndrome hits close to home, especially when doctors' spouses are left to manage and run their office. This behavior usually results in a slowly dying medical practice for sure, if not for real. So remember, satisfying your employees is the gateway to Ultimate Patient Satisfaction. To identify individuals within your practice who are reducing your overall efficiency, performance, and reimbursement you might consider having a confidential survey conducted by a reputable third-party agency that guarantees each employee's anonymity.

A HELPING HAND

We all need a helping hand once in awhile. Though when I first read it, I found it hard to believe, the American Medical Association recommended that medical schools start including acting classes in their curriculum so doctors would be better prepared to interface with their patients. As healthcare professionals, have we come so far as to only distance ourselves from our patients? Remember, distancing is the first step toward divorcing. This acting approach, if accepted, may benefit medical students; however, what about those physicians already practicing? You may wish considering using, "The Fifteen Ways to Lose a Patient" found on page 20 for creating your own colorful, self-help, attention-getting poster for doctors. You can start by hanging the posters in conspicuous locations where physicians are being reminded daily what it takes to lose a patient. Some good locations are in the physician lounge, dining room, reading room (radiologists), medical meeting or classroom areas, medical library, nursing stations, surgical scrub areas, and where physicians check in. Give it a try, you have nothing to lose but your patients.

THE DIFFERENCE

Ken Orton, a sales manager with a national pharmaceutical company, whom I had the pleasure of meeting at a training program I was conducting, shared with me on a small piece of green paper the difference between a specialist and a general practitioner. It read, "A general practitioner knows less and less about more and more until eventually, he or she knows nothing about everything. A specialist knows more and more about less and less until eventually he or she knows everything about nothing." Ponder that for awhile, if you dare. It only goes to prove how easy it is to get so caught up in our own ego and world, we miss the big picture, Ultimate Patient Satisfaction.

On the more serious side, there is another action item I want to suggest you ponder, and that is sending each of your referring physicians one or more of the following books. Any one of the listed books will provide valuable information and thought-provoking realities that will make every doctor a better doctor by helping create the necessary mind-set to ensure Ultimate Patient Satisfaction in their and your healthcare delivery system.

> *Getting the Best From Your Doctor*, Wesley Smith, Doctor Book—
> A nuts and bolts guide to consumer health. ISBN 9621259-5-4
> *Silent Violence, Silent Death*, Harvey Rosenfield, Essential
> Books—A consumer's guide to the medical malpractice epidemic. ISBN 9621259-6-2

A Doctor's Guide to The Best Medical Care, Michael Oppenheim, MD, Rodale—A practical no-nonsense evaluation of your treatment options for more than 100 conditions and diseases. ISBN 0-87857-982-6

Not What the Doctor Ordered, Jeffery Bauer, Probus Publishing— Reinventing medical care in America. ISBN 1-55738-620-X

Try ordering the books over the Internet at www.amazon.com, claimed to be the world's largest bookstore. You can expect to save up to 40% on many books.

TURNING DOCTORS INTO MDs

Most doctors still feel uncomfortable and uneasy about marketing their services to others. Engaging in self-marketing goes against decades of resisting a retail approach to medicine by the premier medical profession, the medical doctor. Many doctors are still relying on and believing the professional's word-of-mouth approach, one doctor to another, to retain their practice's financial solvency. Some physicians are also banking on the old reliable satisfied patient's word-of-mouth advertising to bring in new patients. All well and good I say, that is, if you want to steadily be relinquishing more and more of your dwindling market share to more aggressive physicians, managed care plans, practice management services, local hospital systems, and national healthcare delivery networks. If not, listen up, there's still hope for all but the diehard of passé caregivers.

Physician Excess

By now you should have gained a firm understanding of how important physicians are to achieving Ultimate Patient Satisfaction. Turning doctors into Marketing Disciples (MDs) is an important step on the journey to Ultimate Patient Satisfaction. This is especially important after you realize, especially if you are a doctor, that there is currently a major over supply of physicians in America, as many as 100,000 or more by some estimates. Besides the excess supply of physicians, the nation is confronted with a medical profession that has consistently resisted establishing any serious continuity in practice standards, patient care, and medical outcomes! However, such standardization is not too distant in the future for physicians in fast-growing and aggressively contested managed care and for-profit markets. No matter what happens, no quarter will be given to the meek healthcare providers, including physicians. To survive and prosper physicians have two options. The first is to join a large, progressive group practice and let someone market for them, such as a management service organization. The second is to proactively start marketing themselves. As marketing disciples, more doctors will actively engage in marketing their cost-effectiveness, their benchmark outcomes, and patient satisfaction to patients, managed care plans, employers, and other physicians. One does not need a medical degree and cold stethoscope to take the hot pulse of change. I believe that doctors who change today will be the physicians who control tomorrow's healthcare systems.

Physician Marketing Tactics

Even in a managed care environment, physicians refer to physicians whom they know, like, and respect. Physician-to-physician marketing is a highly personal undertaking requiring good interpersonal and communicative skills. Establishing yourself as the physician-of-choice, the one other doctors know, like, and respect, takes time yet there is no time to waste. So here are 25 action items you can start using in converting yourself into a MD, a marketing disciple. You can effectively start building your practice and marketing yourself physician-to-physician, physician-to-employer, and physician-to-managed care by:

1. Going out of your way to be nice to patients, personnel, and people;
2. Returning phone calls promptly;
3. Losing your adversarial mind-set toward managed care;
4. Managing your time better;
5. Treating all your patients with great respect and dignity;
6. Benchmarking your medical skills and services;
7. Aggressively expanding your personal and business networks;
8. Proactively pursuing self-promotion by actively participating in professional and community activities;
9. Outsourcing practice operations to increase your cost efficiency and quality;

10. Creating an understanding of basic marketing principles;
11. Start associating with, and learning from, market-oriented physicians;
12. Accepting all patients, regardless of reimbursement;
13. Presenting at local, regional, and national meetings or run for office;
14. Making an effort to refer to those physicians referring to you;
15. Creating an image in the medical community as a quality, state-of-the-art physician, and practice;
16. Creating a referral development plan, work the plan, and proactively making things happen, stay with it;
17. Establishing close and friendly relationships with referring physicians' office staff;
18. Creating opportunities to encounter other doctors by attending medical staff meetings, functions, and events, and learning how to work a room;
19. Educating prospective doctors (referral sources) about your skills and how your services will enhance their practice;
20. Volunteering to be on medical committees with potential referral sources and opportunities;
21. Creating and putting on approved continuing medical educational programs for local physicians, conduct a CME luncheon series (your specialty);
22. Direct mailing a one-page, quick-read, colorful, case-history newsletter to area doctors describing the medical situations and conditions that you handle;
23. Writing a letter of introduction and thank you to each new referring doctor, place a special introduction call;
24. Remembering referring physicians' birthdays, anniversaries, and the like with a card or phone call; and
25. Realizing that cemeteries are full of indispensable people.

CAUTION

A few words of caution: physicians must take an open and nonnegotiable position toward wholeheartedly identifying and weeding out those doctors who contaminate the practice of medicine and their chosen profession by engaging in inexcusable social behaviors, fraud, and incompetency. All doctors are not equally created. If our doctors do not come together and proactively start taking back the lost stewardship of their profession by cleaning house, the enraged public will. Aided by digitizing, analyzing, and publicizing technologies, consumer groups are disseminating heretofore proprietary information about physicians to the general public. Many doctors are discovering that a growing number of their patients are better informed about the latest treatments, drugs, and surgery options available than they are, all due to open communications (Internet?) between people having similar medical situations. The Internet alone will snare and dispose of marginal physicians in the future: the handwriting is on the wall, or should I say a monitor. A few closing words, the physician who smokes is a healthcare oxymoron!

6

CHAPTER

Internal Patient Satisfaction

It's not a solo event, it's a team encounter . . .

You can find many marketing definitions in the literature, each a little different from the other; each, however, conveys an underlying theme that marketing is important. Here is my own version or definition of what marketing is: "Marketing is a *battle* for the *mind*, and in part, is accomplished by proactively employing the art and science of identifying and understanding what people's perceptions, needs, and desires are, why, how, and when people and organizations make decisions to satisfy their perceptions, needs, and desires while favorably influencing the decision process. Furthermore, marketing is also the art and science of planning and executing the conception, pricing, promotion, and distribution of ideas, goods, and services to create *internal* and *external* exchanges that satisfy individual and organizational perceptions, needs, desires, and goals." Dissected into its purest meaning, marketing is the ongoing quest for total customer satisfaction that in the end terminates in Ultimate Patient Satisfaction.

I also believe marketing is employing common sense once all the facts are known, or as much as possible under given circumstances. You will be surprised how common, common sense becomes once everyone is well informed. Marketing is also too important to be left to a marketing person or department. Everyone in your organization is in

59

marketing, a marketeer. And finally, from my point of view marketing's primary function is to provide senior management reliable information from which key business decisions can be better made. Marketing to me is simple, so simple that everyone can do it, and needs to do it.

SO WHAT, WHO CARES

When it comes to internal patient satisfaction, who really cares? Sometimes it is really difficult to tell. Saying you care and demonstrating you care are two different things as the following poem by Charles Osgood says best.

Everybody, Anybody, Somebody, and Nobody

There was a most important job that needed to be done, and no reason NOT to do it, there was absolutely none. But in vital matters such as this, the thing you have to ask is WHO exactly will it be who'll carry OUT the task. ANYBODY could have told you that EVERYBODY knew that this was something SOMEBODY would surely have to do. NOBODY was unwilling. ANYBODY had the ability. But NOBODY believed that it was his responsibility. It seemed to be a job that ANYBODY could have done, if ANYBODY thought he was supposed to be the one. But since EVERYBODY recognized that ANYBODY could, EVERYBODY took for granted that SOMEBODY would. But NOBODY told ANYBODY that we are aware of, that he would be in charge of seeing it was taken care of. And NOBODY took it on himself to follow through and DO what EVERYBODY thought that SOMEBODY would do. When what EVERYBODY needed so did not get done at all, EVERYBODY was complaining that SOMEBODY dropped the ball. ANYBODY then could see that it was an awful crying shame and EVERYBODY looked around for SOMEBODY to blame. SOMEBODY should have done the job and EVERYBODY would have, but in the end NOBODY did what ANYBODY could have.

Need I say more, when Osgood said it best of all?

INTERNAL MARKETING

Internal marketing is the ongoing commitment and effort of ensuring that your organization is delivering with consistency, dedication, and enthusiasm the highest level of quality and service necessary to achieve the highest level of customer satisfaction. Easy to say, but more difficult to do, you say. Well I say, with the right mind-set, difficulties become less difficult. Regardless of the industry, you will find that internal marketing has two major components: employee satisfaction and customer satisfaction. You will learn more about the employees' satisfaction component in Chapter 9. The focus of this chapter will explore and address patient satisfaction, the core segment of total customer satisfaction in the healthcare industry.

Patient Orientation

The very foundation for achieving patient satisfaction is a patient-friendly environment. However, a patient-friendly environment or oasis does not come with the bricks and mortar. Caring people have to convert the realities of life into the comforts of life. This is accomplished internally, over time, starting at the top and demonstrating its way to the bottom of an organization. Creating such an environment means that all your employees, policies, and procedures are employed from the perspective of the patient and their family members. Internal ease has to give way to your patients' needs, if you want to please. Everything said and done is oriented toward the patient. Just like a house is not a home, a hospital or medical practice is not a patient-friendly environment without considerable effort and commitment by all concerned parties, including the patient. To that end, I have listed what I refer to as the 24 C's of healthcare. A strategical patient orientation means you are addressing and acting on each of the 24 C's from a position that is benefiting your patients. Please note that the 24 C's are in eight strategic groups of related three issues as follows:

Healthcare Providers' Guiding "C"s

1. Capital	7. Costs	13. Computers
2. Course	8. Charges	14. Communications
3. Commitment	9. Collections	15. Continuum
4. Customers	10. Competition	16. Convictions
5. Customs	11. Coalitions	17. Courage
6. Change	12. Capitation	18. Consistency

19. Caring   22. Connections
20. Community   23. Consultants
21. Conscious   24. Congress

Patients Have Needs

You can not do it alone. You need to be encouraging your patients to help you deliver your services to their expectations and beyond. Only through understanding your patients' needs can you successfully and constantly improve the quality and delivery of your services. Your patients have many needs, the exact same needs you expect if you were a patient. The more of your patients' needs you can meet, better yet, exceed, the greater are your chances of delivering Ultimate Patient Satisfaction. The nine most common patient needs are as follows:

1. To receive professional care;
2. To be understood, appreciated, and respected;
3. To be shown empathy;
4. To be kept honestly and well informed;
5. To receive timely and friendly help and assistance;
6. To be physically and mentally comfortable;
7. To be and feel safe and secure from medical harm;
8. To sense a caring staff; and
9. To be treated with dignity.

Keeping PACE

Providing Ultimate Patient Satisfaction is not an event, it is a team event and process. By constantly evaluating how well you and your organization are currently delivering patient satisfaction is a critical fine-tuning step in the process. I call this concept or approach Proactively Analyzing Customer Encounters (PACE). By keeping pace with your patients' needs you stay on track toward reaching Ultimate Patient Satisfaction. Here is how it works. Each manager, employee, and department conducts frequent patient encounter analyses on their own or as a team. An important point to remember is that the level of patient satisfaction is only as high as the lowest delivery value. You are only as strong as the weakest customer service representative link. In other words, all the good being done by one department or individual can quickly be compromised by another department or individual. You have to be proactively reviewing each of the processes you are involved in, are responsible for, and are accountable for from the patient's perspective. This is a very important concept; read it again before going on. Consider the following PACE example for analyzing a typical patient office visit to a cardiologist's office. For brevity, the example has been kept to 29 steps. Take a few moments to review the 29 steps described:

Proactively Analyzing Customer Encounters

1. Patient is contacted;
2. Patient information is collected;
3. Patient provides information;
4. Patient arrives at facility;
5. Patient finds a parking space;
6. Patient arrives at facility entrance;
7. Patient arrives at check-in area;
8. Patient (and escorts) are greeted;
9. Patient information is verified;
10. Patient's medical history is collected;
11. Patient registration is completed;
12. Patient signs consent forms;
13. Patient is waiting;
14. Patient is called;
15. Patient meets staff members;
16. Patient receives instructions and has any question(s) answered;
17. Patient is escorted to examination room;
18. Patient meets the physician(s) and/or the technologist;
19. Patient is taken to procedure room;
20. Procedure is finished;
21. Patient receives post-procedure instructions;
22. Patient receives medication and/or prescription;
23. Patient is escorted to checkout area;

24. Patient's copayment and deductible is reconciled;

25. Patient's follow-up visit is scheduled;

26. Patient is encouraged to ask any last minute questions;

27. Patient is given the option to complete a satisfaction questionnaire;

28. Patient leaves facility; and

29. Patient receives post-visit follow-up call.

You will find using the PACE method easy. Start by listing the patient encounters in sequential order as shown. Next begin dissecting each encounter by analyzing it into finer elements. This is done by asking and answering who, what, when, where, how, and most important, why. Analyzing each encounter enables you to better understand the microdynamics within the total process. Power is knowledge. Once you truly understand the process, the easier it will be to change. As an example, consider the previous PACE patient encounter #13: the patient and possibly an escorting family member is waiting to see the cardiologist. Let the analysis begin.

Patient Encounter #13 . . . Patient waiting:

Who:	The patient and family member
What:	Waiting to see the cardiologist
When:	After completing registration
Where:	Patient reception area
How:	Sitting and watching TV, reading, and talking with an escort
Why:	A patient is scheduled every 15 minutes, though the doctor spends on average 30 minutes with a new patient; waiting is common and expected

You now analyze each of the six elements:

Who:	Our average patient is over the age of 40, male, has healthcare insurance, is well educated, and comes with another person, usually their spouse.
What:	The patient comes to see Dr. Meade, but may also spend time with the lab technologist, sonographer, office nurse, and administrative staff.

When:	Typically the patient may have to wait before registering, before seeing the physician, and before checking out, depending on staff availability, and for any unforseen emergency, though the longest waiting period is to see Dr. Meade, the cardiologist.
Where:	Our patient reception area is clean, in a good state of repair, and spacious enough to accommodate on our busiest days all patients and one guest each, furnishings are comfortable and clean.
How:	The patients have several time-passing choices while waiting, such as current reading material suitable for our patient base, television, radios with headsets, a soothing fish tank, and an appropriate assortment of snacks and beverages.
Why:	Patients are scheduled every 15 minutes to compensate for no-shows and projected revenue goals.

Under the given scenario, to enhance your patient's waiting experience, you might consider:

Who:	Ensure the office decor is reflective of your typical patient profile.
What:	Start building rapport by displaying an introduction photograph of Dr. Meade in the office area, including a small bio, also display photographs of key staff members the patient will most likely meet. Use photographs with smiling faces only, please.
When:	Preregister patients over the telephone before their appointment, prepare checkout documentation in advance, and place a sign reading in effect, "We are all sorry for any inconvenience waiting may have caused you. Please try and be understanding and patient with me and my staff. We are sure you would want us to spend the necessary time with you to ensure your well-being as we are currently doing now with another patient. Your patience is greatly appreciated. Thank you. Dr. Meade."

Where: Let them wait elsewhere by offering a pager to
                notify the patients or their family members that
                the doctor will see them in five minutes.

How: Install a wide screen television, high-end stereo
                system, keep patients and family members
                informed, tell them why they are waiting, how
                long it will be, tell them longer than you expect,
                have staff bringing the patient back to see the
                doctor explain the reason for the delay and
                apologize and also have the doctor apologize.

Why: Start scheduling patients every 20 minutes apart,
                look for ways to speed up mundane and timely
                processes, conduct a time management study, set
                task time standards that do not compromise care.

The preceding example is intended to provide you with a conceptional understanding and the guidance necessary for conducting your own PACE evaluations. Give PACE a try. I know you can do it.

DISSATISFACTION: PATIENT-PULSE POINTS

Any patient encounter, procedure, and area that have the tendency for producing stress, psychological trauma or emotion, problems, pain, or anxiety is a candidate for producing patient and visitor dissatisfaction. You need to start focusing on identifying, analyzing, and enhancing all patient-encounter points, or what I call, dissatisfaction patient-pulse points (DPPP) that possess one or more of the following nine attributes:

1. High volume;
2. High-risk procedure;
3. Procedure associated with probing, sticking, and pain;
4. Prone to long delays and waiting;
5. Multiple and different patient-staff encounters;
6. Senior-citizen patient load;
7. Staff with poor English and communication skills;
8. Treating a chronic medical condition; and
9. Poor outcomes.

Figure 6–1, Patient Encounter Table, provides nine examples of possible areas, procedures, and encounters that are prone to generating patient dissatisfaction. You need to create your organization's own list of dissatisfied patient pulse points.

CULTURAL SENSITIVITY TRAINING

Without the effective use of cultural sensitivity and language, the employee-patient and physician-patient encounters and relationships are seriously impaired and compromised. This is also true regarding visitors. Typically, language differences among employees, physicians, and patients are indicative of cultural differences that can significantly affect medical intervention, care, and outcomes. You will also discover that dealing with upset patients and family members, especially those with cultural and language barriers, is difficult, if at all possible at times. I strongly recommend providing cultural sensitivity training to your employees, physicians, volunteers, or anyone dealing with patients and their visitors. Consider including the following 10 basic elements in your cultural sensitivity training program:

1. Identify cultural and religious differences within your service area;
2. Significant differences that are prone to cause confusion, difficulties, poor communication, and compliance problems;
3. Common medical conditions and treatment practices;
4. Concept of death;
5. Concept of time;
6. Tolerance to pain;
7. Medical language interpretation barriers;

FIGURE 6–1

Patient Encounters

Area	Procedure	Encounter
Emergency department	Receiving an injection	Admissions
Surgery	Lower G.I. study	Discharge planning
Parking	Giving blood	Bodily waste removal

8. Food preferences and dislikes;
9. Self-esteem, pride, and honesty; and
10. Family dynamics and decision making.

INNOVATION

To deliver Ultimate Patient Satisfaction you must become creative, progressive, and proactive. Success in healthcare is born of innovation and initiative, not imitation. Start looking for new ways to do old things. Search for and start using enabling technologies to speed up your processes, increase accuracy, and respond quicker to customer and patients' needs. Three such technologies are wireless communications, interactive-voice-video-response systems, and digital data collection, processing, and management networks. Enabling technology does not have to be state-of-the-art, just enabling. As an example, consider the existing and enabling technology already found in most hospital patient rooms, the television. For the most part, inpatients spend their hospital stay in their room, except for brief catacomb forays to mysterious departments. You know the departments, the boredom busters, rehabilitation, respiratory, radiology, and the laboratory. However, when the patient is in their room, you have a captive audience and a great opportunity to build expectations and educate the patient to the world around them. This holds true for their visitors as well. Many hospitals never use the in-room television to its fullest potential. To help you out, I have listed the following 31, realistic ways you can start using in-room televisions for building great expectations and educating your patients. You may want to consider using your in-room televisions to provide:

1. In-service education regarding self-care, preventive healthcare, and specific procedures;
2. Facility and department tours, narrated by the president, chief executive officer (CEO), or administrator;
3. Introductions to key personnel, such as the floor nurses, resident doctors, administration, and other people they are likely to encounter during their stay;
4. History of organization, hospital, or facility, interesting facts and figures;
5. Explaining major healthcare issues;

6. Explore gift shop, cafeteria, and chapel;
7. Reading the daily meal menu, viewing prepared food items, and even selecting the meal;
8. Provide nutritional information about hospital food;
9. Provide a medical glossary for inquisitive minds;
10. Information about your development fund and how to donate;
11. Recruiting volunteers and auxiliary members;
12. Explain your healthcare delivery system;
13. Mission statement, patient rights, and other informative tidbits;
14. Managed care issues and protocols affecting patient care;
15. Explain the hospital's billing process, give examples, walk the patient through the process;
16. Provide information about the discharge process and social services;
17. Review Medicare and Medicaid guidelines from a beneficiary's viewpoint;
18. Explain the processes for registering a complaint or making a suggestion;
19. Introduce the hospital's medical staff, via picture and short video or bio;
20. Introduce your seniors' program, upcoming events, and special activities;
21. Answers for the most commonly asked patient questions;
22. Show testimonials;
23. Create inter-room activities, such as bingo, video games, and self-purchased movies;
24. Explain medical technology, such as computed tomography (CT) or magnetic resonance imaging (MRI), or show how to do a self-administered breast examination;
25. Tell the patient when to have certain checkups and tests, such as a mammogram, prostate test, or stress test, help the patient or a family member self-refer;
26. Dial a movie like hotels offer their guests;
27. Complete a patient satisfaction survey;

28. Talk to the patient down the hall, or make an IVVR doctor office visit;

29. Access the Internet;

30. Tune into prerecorded spiritual messages, words for the day, or stress release techniques; and

31. Explain that mistakes can and do happen in hospitals, the steps you take to minimize mistakes, and that you will be honest and forthcoming about all mistakes.

You may want to provide, or rent, patients a VCR too so they can watch a free movie from your library, one a visitor brings, or they can rent from the gift shop. The uses are only as limited as our minds. Enabling technology exists today to make all the above possible. So besides using in-room televisions as a means of passive entertainment, start converting those boob tubes into effective entertainment and educational tools. Remember, an educated patient makes everyone's job easier and less stressful.

Focus on Your Delivery System

The secret to differentiating your services from the competition in a me-too provider market is to deliver your services better than the competition. Remember, think retail, not healthcare. Ask yourself how would Nordstrom, Niemann Marcus, or Tiffany deliver your service. As an example, two competing imaging centers have identical MRI units and the images are read by the same radiologist. Imaging center "A" is providing free transportation, while imaging center "B" is not. Which of the two imaging centers is delivering its services better that the other? Focus on your delivery system by thinking retail.

Quality

Quality is a given. Your patients and their family members simply assume that you will and are providing quality care and services. In fact, as a healthcare provider, one has to make a serious effort and go out of their way to deliver an inferior product or service with consistency in today's highly regulated, accredited, and certified industry. To the patient, though, quality is measured in terms of easy access, low out-of-pocket costs, and feeling better. Your patients on average are not medically suave. Most do not understand how the healthcare system works, how the human body works, how medical technology works, and how medical intervention works. However, they will judge you and your performance by what does not work. Patients will judge you for the most part based on their retail experiences. Your patient will be more likely to evaluate you and your services using the same criteria they will judge a restaurant, hotel, and department store by, a retail perspective. All of us know what to expect and demand from a retail establishment. We can all judge the level of service received by a retailer by evaluating the following 16 common denominators:

Parking	Process	Product
Place	Paperwork	Payment
Pleasantries	Price	Problems
Personnel	Proprietor	Prestige

So, when you are trying to deliver patient satisfaction, remember the 16 P's of retail and think retail, not healthcare, and you will have a head jump on the competition.

Patient Parking

As an example from the above list, consider parking. It seems that the simple act of parking one's automobile, that is if you can find a parking space, starts many patients, their family members, and visitors off on the wrong foot when it comes to Ultimate Patient Satisfaction, though many things have been done to improve the parking experience (crisis?): valet parking, shuttle buses, and a front door drop-off area. However, depending where you have to go for medical care, parking issues and problems may still exist, especially at many large healthcare facilities and medical centers. However, even a small office practice can experience parking issues that adversely impact patient satisfaction, often without knowing so because the patient did not want to upset the doctor or office staff. With an Ultimate Patient Satisfaction mind-set, however, you would be pursuing enhancement of your patients' and visitors' parking experience. Here are a few parking enhancement strategies and tactics you may want to consider:

1. Provide free parking;
2. Provide patients with parking discounts;

3. Arrange discounted taxi services for your patients;

4. Ensure your parking areas are well lit, safe, and provide an escort if requested;

5. Provide loaner umbrellas on rainy or inclement days (inexpensive advertising);

6. Increase the number of available spaces by eliminating unnecessarily reserved slots, such as clergy, physician, executives, and employee of the month. Monitor reserved slots and if not used, reduce. For example, 15 physician slots are available, the maximum in use on any given day (peak hours) over a five-day test period was nine, so reduce your number of physician slots to 10, freeing up five parking spaces for patients and visitors;

7. Make the closest parking spaces available for patients and visitors, everyone else can walk, including doctors;

8. Institute cleanup patrols to walk the parking area and pick up and dispose of unsightly trash and debris, patrol first thing in the morning and at lunch;

9. Beautify the parking area with flowers, trees, and shrubs that add cheerful color, convert several, strategically located parking spaces into oases of living color, change with seasons;

10. Install an entrance canopy to provide a sheltered loading and unloading area for patients;

11. Pursue having a city bus stop at your front door or within close proximity; and

12. If you have a multi-level parking deck, consider selling advertising space within the parking deck where national and local businesses can promote their products and services, such as Drink Dr. Pepper. With the extra money you can now afford giveaway umbrellas and free parking. Also consider using your parking deck and elevators as marketing tools for communicating and educating the public about your services.

KICKING CATS

Many years back, I attended a Zig Ziglar self-motivational training program for managers called, "See You at the Top." The program was presented through the Zig Ziglar Corporation. If you are familiar with Zig Ziglar, you will recognize him as a great salesperson, motivational speaker, and mentor. Mr. Ziglar wrote the book, *See You at the Top*, which was used for all practical purposes as the program manual. In the book on page 220, a reference is made to kicking the cat. In essence it means, taking your anger or frustration out on someone else, the symbolic kicking of the hapless cat. Hence, aggressively venting on an innocent party became known as kicking the cat. While pondering over the "kicking the cat" analogy, I was doodling. People who know me know I draw a lot. Drawing conjures forth my creative powers. Anyway, I drew a picture of a stomped cat. If you have never seen a stomped cat, try picturing in your mind a cat that resembles a sway-backed horse. You know, horses with backs that droop in the middle. A stomped cat is just shy of a kicked cat, but it still hurts. Scribbling away, I went on to draw a pile of kicked cats, dead cats really. Then it dawned on me. Kicked cats do not purr. Zig's message was becoming much clearer to me. Not too many of us feel good after being kicked around for something we had no control over. I felt so creative that day that I wrote Zig a letter shortly thereafter, introducing him to "kicked cats don't purr," and sent along a black tee-shirt I designed depicting a pile of kicked dead cats on the back. The cats were pink. One day, late in the afternoon, my secretary ran into my office yelling, "Zig Ziglar is on the phone and wants to speak with you. Quick, pick up the phone," she shouted! Immediately, I figured this was a setup and refused to take the call, though I uneasily eyed the flashing on-hold button. I will show them, I thought. You can not trick the boss. I am too smart, but curiosity killed the cat. After about 15 minutes of downright serious begging on the part of my secretary and the other people who started gathering around my desk, I finally answered the phone. As soon as I heard that deep, commanding, yet friendly signature voice, I knew it was Zig Ziglar. Holy cow, I had Zig Ziglar on hold! Believe it or not, we talked to each other for about 25 minutes. Zig went on to thank me for the "kicked cats don't purr" tee-shirt and wanted to personally visit our hospital. Though we tried, our schedules never permitted us to arrange a mutually convenient meeting; however, in its place, Zig did make a special "See You at the Top" videotape for our management team, in which he was proudly wearing my tee-shirt. I really felt special that day, showing that custom Zig-tape to the hospital's management team. Today I reflect back and realize Mr. Ziglar gave generously of his time, I figure about $10,000 for the phone call and another $30,000 for the tape. Wow, $40,000, you can bet I was purring. However, there is a lesson to learn and remember, just like kicked cats don't purr, kicked patients don't purr neither. Ultimate Patient Satisfaction means never venting your anger or frustrations out on others, especially your patients. Become a cat lover and repeat after me, here kitty-kitty-kitty.

CATS—CUSTOMER ACTION TEAMS

Speaking of cats, you may want to consider creating customer action teams (CATs). It is fun watching them prowling around your delivery system department by department, searching for rats and ratty things that carry the fleas of dissatisfaction to your patients. People start looking scared, scurrying about looking for a hole to hide in. Empower your CATs to do more than just scratch at the surface looking for dissatisfaction's breeding grounds. Your CATs must corner the hosts, pouncing on negative attitudes, poor service, and hassle-riddled processes, ending their plaguing destruction to Ultimate Patient Satisfaction and the organization.

HEALTHCARE PROFESSIONALS AND SMOKING

What do you think the message is that you are communicating when patients and their companions witness your employees smoking? Smoking healthcare providers is a real but deadly oxymoron. Healthcare personnel that smoke, especially physicians, are sending the wrong message to your patients, visitors, and children. Can you trust a healthcare professional that smokes to tell you how to live a healthy life? Smokers have a right to smoke, but not to subject others to the health hazards and offensive side-effects of secondhand smoke. Instead of congregating about and hogging the front, side, and back entrances to your facility, your smokers need to smoke in highly restrictive and secluded areas that isolate them from your patients' eyes (seeing an unhealthy habit in a healthcare facility), their ears (hearing hacking sounds), and their nose (smelling the offensive tell-tale odor on clothing and breath). As healthcare providers, we owe it to the communities we serve to demonstrate healthy lifestyles. What message are you sending to the countless children visiting your facility, seeing doctors, nurses, and other healthcare professionals smoking? It is simple, the wrong message! Smoking in and around a hospital, medical building, or private practice is just as wrong as smoking in and around our childrens' schools, sporting events, and playgrounds. You will see the day when employees who want, and continue to smoke, will be paying a higher share of their healthcare benefits package. Less than 30% of the population smoke and use tobacco products, yet smoking is the leading cause of heart attacks, strokes, and respiratory problems that cost hundreds of billions of dollars in medical intervention annually. The smoking message we send as healthcare professionals today will either plague or help cure tomorrow's healthcare.

"Empowered and entrusted employees excell"
John F. O'Malley

CHAPTER

Finding Time for Patients

It's always the right time
to help a patient . . .

One common complaint I hear all too frequently is, we do not have enough time. Well, that is what patient satisfaction is all about, having time to properly serve and care for your patients. Time is everything to patients and fundamental to their care. Patients want to know how long they have to wait, when will they see the doctor, how long the surgery will take, when will they leave the hospital, when to take their medication, when is their next appointment, and when will they get better. Ultimate Patient Satisfaction takes time, time for creating benchmark patient services, time for enhancing patient encounters, and time for evaluating and improving those encounters. Running out of time is no excuse for not having time. Besides, one never runs out of time. We run out of available time. Most of us find ourselves spending time losing time. Instead, you need to start managing your time better so you have more time available to complete time-consuming tasks in a timely fashion. So remember, it takes time to make quality time. You may even have to start taking timeouts for making more available quality time. It is time to get you more time so you can finish reading this timely book.

TIME MANAGEMENT IS SELF-MANAGEMENT

Managing one's time is really self-managing one's activity. In a busy, often stressful healthcare environment, time can seem like a luxury and is usually reserved for people with nothing to do. However, this chapter will show you how to capture more quality time out of those endlessly short days. The best way to start is to evaluate your self-management skills. You will find that the following self-evaluation uses 12 questions that will help in determining your skills. To get an honest insight into your self-management skills, you have to be honest, so tell the truth and shame the devil.

Self-Management Evaluation

To each of the following self-management declarations, select and check the most appropriate of the four given responses that best characterizes your self-management style:

1. I write down my goals, tasks, and deadlines.

   ❐ rarely   ❐ sometimes   ❐ often   ❐ almost always

2. Each workday I set aside a block of time for preparations and planning.

   ❐ rarely   ❐ sometimes   ❐ often   ❐ almost always

3. Each workday I delegate everything that can be delegated.

   ❐ rarely   ❐ sometimes   ❐ often   ❐ almost always

4. I work on each document received only once and thoroughly.

   ❐ rarely   ❐ sometimes   ❐ often   ❐ almost always

5. Each workday I establish a prioritized list of tasks and activities to be completed.

   ❐ rarely   ❐ sometimes   ❐ often   ❐ almost always

6. I work my prioritized list, starting with the top priority task first.

   ❐ rarely   ❐ sometimes   ❐ often   ❐ almost always

7. I arrange my workload and activities so that I can concentrate on a few key issues or matters.

   ❑ rarely   ❑ sometimes   ❑ often   ❑ almost always

8. I schedule flexible "windows-of-response" to address sudden issues or important matters.

   ❑ rarely   ❑ sometimes   ❑ often   ❑ almost always

9. I try to schedule my daily workload according to my most productive performance periods.

   ❑ rarely   ❑ sometimes   ❑ often   ❑ almost always

10. Each workday I take actions to minimize unnecessary interruptions, such as: telephone calls, appointment-less visitors, and unscheduled meetings.

    ❑ rarely   ❑ sometimes   ❑ often   ❑ almost always

11. I can say "no" if others want to wastefully consume my time, when more important things need my attention.

    ❑ rarely   ❑ sometimes   ❑ often   ❑ almost always

12. Each workday I take planned breaks.

    ❑ rarely   ❑ sometimes   ❑ often   ❑ almost always

Self-Management Evaluation Analysis

To determine your total score, assign the response value shown to your selected responses and add the values together.

(0) rarely   (1) sometimes   (2) often   (3) almost always

Your total score is suggestive of your self-management skills. Locate your total score below:

36-32 Congratulations! You are a self-management superstar. Actively share your knowledge and expertise in self-management with others, especially those individuals with scores below 26.

31-26 Good work. Your self-management style is commendable. With a little extra effort you can improve your time management skills and move up to the next level, superstar.

25-19 It is apparent you are making an effort to gain control of your time. However, because you lack any consistency, your overall success will be marginal. Focus on habitual consistency if you want to experience a significant improvement.

18-0 You are not planning your time effectively. There are too many distractions in your workday, and you are letting yourself be too influenced by others. Major opportunity for improvement does exist, so take a timeout and figure out how you are wasting time.

Self-Management Control

There are four basic areas (Table 7–1) you need to start focusing on if you want to gain and maintain the highest level of self-management. The four areas of self-management control are determining, optimizing, planning, and eliminating (DOPE). You can quickly become smarter at managing your time by using the DOPE self-management technique immediately. You would be a dope if you did not.

TABLE 7–1

Self-Management Control Techniques

Determining	Optimizing	Planning	Eliminating
Determine your goals.	Make optimum use of your peak performance periods.	Schedule the use of your time on a daily, weekly, and monthly basis.	Abrogate and delegate as much as possible.
Establish related responsibilities, priorities, and objectives.	Use enabling technology, such as wireless communications.	Be flexible, include "windows-of-response" time.	Avoid unnecessary and inappropriate people and activities. Just say NO!

Self-Management Tips

You can start using the following (Table 7–2) self-management time wasters and saver's tips to immediately take control of your time, your career, and the people and things around you.

Improving Your Self-Management by Analyzing Your Actions

To help you better understand your self-management and time utilization and make timesaving improvements, collecting and analyzing specific data and information is crucial. However, you must be honest and

TABLE 7–2

Self-Management Tips

Time Wasters		Time Savers	
Controllable	**Uncontrolled**	**Habits**	**Technology**
Being disorganized, unfocused, forgetful and unprepared	Unscheduled waiting for people, staff, and boss	Learn to skim read, throw out or recycle files, documents, and reports	Pager Voice mail E-Mail
Procrastination, minimal delegation	Trash mail, E-mail, S-mail, no mail	Decide immediately, handle documents only once, twice at most	Car telephone Cellular telephone Wireless
Self-assertiveness, do not passively accept a non-realistic deadline	Non-productive meetings, scheduled or otherwise	Place like things together, files, supplies, and tools	Facsimile machine Answering machine Copier
Gossip, accommodate, and pass on negative office talk	Work environment and associates	The more frequently used, the closer, the better	Laptop computer Optical scanner Color laser printer
An attitude that is negative, defeatist, and distracting to others	Unscheduled events, encounters, visitors, and vendors	Use a calendar, make lists, prioritize tasks, and follow through	Calculator Tape recorder

commit the time required for conducting your personal self-management analysis to reap the benefits of more quality time. Like anything and everything you do, you only get out of it what you put into it. If you make an honest effort, I guarantee you will have more quality time on your hands, enough maybe to even call me and thank me. And keep in mind this is a private analysis; only you have access to the recorded data. So without wasting any more time, here is my nine-step approach:

1. Select a week where there are no planned major interruptions, such as holidays, vacations, seminars, training, and major scheduled meetings.

TABLE 7-2

Self-Management Tips—cont'd.

Time Wasters		Time Savers	
Controllable	Uncontrolled	Habits	Technology
Perfectionism beyond necessity, complexity	Telephone interruptions	Set goals, plan, and complete each project, task, and assignment	Digital data collecting, analyzing, and management software
Work station clutter, a "Thank God" filing system	Organizational clutter, restrictive policies, and archaic procedures	Take action, monitor results, and revise. Followup quickly	Answering service Information service
Lack of self-confidence and esteem	Crisis intervention, internal and external troubleshooting	Keep it simple, organized, and updated, break up large projects into smaller tasks	Electronic card file Electronic calendar
Unorganized vehicle storage area	Dependent peers, associates, and staff	Pick up your work area at day's end	Internet Intranet
Knowingly wasting time and taking unnecessary time off	Lack of customer service orientation	Hire and fire attitude, train your people well, and delegate often	Teleconferencing Video-conferencing Telephone speaker

2. Using your Daily Time Analysis Log (Figure 7–1) record each of your daily activities. Record your activities every 30 minutes. Detail is important, so be as specific as possible.

3. Take the time to include an insightful comment about each activity, such as any duration, distractions, difficulties, persons, location, waiting, and anything else that will help you analyze the data later.

4. Determine and record the type of workday you experienced. Was your day a typical day, slower than usual, or busier than usual?

5. At day's end, review the log and group your recorded activities into categories. Some category examples are internal and external meetings, telephoning, driving, a specific project, planning, preparations, coaching, administrative, mail, customer service, vendors, or troubleshooting. I think shooting-the-bull was left out. The provided Activity Category Log (Figure 7–2) will help you categorize your activities.

6. Using the Activity Category Log, record your daily hours under the appropriate day and category. Total the hours per day and week, and calculate each activity category's total hours as a percent of total hours for the week.

7. Now analyze your Activity Category Log to determine where you are not maximizing your time. List the categories, actions, or persons wasting your valuable time.

8. Next create a self-improvement action plan (Figures 7–3, 7–4, and 7–5, and set self-management improvement opportunities for yourself based on your activity analysis. Pick a maximum of three categories to improve in, set your goals, and work at it, and before you know it you will have more quality time.

9. Periodically, check the progress you are making in achieving your self-management improvement goals; in 90 days or so, conduct another activity analysis. Remain committed, self-improvement is an endless task for people who want to do their best.

FIGURE 7-1

Daily Time Analysis Log   Date:

Weekday: ❑ M ❑ T ❑ W ❑ T ❑ F Day Type: ❑ Slow ❑ Typical ❑ Busy		
Time	**Activity**	**Comments**
06:30 a.m.		
07:00		
07:30		
08:00		
08:30		
09:00		
09:30		
10:00		
10:30		
11:00		
11:30		
12:00 Noon		
12:30 p.m.		
01:00		
01:30		
02:00		
02:30		
03:00		
03:30		
04:00		
04:30		
05:00		
05:30		
06:00 p.m.		

FIGURE 7-2

Activity Category Log   Week of:

Category	M	T	W	T	F	Total	%	Analysis Comments
			Hours					
Internal meetings								
External meetings								
Planning								
Preparation								
Telephoning								
Customer service								
Crisis management								
Coaching								
Project A								
Project B								
Project C								
Driving								
Waiting								
Administrative								
Mail								
Correspondence								
Lunch								
Interruptions								
Person A								
Person B								
Totals								

Self-Management Self-Analysis

Once you have finished completing your Daily Time Analysis Logs and converting the data to your Activity Category Log, the next step is to spend some quality time evaluating the information and determining the following:

1. Which part of each workday was the most productive?
2. Which part of each workday was the least productive?

FIGURE 7-3

Self-Management Improvement Opportunities

#	Personal Opportunity	Time Saved per Week	Date to be Accomplished
1			
2			
3			

FIGURE 7-4

Self-Management Improvement Opportunities

#	Personal Opportunity	E	D	R	Action Plan
1					
2					
3					

3. Which part of the week was the most productive?

4. Which part of the week was the least productive?

5. What activity categories appear to be most self-management efficient?

6. What activity categories appear to be wasting valuable self-management time?

7. What did you do that you wished you had not done?

8. What activity categories do you think can be improved? Prioritize activity categories.

9. Which of the week's activities did not contribute to you achieving any one of your goals?

10. What part of your work time is productive, per day and week?

11. What activities did you enjoy the most? Prioritize activities.

12. What activities did you enjoy the least? Prioritize activities.

13. Were you truly honest with yourself in recording daily activities?

F I G U R E 7 – 5

Taskmaster Log

#	Task	P	Deadline	Time	Delegated to	Date Completed	Comments
1							
2							
3							
4							
5							
6							
7							
8							
9							
10							
11							
12							
13							
14							
15							

P = Priority ranking.

Self-Management Improvement Plan

Now that you have determined self-management time wasters and identified areas for saving time, the next step is to develop a self-improvement action plan. The following process is easy:

1. Determine your self-management improvement opportunities. Be specific in describing the opportunity. Identify and prioritize no more than three activity categories. Now, estimate the time you will save per week, and when the improvement will be accomplished.

2. Determine which personal opportunities can be eliminated, delegated, or reduced. Here is your opportunity to save time by getting rid of an opportunity.

3. Create a personal self-management improvement action plan that includes at minimum the following: objectives, starting dates, action steps required, additional people involved, and a completion date. Refer to Chapter 10 on goal setting.

4. Execute your action plan and track your progress. Reevaluate your progress by repeating the self-management analysis again. Compare results and conclusions.

Task Management

One of the secrets to self-management is to keep and work a task management log. A sample task management log is provided for your convenience (Figure 7–5). A task management log is more than a list of things to do. It helps you stay focused on important tasks. In the event you are interested in automating the task management process, try one of the numerous software programs on the market. To become more organized, you can start using a task management log like the sample provided or of your own design.

Peak Performance Cycle

How often have you heard someone say, I am a morning person? They are at their best in the morning. We all have one or more daily peak performance periods during our day. During the day, the degree by which your performance proficiency rises and falls determines (Figure 7–6) your peak performance cycle. You need to determine

FIGURE 7-6

Peak Performance Cycle

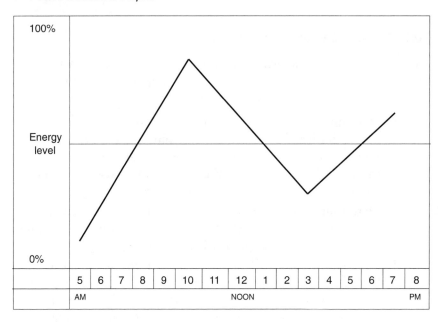

FIGURE 7-7

Peak Performance Cycle

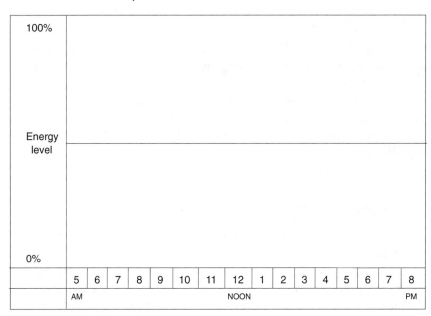

FIGURE 7 – 8

Prioritizing Self-Management Activities

Rating	Pressing	Non-Pressing
Important	Patient satisfaction, deadline-driven tasks, internal and external strategic crises, developing routine systems and procedures, personnel problems, and personal well-being.	Maintenance activities, planning special events, preventive tasks, training, relationship building, goal setting, networking, and market research.
Non-important	Some people, calls, meetings, mail, reports, projects, developing contingency plans, and administrative activities.	Administrative duties, mail, meetings, interruptions, phone calls, and special activities.

your peak performance cycle and identify your peak performance periods. Organize your workday so those tasks and activities requiring maximum concentration, effort, and creativity are scheduled during one or more of your peak performance periods. Use Figure 7–7, Peak Performance Cycle Graph, to plot your hourly energy level. It is simple, but effective in helping self-manage your time and energy.

Self-Management Means Prioritizing Activities

You can better self-manage yourself by prioritizing your time and activities. Figure 7–8, Prioritizing Self-Management Activities Table provides examples of some common activities and tasks within a typical priority rating matrix to help you prioritize your time. Start using the priority matrix as a guide or create your own; you now have the time.

8

CHAPTER

Patient Personality Types

Patients come in all shapes, sizes, and types . . .

When caregivers are encountering and dealing with patients, personality comes into play, both theirs and yours. Knowing how to read a patient's personality can often be one of your greatest interpersonal communication tools in developing rapport and resolve issues. Much has been written on the subject of personality typing, and most experts routinely place human personalities into four major groups. And as you might expect, each expert coined their own personality group names. I am no expert, yet, since I teach personality selling to salespeople, I also developed my own group's names. My own classifications are bolded in Figure 8–1. However, I used Carl Gustav Jung's (1875-1961) conceptional theory as my core classification because of his scientific reputation and a theory that a rose by any color is still a rose.

To my way of thinking, as you could probably have guessed by now, most patients' personalities fall within four major groups or types. It has been found by researchers that each of us has various personality characteristics formed by our past experiences. By placing these common or basic characteristics into distinctive groupings, researchers discovered that four personality types emerged. Understanding these characteristics will enable you to better personality type your patients and their family members. Once a patient's personality type is known, you can improve your communicating effectiveness.

FIGURE 8-1

Patient Personality Types

Explorer	Connecter	Gatekeeper	Organizer
Intuitor	Feeler	Pragmatic	Analytical
Extrovert	Amiable	Sincere	Thinker
Bold	Friendly	Sensor	Competent

Knowing the patient's personality enables you to start adjusting your communications style, your encounter interactions, and your approach to problem solving accordingly for achieving desired results and maximizing patient satisfaction. Before going any further, you can discover your own personality type by completing the following self-analysis. This is not a test. Take your time and read all the characteristics before making your choices.

PERSONALITY SELF-ANALYSIS

To determine your personality type, check 20 of the 72 characteristics in Table 8–1 that you feel BEST describes you as a person. Do not rush, take your time, be honest, and think about your choices. Remember, you are only permitted 20 characteristics out of the 72 listed.

Once you have made your 20 choices, find and mark each on Figure 8–2, Personality Group Characteristics Table. After finding and marking all your 20 characteristics, count the checkmarks up in each column. The column with the most checkmarks suggests your most dominant personality type. Your overall personality might consist of more than one group; however, most people will be in a dominating group. An interesting and often more revealing approach is to have several of your coworkers select 20 characteristics from the list that they think best describe you. Now compare results. Surprise!

Personality-Defining Characteristics

You will be happy to learn there is no right or wrong personality group, let alone a set of characteristics or traits. As you can see, each of the four personality groups has what most of us would consider

TABLE 8–1

Personality Self-Analysis

❏ Pioneer	❏ Trusting	❏ Service-oriented
❏ Initiator	❏ Enthusiastic	❏ Long fuse
❏ Outspoken	❏ Persuasive	❏ Compromiser
❏ Short fuse	❏ Likes attention	❏ Consistent
❏ Likes measurements	❏ Good first impression	❏ Stable
❏ Self-sufficient	❏ Articulate	❏ Problem solver
❏ Strong ego	❏ Seeks variety	❏ Pragmatic
❏ Seeks responsibility	❏ Spontaneous	❏ Assertive
❏ Apathetic	❏ Empathetic	❏ Very decisive
❏ High energy	❏ Traditional values	❏ Impatient
❏ Creative	❏ Impulsive	❏ Present orientation
❏ Charismatic	❏ Past orientation	❏ Looks for change
❏ Future orientation	❏ Resists Change	❏ Perfection seeking
❏ Forces change	❏ Manipulative	❏ Technically skillful
❏ Abstract thinker	❏ Sentimental	❏ Not long-range visionary
❏ Poor listener	❏ Stirs up conflict	❏ Status seeking
❏ Dogmatic	❏ Subjective	❏ Neat
❏ Knowledgeable	❏ Systematic	❏ Humble
❏ Extrovert	❏ Methodical	❏ Sensitive
❏ Apprehensive	❏ Past, present, and future	❏ Reserved
❏ Likes structure	❏ Resists change	❏ Unemotional
❏ Looks for backing	❏ Rational	❏ Prudent
❏ Suspicious	❏ Analytical	❏ Highly organized
❏ Verbose	❏ Objective	❏ Conservative dresser

both good and bad traits. While most of us will have traits in more than one group, the majority of our characteristics will usually fall within one of the four primary groups, suggesting our personality type.

Personality Perception and Differentiating

Studying the personality guide (Figure 8–3) will give you valuable insight, making it easier for you to distinguish among the four patient personality groups or types by understanding their style, their orientation, their strengths and weaknesses, and their needs.

FIGURE 8-2

Personality Group Characteristics

Explorer	Connecter	Gatekeeper	Organizer
Pioneer	Extrovert	Tradition prevails	Neat
Initiator	Trusting	Methodical	Humble
Outspoken	Enthusiastic	Service-oriented	Sensitive
Short fuse	Persuasive	Long fuse	Apprehensive
Likes measurements	Likes attention	Compromiser	Likes structure
Self-sufficient	Good first impression	Consistent	Looks for backing
Strong ego	Articulate	Stable	Suspicious
Seeks responsibility	Seeks variety	Problem solver	Reserved
Apathetic	Spontaneous	Pragmatic	Unemotional
High energy	Empathetic	Assertive	Prudent
Creative	Traditional values	Very decisive	Highly organized
Charismatic	Impulsive	Impatient	Conservative dresser
Future orientation	Past orientation	Present orientation	Past, present, and future
Forces change	Resists change	Resists change	Open to change
Abstract thinker	Manipulative	Perfection seeking	Rational
Poor listener	Sentimental	Technically skillful	Analytical
Dogmatic	Stirs up conflict	Not long-range visionary	Objective
Knowledgeable	Subjective	Status seeking	Verbose

Keep in mind that the four personality groups presented herein are just as effective in determining and differentiating the personality types of other people you come in contact with, such as your supervisor, significant other, friends, and coworkers. And what holds true for the patient is also valid for the other people in your life, both internal and external to your organization.

Environmental Personality Secrets

By studying a person's surroundings, environment, or space, you will be gaining insight into their personality type. The following

FIGURE 8–3

Personality Guide

Style	Orientation	Strengths	Weaknesses	Needs
Explorer Valiant, Bottom Line, Straight Forward	Action Results Challenges	Goal achieving Problem solving Decision making	Finds fault Lacks caution Overruns people	Status Control Authority
Connecter Amicable, Friendly, Gregarious	People Networking Relationships	Participating Finds good Communi- cating	Time control Follow- through Lacks objectivity	To talk Acceptance Recognition
Gatekeeper Genuine, Sincere, Down-to-Earth	Team Department Organization	Loyalty Listening Patience	Overly possessive Avoids risk taking Avoids conflict	Time Security Appreciation
Organizer Efficient, Thinker, Competent	Detail Quality Systems	Analyzing Accuracy High standards	Rigid Procrastinates Overly critical	Facts Time Precision work

Personality Environment and World Table (Figure 8–4) will help you better understand specific characteristics about a given personality group's dress, working area, and the world they live in. This information can be very helpful in further determining a person's personality type.

Personality Emotional and Assertive

Personality types also have an emotional and assertive side. Explorers and connecters are highly emotional, while on the other hand, gatekeepers and organizers are highly assertive (Figure 8–5). Explorers interface well with organizers, connecters with gatekeepers.

FIGURE 8–4

Personality Environment and World

Type	Attire	Work Surface	Work Area	World
Explorer	Mod or rumpled, sometimes colorful	Reference and theory books, semi-neat	Abstract art, book cases, planning charts, and trend graphs	Future
Connecter	Dress less formal, current, trendy, cheerful colors	Family pictures, mementos, almost cluttered	Warm, inviting, personal recognitions, scenic pictures, antiques	Past
Gatekeeper	Dress less formal, more functional work clothes, short sleeve shirts, loose tie, no jacket or suit outfits, drab	Messy, unkept, find it if you can stacks	Business-related pictures of plant and products, piles of papers and magazines, action and sports pictures	Present and past
Organizer	Well groomed, neat, conservative	Neat, everything in its place	Organized, a computer, calculator	Past, present, and future

FIGURE 8–5

Emotional and Assertive

	Highly Emotional	
EXPLORER		CONNECTOR
GATEKEEPER		**ORGANIZER**
	Highly Assertive	

FIGURE 8-6

Customizing Patient Communications

Type	Approach Style
Explorer	Be direct, concise, innovative, concentrate on what, get to the point, fast pace, but allow ample time, concepts, futuristic thinking, quick decision makers
Gatekeeper	Earn trust, go slow but be brief, verbal communications, visual aids well received, reassuring presentation and demeanor, answer all questions, formal, fast decisions
Connecter	Socialize, small talk, personal presentation, new things, spare details, follow-up, slow pace, impact on people, conduct business off-site, no high pressure tactics, slow decisions
Organizer	Stress evidence, testimonials, proof, supporting data, facts, focus on how, structured presentation, logic, systematic inquiries, no loose ends, provide time to think it over, slowest decision makers

FIGURE 8-7

Personality to Personality Dealings

Type	Explorer	Gatekeeper	Connecter	Organizer
Explorer	**Be you, concentrate on listening**	Easy does it, no high pressure	Socialize, be empathetic	Provide data, facts, and proof
Connecter	Stay focused, display self-confidence	**Remain formal, reassuring and knowledgeable**	Socialize, conduct meeting in neutral but inviting friendly place	Show data, facts, and proof
Gatekeeper	Limit small talk, get to the point, by dynamic	Build trust, talk organizations, do not waste time	**Remember your purpose, ask for their opinion**	Emphasize evidence, use testimonials, visual aids
Organizer	Be direct and confident, use abstract examples	Do not rush the process, show your appreciation	Do not become bogged down in detail, exhibit friendliness and caring	**Discuss details, use facts, charts, evidence, and graphs**

Customizing Patient Communications

You will find that communicating effectively with patients becomes much easier when you know the personality you are dealing with and customize your approach accordingly. When communicating with a patient, try using the appropriate personality approach style as indicated in Figure 8–6, Customizing Patient Communications Table. The right approach is especially effective when providing training, education, and instructions to the patient.

Dealing With Different Personalities

When you are dealing with a patient, you are also dealing with their personality. Be careful, your personality may be just the opposite of theirs, making communications difficult unless you know your personality can best deal with another personality. Figure 8–7, Personality to Personality Dealing cross-reference will help you master the dealing with the four different personality types.

> "You can tell the character of the person by the choice made under pressure."
>
> *Churchhill*

9

Creating Patient Satisfaction Teams

One for all, and all for the patient . . .

Within any healthcare organization you can find incidents of great customer service being delivered. You will also discover in time that great episodic service is inadequate at propelling your organization into the competitive realm of Ultimate Patient Satisfaction. I refer to episodic service as "oops-service," oops, we are sorry. The patient experienced you at your best. Enjoy it as best you can, for tomorrow is another day and great patient satisfaction may not happen again in your lifetime. Patient satisfaction is not an "oops" event, but an "ah" process. Ultimate Patient Satisfaction is a delivery process dovetailed together by a system-wide matrix of interlocking patient encounters and positive experiences. Contrary to episodic encounters, delivering Ultimate Patient Satisfaction consistently is a team effort, a system-wide undertaking. In healthcare organizations where only a few managers and employees are self-motivated in having a patient and service orientation, customer satisfaction will be spotty, and at best, superficial in nature. While most healthcare professional and support people take pride in delivering patient care and have the "golden rule" attitude toward service, there are always individuals and coworkers who are lacking this personal dedication and special feeling. The bad apples in the barrel of patient satisfaction. In time, you will realize that patient satisfaction is too important to be left to a few determined individuals and a few bad apples. When you are serious about patient satisfaction, it becomes a team event, an organizational commitment. So what can you do? You can start thinking like a patient, doing so from a team's perspective. You can start delivering service as a team, a well-disciplined team of dedicated, caring, and empowered individuals. One for all, and all for the patient!

TEAMS

There are no hard set rules for building Ultimate Patient Satisfaction teams. Dozens of team dynamic books are available to the inquisitive. A team, however, is usually two or more people who perform a specific function or group of tasks with one end goal in mind. Each team member has individual responsibilities for achieving interdependent objectives based on the team's goals. Regardless of the team's size, a small two-person, a large department size, or the ultimate maxi-team, the organization itself, each team member must be performing for the betterment of the team and its individual members. Ideally, the team is the organization. In their truest form, teams are a well-knitted society of sharers, wherein its members openly share the team's successes and failures together. Individualism is a way of life for individualistic individuals. Teams need individuals, but not individualism. You will also find that teams function as an instrument for participation learning, the supportive environment for unleashing one's individual abilities and skills. A team also takes on a dynamic culture and life of its own, not that of its leader.

ULTIMATE PATIENT SATISFACTION TEAMS

Ultimate Patient Satisfaction (UPS) teams are charged with listening, observing, collecting, analyzing, and using customer service, patient satisfaction, and related information such as clinical outcome, financial, and operational data in creating a patient satisfaction action plan for their assigned areas. A healthcare facility or organization may have one or more UPS teams depending on its internal structure and needs. When there is more than one UPS team, special arrangements are necessary to ensure multi-path communications among the various teams' members working toward a common primary goal in concert.

In the example in Figure 9–1, the organization has four UPS teams, one primary and three secondary teams. Team leaders from the secondary teams are members of the primary team. The B-Team has six members, each having direct, open, and free communications with each other. A hospital typically has multiple UPS teams, while a solo practice may have only one UPS team. Your UPS team(s) should meet formally on a predetermined basis as needed to review its performance, to evaluate its progress, and to make any adjustments necessary to achieve its assigned objectives and goals. When the time comes to create or lead a UPS team, will you be prepared with the necessary mind-set and skills? Does your management style support group or team dynamics? Let us find out.

FIGURE 9–1

UPS Team Structure

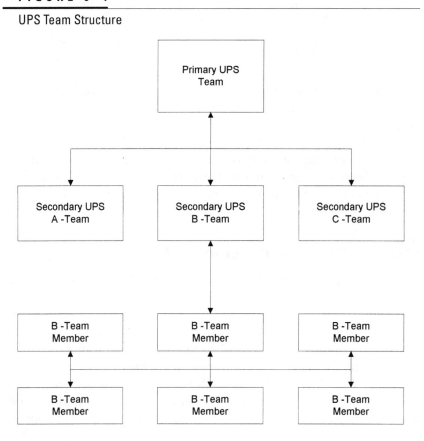

Management Style Self-Analysis

A short self-analysis questionnaire is provided to help you in determining your aptitude for managing an UPS team. You begin the self-analyst, by comparing the group and team numbered orientation statements, and checking the statement that best reflects your current approach to managing people. Be honest with yourself. Only you will see the results and benefit from the self-analysis. Determining your management style or orientation is very important to leading an UPS team.

Once you have completed your self-analysis (Figure 9–2) total the number of checkmarks in each orientation column. The column with the most checkmarks suggests your orientation. If your current management style favors a team orientation, your chances for succeeding are greater than a team leader having a group orientation. In the event your self-analysis suggests you have a group orientation, do not despair. You will find that changing your management style from a group to a team orientation is not difficult, especially if you are committed to do so, to adhere to the principles presented in this chapter, and to put forth the required effort.

Team Type Analogies

As mentioned earlier, many books have been written on the subject of teams and their dynamics, even books on why teams fail. Anyway, the team concept is not new to healthcare. We had teams before teams became buzzwords and fashionable. Our industry is full of teams, large and small, effective and ineffective, medical and nonmedical, and various combinations thereof. However, what is important is determining the type of team and team behavior best suited for achieving Ultimate Patient Satisfaction. To help you in making that determination, I will be using several sports' team analogies to facilitate conceptual understanding. Close your eyes for a minute. Now, envision your favorite professional sports team playing their arch rival. Can you see the players interacting with each other during the game? You may have to pretend the players are not on strike. Striking team possibilities brings to mind an interesting healthcare provider situation. What if all physicians went on strike? What would happen to the many healthcare teams or current delivery system as we know it? Who would be

FIGURE 9-2

Management Style Self-Analysis

Group Orientation	Team Orientation	
1 ☐ Overriding concern to meet current goals inhibits thought about what might be accomplished through reorganizing to enhance people contributions.	Current goals are taken in perspective. Can be a visionary about what people can achieve as a team. Can share vision and act accordingly. Can steer or row the boat.	1 ☐
2 ☐ Reactive to upper management, peers and employees. Find it easier to go along with the crowd. Tries hard not to rock the boat.	Proactive in most relationships. Exhibits personal style. Can stimulate excitement and action. Inspires teamwork and mutual team member support.	2 ☐
3 ☐ Willing to involve people in planning and problem solving to some extent, but not without controlled limits.	Can get people involved and committed. Makes it easy for people to see opportunities for teamwork. Can step back and allow people to perform.	3 ☐
4 ☐ Resents or distrusts people who know their jobs better than the manager.	Looks for people who want to excel and can work constructively with others. Feels their role is to encourage and facilitate this cooperative behavior.	4 ☐
5 ☐ Sees group problem solving as a waste of time or a surrender of managerial responsibility and eroding power.	Considers problem solving a joint venture and the empowerment of team's responsibility.	5 ☐
6 ☐ Controls information and communicates only what you feel people need or want to know.	Communicates fully and openly. Welcomes questions. Allows team members to do their own filtering.	6 ☐
7 ☐ Ignores conflict between coworkers, team members, management, and others.	Mediates conflict before it becomes destructive to individuals, organization, and achieving team goals.	7 ☐
8 ☐ Sometimes slow to recognize individual or overall team achievements.	Makes an effort to see that both individual and team accomplishments are recognized at the right time in an appropriate manner.	8 ☐
9 ☐ Sometimes revises team agreement to suit personal convenience or agenda.	Keeps commitments to team members and others and expects the same in return.	9 ☐

permitted, if at all, to practice medicine under our existing laws? Would the practice of medicine become more of a corporate undertaking, if it has not already happened, or possibly yet, by group consensus? If the latter are true, managed care will really be taking on a new meaning, team care. Imagine, if you will, the day when all doctors will be required by law to apply for a medical team license before practicing medicine. The medical team license is used to certify that doctors and their practice staff meet minimal education and competency levels and qualify to practice medicine as a team. Do not laugh it off as science fiction. In time, fiction often becomes reality. Why not eliminate individual state medical licensing and replace the same with one federal program? I think there are more pros than cons to pursuing such a national medical licensing system. Hopefully the doctor team practice detour did not derail your train of thought. Upon closer analysis there is a strong analogy that can be drawn between playing certain sports and delivering healthcare. Several types of sports teams, specifically, football, baseball, soccer, and tennis closely emulate many of healthcare's teams. You will find that Figure 9–3, Sports Team Analogy Table identifies the dynamics and similarities between healthcare and sports teams.

To me, of the four sports teams, tennis-doubles best reflects the team dynamics necessary to deliver Ultimate Patient Satisfaction. When playing tennis-doubles, each player knows their own skill level of play and court responsibilities. Each also knows the strengths and weaknesses of their partner's game. In the event the ball is played to your partner's side of the court, and for whatever reason your partner is out of position to return play, would you stand by and watch the ball blur by? Or would you make your best effort to quickly position yourself to return the ball from your partner's side of the court and quickly return to your area of responsibility? The latter, of course, if you want to win more tennis-doubles games than lose. You are responding to your partner's need without being asked, that is the true secret to team success. You are helping without being asked, because you are more caring about the team, not just how well you are playing on your side of the court. To win, you have to care how well the team plays on the court, period. Your success is to ensure all team members (players) are self-empowered to quickly respond to the situation at hand and feel comfortable in giving a helping hand without being asked or told. Team members, when their whole being is for the

FIGURE 9-3

Sports Team Analogy

Sport	Team Dynamics	Resulting Behavior	Healthcare
Football	Micro teams within the team, each member has a fixed position, limited backup, a specific role to execute in support of another, performance is dependent on other members' support, creates superstars who usually receive all the credit.	Focuses on the performance of a few individuals. A few carry the team. Coach makes most of the decisions.	Doctor's office, group practices, independents, university medical centers
Baseball	Each member has a fixed position, limited backup, becomes involved as needed, performance not usually dependent on other members, players seldom help each other out. Mostly reactive in nature.	Great at repetitive tasks, the focus is on individual performance, perform as a loose team. Slow to respond.	Typical hospital, departments, clinics, radiologists
Soccer	Each member has a fixed, yet flexible position, there is backup, each player becomes involved and directs play as needed, scoring is usually dependent on assistance from other members, players try to help each other out.	Great responsive speed, individuals move and work as a team, any member can direct play, empowered, quick to change strategies on the move.	Surgical team, emergency departments, radiologic technologists
Tennis (Doubles)	Small number, quick, preferred position, yet very flexible, quick to backup teammate without being asked, requires great self-discipline from each member.	Responsive decision making, team members compensate for each other's strengths and weaknesses. Fast and focused.	Emergency department, EMT, code blue team, UPS team

betterment of the team effort, that is team play. When was the last time you helped a coworker or a patient without being asked or told? Did you have to give it some thought? If you did have to think about it, think about this. In providing Ultimate Patient Satisfaction, there are no timeouts, the game goes on. Your UPS team players have to be in shape physically and mentally to deliver Ultimate Patient Satisfaction with consistency.

Team Philosophies

If people in organizations and groups are empowered and entrusted to make a difference, they will, and in the process become a winning team. If you want to achieve Ultimate Patient Satisfaction, you need to turn your people and organization into fine-tuned teams of patient advocates, regardless of their administrative, management, supportive, or technical role. You will find that having insight into the differences in how organizations and team members are communicating, empowering, and cooperating with each other will make you more effective in turning an organization, a department, or a group of people into an UPS team. Using Figure 9–4, Organization Versus Team Dynamics Table as a guide, you will better understand the internal communications and cooperation relationships necessary to have effective teams. You may want to consider distributing a copy of the Organization Versus Team Dynamics Table at your next team meeting and openly discuss the differences.

Improving Your UPS Team's Productivity

A lot has been written regarding team productivity and the reasons teams fail. However, over the years I have come to believe that people, not things, fail. It is the human factor. Like most things involving human beings, the lack of communication tends to be the underlying culprit and fundamental reason for failure. Consider the following eight reasons teams fail as outlined in the cover story, "Why Teams Fail," published in *USA Today*, February 25, 1997:

1. Goals unclear - 55%
2. Changing objectives - 55%
3. Lack of accountability - 51%
4. Lack of management support - 49%
5. Lack of clarity - 47%
6. Ineffective leadership - 45%
7. Low priority of team - 40%
8. No team-based pay - 30%

FIGURE 9-4

Organization Versus Team Dynamics

Organization and Group Dynamics	Team Dynamics
People think they are grouped together for administrative and management purposes only. The individual person works independently; sometimes at cross purposes with other people within the group and organization.	Members recognize their interdependence, and understanding both personal and team goals are best accomplished with mutual support. Time is not wasted struggling over "turf" or attempting personal gain at the expense of others.
People tend to focus on themselves because they are not sufficiently involved in planning the group's objectives. They approach their job simply as an employee or hired hand.	Members feel a sense of ownership for their jobs and team because they are committed to goals they helped establish.
People are told what to do rather than being asked what the best approach would be. Suggestions are not encouraged or taken seriously.	Members contribute to the organization's success by applying their unique talent and knowledge to team objectives. The right people for the right assignments. The right teams for the right goals.
People often distrust the motives of associates because they do not understand the role of the other people. Expressions of opinions or disagreement are considered challenging or nonsupportive.	Members can work in a climate of trust and are encouraged to openly express ideas, opinions, disagreements, and feelings. Input is wanted and actively and openly solicited from each member.
People are very cautious about what they say, and do not say, hence real understanding is not possible. Game playing and competitive traps set to catch the unwary may occur.	Members practice open and honest communications. They make an effort to understand each other's point of view. Information is freely shared.
People may receive good training but are limited in applying it to the job by their supervisor or coworkers.	Members are encouraged to develop skills and apply what they learn on the job. They receive the support of the team and management.
People find themselves in conflict situations that they do not know how to resolve. Their supervisor may wait putting off intervention until serious damage is done.	Members recognize conflict is a normal aspect of human interaction but they view such situations as opportunities for new ideas and creativity. The team works to resolve conflict quickly and constructively.
People may or may not participate in decisions affecting the organization/group. Conformity often appears more important than positive results.	Members participate in decisions affecting the team but understand their leader must make a final ruling whenever the team cannot decide, or an emergency exists. Positive results, not conformity, are stressed.

To my way of thinking, six out of the eight reasons for teams failing are communications-based. The lack of appropriate communications is the root of all evil, not money. Important values like honesty, ethical behavior, and self-worth were not effectively communicated to us as children and reinforced throughout our lives. So, on occasion, the dark-sided undisciplined human factor takes over. There I go off on another tangent. If you want to improve any team, but especially your UPS team's productivity, consider using my seven guidings D's of team productivity. The D's are presented in Figure 9–5. Over time I have come to rely on and found the "D" approach to be very helpful and effective in keeping teams' productivity high and in making significant contributions to an organization's success. And one last thing on productivity, as pointed out earlier a person's behavior, not their experience, tends to be the great single factor impacting productivity. Attitude and performance go hand-in-hand. People with bad attitudes usually have the performance to match.

FIGURE 9–5

Improving Team Productivity

Step	Action
Define	Defining the team's goals, and each team member's objectives, expectations, and performance levels.
Determine	Determining the availability and allocation of resources, critical dates, and work flow the team will operate under.
Delegate	Delegating appropriate empowerment, responsibility, and accountability to each team member.
Deregulate	Deregulating working contraints, free the spirit and mind, focus on the objectives, achievements, and especially rewarding success.
Dedication	Dedicating the necessary time, resources, and management support to achieve assigned team goals, especially on personal basis.
Dissolve	Dissolving disruptive internal and external conflict in a timely fashion.
Demonstrate	Demonstrating a sense of importance in achieving team's goals and individual member's worth personally and to the team effort.

Resolving Conflict

Team leaders and members are often called upon to address specific issues, conflicts, and problems, both internal and external, to the team. You will be more effective in resolving conflict once you have a better understanding of the five approaches to resolving conflict and the associated dynamics. With this knowledge, you will find confidence in choosing the best conflict resolution approach and the self-confidence to succeed. Spend the necessary time reviewing Figure 9–6, Conflict-Problem Resolution Table and you will have no problem in determining the right approach to resolve a conflict.

FIGURE 9–6

Conflict-Problem Resolution

Style	Root Reasons and Behaviors	Justification
Evading	Non confrontational. Ignores or passes over issues or poor performance. Denial issues are not seen as a problem. Avoids confrontation at all costs.	Differences too minor or too great to resolve. Attempts might damage status quo, relationship, or result in even greater problems. Resolving will seriously challenge the group's ideology.
Appeasing	Agreeable, nonassertive behavior. Cooperative even at the expense of compromising established goals. Overall fairness may be compromised.	Not worth risking damage to culture, customs, relationships, or creating general discord.
Domineering (Win-Lose)	Confrontational, aggressive. Must win at any cost. Ego, power, status, or perceived self-survival driven.	Survival of the fittest. Must prove superiority. Most ethical or professional choice rational.
Negotiating	Important all parties achieve their basic interests or goals and maintain good relationships. Aggressive, but cooperative.	No one person or idea is perfect. There is more than one good way to accomplish an objective. You must give to recieve.
Teaming (Win-Win)	Needs of both parties are legitimate and important. High respect for mutual support and open resolution. Shared information. Assertive and cooperative.	When parties will openly discuss issues, a mutually beneficial solution can be found without anyone making a major concession or losing face.

UPS Team Training

As a manager, one of your more important responsibilities is coaching and developing people; the same holds true for UPS team leaders. There are times when a team needs special training before it can successfully carry out an assigned objective. Consider using the UPS approach for training your team members (Figure 9–7). You will also find the training guidelines are effective for all your training needs

FIGURE 9–7

UPS Team Training

Basics	Principles	Elements	Reinforcement
Tell the person how	Present meaningful information	Team manager must have both knowledge and experience in the subject	Refresher courses
Show the person how	Present only one idea or concept at a time	People must be motivated to pay attention	Progress journals and daily activity logs
Let the person practice what they learned	Present information in a way that is easily comprehended and mastered	Use plain, intelligent, and understandable English	Training and performance aids
Ensure the person is doing it correctly	Present frequent summaries and get feedback to ensure understanding is achieved	New information and material must be associated to something the person is already familiar with	Follow-up activities, testing, and performance reviews
			Failure analysis
		The best learning process challenges people to study for themselves	
		Make material applicable to the job. Review the material to ensure that people fully understand it.	Positive reinforcement

UPS Team Test

✔ the True or False box that best reflects your understanding of
UPS team dynamics.

T F

□ □ 1. UPS team leaders emphasize each person's
involvement and expect that team member to take
responsibility for their contributions and actions.

□ □ 2. If you plan to build a strong UPS team and use
individual people's skills to the maximum, you also
need to improve your own.

□ □ 3. UPS team members are more productive when they
feel a sense of ownership of the task or of the
organization.

□ □ 4. When an UPS team achieves success, so will all of its
members.

□ □ 5. Selecting qualified people who work well with others
at the outset is important to UPS team-building
success.

□ □ 6. Commitment to a specific task is accomplishment
when the team leader involves team members in
planning, goal setting, and problem solving.

□ □ 7. UPS team leaders facilitate training for people and
coach individual people to apply what has been
learned.

□ □ 8. UPS teams are more concerned with getting positive
results than they are with "turf" battles.

□ □ 9. Trust is a critical factor among UPS team members.

□ □ 10. UPS team members need to know everything that
affects their work and ability to achieve the team's
goals.

□ □ 11. Competition and conflict in an UPS team are
healthy, only if they are properly controlled and
quickly resolved.

□ □ 12. Open communication in an UPS team will promote
understanding, a recognition of individual differences,
and encourage mutual support.

  ❐ ❐ **13.** UPS team members participate in decision making, but also recognize their team leader must act on his or her own if a consensus cannot be reached, or in the event of an emergency or crisis.

  ❐ ❐ **14.** UPS teams need to receive recognition and praise to be successful.

  ❐ ❐ **15.** Personal self-control and good discipline are by-products of UPS team building.

  ❐ ❐ **16.** UPS teams do not compromise or cause their team leader to abdicate their responsibilities.

The answer to each of the UPS Team self-analysis questions is true. Congratulations if you got all 16 questions correct. If on the other hand you scored less than 16, read the chapter over again.

"Your Future depends on today's patients' satisfaction."

John O'Malley

10

Getting Results by Setting Goals

Setting yourself up for success means setting yourself goals . . .

The road to Ultimate Patient Satisfaction will constantly be testing your aptitude and creativity in identifying and solving problems, along with your ability to set realistic goals and obtain the same. Every successful person has achieved their success by setting and achieving goals. Though failing is part of being successful, this chapter focuses on helping you in analyzing and solving problems, and setting goals.

CREATIVITY

You will be glad to know that experts agree and research shows that when it comes to creativity, all people of normal or higher intelligence have the ability to be creative. Put another way, that is just about everyone, including you and me, can be creative. If creativity is not limited to a few, but distributed among the multitude, then everyone in your organization can participate in creative thinking and problem solving. To my way of thinking, creativity and problem solving are the same. And, the best part being, with a little help, you can start increasing your creative and problem-solving abilities, especially when you are focusing on achieving and maintaining Ultimate Patient Satisfaction. But before we start learning more about being creative, solving problems, and setting goals you will find learning more about your cerebral vault far from an empty experience.

THE GRAY STUFF, YOUR BRAIN

In a nutshell, your brain is the internal neuro-chemical engine driving your very existence, including your creative thinking, analogical and abstract problem-solving abilities, and your love affair with daydreaming. No matter what anyone says, daydreaming is one of the most healthy and stimulating undertakings people can do with their gray matter. And daydreaming takes considerable brain power. To explain neurological anatomy in a fundamental premise, if unthinkable simplicity, your brain is divided into two major chemical tanks or hemispheres. The hemispheres each have a large neurological area in the front called the frontal lobe that oversees our conscious being and functions. The left hemisphere controls the right side of your body and the right hemisphere dictates the actions of the left side. Right-handed people are left hemisphere-dominant, while the opposite is true for left-handed people. Statistically, you could wager successfully that the reader of this book is right-handed. Your left hemisphere is your logical or reasoning side of the brain, where you process things in a logical, linear, step-by-step, and analytical manner. You might say that your brain's left hemisphere's gray matter sees the black and white of things. The left side also likes to process data and information sequentially. If you are left side-dominant, you more than likely excel at using words and working with numbers. The chances are you also have a knack for analysis and convergent thinking. However, you are not very good at gap-jumping, getting from point "A" to point "C" without first knowing where point "B" is located. The left hemisphere also controls speech and verbal communications. Now, your right hemisphere is the creative or dreaming side of the brain, where your thinking is more intrinsic, abstract, holistic, and spacial. Right hemisphere-dominant people tend to excel at processing information as imagery, patterns, and relationships, seeing beyond the data at hand. The next time you watch the television show, Jeopardy, notice how many of the contestants are left-handed. Right-hemisphere people are also great at synthesis and divergence thinking, which increases their gap-jumping abilities, getting from point "A" to point "C" without ever visiting point "B."

However, the same people often exhibit difficulty in handling verbal information. Subconsciously, and about every 90 minutes, your brain is actually moving back and forth between its right and left hemispheres. No, you can not feel or hear the clunk, but it is happening. When you were balancing your checkbook, the chances are your left hemisphere was engaging in mental gymnastics. But the last time you were daydreaming, your right hemisphere was dominating your thinking. However, balancing a checkbook on occasion requires creative skills, just ask the many healthcare executives behind bars for creative accounting. You will discover that maximizing your problem-solving ability requires getting your right and left hemispheres working collectively.

SWITCHING SIDES

To keep you from wearing out your gray matter, simplistic explanations are again in vogue. The left hemisphere of your brain is the logical side and the right hemisphere the creative side. Depending on your thinking requirements, logical or creative, there are things you can do to cause your brain to switch to the more appropriate and advantageous neurological hemisphere. The switching process usually takes 10 to 15 minutes and is quite painless for most of us. The next time you are thinking and want to mentally move from the right to left side of your brain, or vice versa, try using one or more of the following hemisphere-switching techniques. The process really works, no matter how silly it sounds or seems. As an example, if you are normally a left hemisphere-dominant person attending a creative brainstorming session, you want your creative juices flowing freely. You want your creative hemisphere fully engaged. What side is your creative side? I was just testing your reading comprehension. To switch sides consider any of the following approaches:

   1. Hand Switching—Switch to using your hand that is opposite to the side of the brain you wish to engage. In this case, using your left hand will force your brain to shift to its right hemisphere, your creative side. To force the switch you can start scribbling, doodling, rolling small objects or balls in the palm of your hand, playing with a small object, are just tapping a pen or pencil.

   2. Nostril Switching—Do not laugh, but holding your right nostril closed and only breathing through your left nostril will force your brain to shift to its right hemisphere, your creative side. Silly sounding I know, and it looks ridiculous, hence preferably executed in seclusion, but let me assure you it works. So the next time you meet a person holding one of their nostrils closed, it does not mean they are tripping, just switching.

3. Visual Switching—Viewing pictures and photographs, especially those of an abstract-, people-, action-oriented nature, will have the tendency of forcing your brain to shift to its right hemisphere, your creative side. Instead of looking at spreadsheets and numbers all day, take a creative visual break, and start viewing your work using more adventurous gray cells. After all, is that not how creative reimbursement (bundling and unbundling) came to be? Someone, somewhere, started daydreaming about milking the healthcare cow and skimming the cream. I am just kidding?

4. Spacial Switching—When it comes to creative empowerment, you will not be barking up the wrong tree by taking your brain for a walk in the park. Creativity and a spacious outdoor or indoor environment go together like Einstein and the speed of light, relatively speaking, that is. Leave confining offices and work spaces to the more analytically demanding chores.

SEEKING SOLUTIONS

Your ability in finding solutions and solving problems is very important and pragmatic in everyday life, more so in healthcare. Working in a business environment that is constantly changing and challenging requires good problem-solving skills at all levels within a healthcare organization. Whether individually or as a team, there are many creative ways you can approach solving a problem, regardless of its complexities. The next time you or your team are working on what appears to be a difficult problem, try thinking from a different perspective, or taking an unconventional approach to coming up with a solution using one or more of the following methodologies:

1. Transpose Thinking—Placing your problem in another industry, different environment, and as a competitive threat can often break the creative ice, thus enabling you to see the problem from another perspective. This transposing action tends to create solutions you would never think of in your own backyard. Another form of transposing is having non-company and industry people working at solving your problem. Such consultants and outsiders are usually not affected or impeded by a corporate culture and industry mind-channeling baggage as you might be, consciously or subconsciously.

2. Analyze Assumptions—Consider revisiting the problem and analyzing the assumptions you make in determining why the given situation is a problem. Reevaluate the real magnitude of the problem. You may discover some new insight into the cause of the problem, which in and of itself may very well propel or lead you toward alternative thinking and springboard solutions by challenging your previous assumptions.

3. Tiny Thinking—Try breaking your problem down into smaller elements or pieces. Start solving each piece individually, one at a time. This micro approach often enables you to solve those frustratingly complex problems. You will also discover that large overwhelming problems become more manageable and less threatening in nature.

4. Diligent Daydreaming—Turn your constitutional right and God-given daydreaming talents into a creative dynamo for pondering problems. You can start unleashing your creative thinking by focusing on solving a specific problem and identifying possible solution options. When it comes to creative thinking, gazing out a closed window can open your mind.

5. Seek Solitude—Find the time to be alone with a problem. Start by avoiding business distractions, contagious negativism, and the cluttered and closed minds so often spawned in fast-paced environments. By seeking mental and physical solitude, you can better encourage a stressed-out mind into being more relaxed and open, rejuvenating itself to new ideas and challenging concepts. You will discover that being alone with a problem can be a fulfilling experience.

6. Crack Up Conservatism—Looking at a serious problem with a less than serious view can be a rewarding approach for the conservative mind. Start loosening up your thinking by taking hold of a problem from another perspective, poking fun at it. Try proposing ridiculous solutions and laughing out loud. Break the tension of the moment. Relax. You will often find that turning the serious into the not so serious can be a very effective approach to solving problems. Humor helps reduce the built-up and often debilitating stress to which we often succumb while trying to solve a serious problem.

7. Brainstorming Blitzing—Brainstorming is a common approach to solving problems. The brainstorming blitzing process has everyone in your organization thinking together on how to solve a specific problem. You may also find it rewarding going outside your organization to bring in new thinkers when brainstorming blitzing. Consider brainstorming your way to solving problems by creating brainstorming teams. Each team comprises people with diverse backgrounds, education, and experiences. Competing against each other for the best solution, each team drives the other teams to excel. Once you have your solution, do not forget to reward the winning brainstorming team's members. And if after all this you are still not sure what the reward should be, Brainstorm Blitz it.

8. Spinning Solutions—Once you have a solution for a given problem, go back and analyze the solution. The problem takes on a different presence once you have identified a solution. However, by dissecting each element of the solution further, you will more than likely start spinning off additional solutions from the initial solution. Start spinning and pushing your creative envelope for the best solutions.

Brainstorming Basics

You will discover that achieving Ultimate Patient Satisfaction requires a lot of soul searching, creative thinking, and the ability to solve complex issues. At one end of the spectrum is changing a corporate culture, at the other end, changing the way the business telephones are answered. Brainstorming for ideas and solutions is an invaluable creative springboarding tool. When properly executed, brainstorming sessions are a very imaginative and effective method for exploring, identifying, creating, changing, and clearing up things. You will find it effective in determining the ways and means for accomplishing your goals and for solving difficult problems. Brainstorming sessions usually consist of more than one person. However, one person can engage in solo brainstorming. Solo brainstorming is another name for daydreaming. However, regardless of the number of people comprising your brainstorming session, you can bet not everyone will think alike. In fact there are eight types of thinkers as shown in Figure 10–1. What kind of thinker are you? Figure 10–1 also shows those thinkers who are better working together. You will discover that having different types of thinkers participating in a well-facilitated brainstorming ses-

FIGURE 10-1

Types of Thinkers

No.	Type	Orientation	Works Best With
1.	Visionary	Fast track, futuristic orientation	2, 6, 5
2.	Changers	Let's do it, improvement orientation	1, 6, 5
3.	Status Quo	Easy does it, traditional orientation	5, 7
4.	Missourian	Prove it, tangible orientation	3, 7
5.	Fluid	Easy going, flow orientation	1, 2, 3, 4, 6, 7, 8
6.	Gap jumper	Visualizes it, succession orientation	1, 2, 5
7.	Analytical	Time out, data orientation	3, 4, 5
8.	Preservationist	For-me agenda, personal orientation	Whoever best serves their personal interests

sion has great value. However, lose control and you will lose the creative process. It is that simple. When brainstorming, you will find it very helpful in having several different brainstorming teams working on the same issue or problem. Formulate each team with different types of thinkers, such as bringing visionaries, changers, and gap-jumpers together to solve a problem. Now take their suggested solution(s) and charge another brainstorming team with evaluating the solution(s). Such an evaluation team might be composed of status quo, analytical, and Missourian thinkers. Mixing and matching your thinkers often produces the best results quicker, as opposed to just throwing a group of people together. So next time you are thinking about conducting a brainstorming session, give some serious thought about the types of thinkers who go into your think-tank sessions.

Brainstorming Phases

A well-planned and facilitated brainstorming session goes through three distinct phases: (1) Generating Phase, (2) Prioritizing Phase, and (3) Executing Phase. By adhering to the three phases, your brainstorming sessions will, in the end, produce better results. Here are the phases:

1. Generating Phase—The generating phase is how most people typically perceive the brainstorming process in its entirety. However, the generating phase has two purposes. First, set the scope for generating ideas and solutions, and second, generate and record those ideas and solutions. You will find that by defining the scope of your brainstorming efforts prior to commencing the session, the whole process will be more time-efficient and productive in nature. Consider using one of the following generating phase designators:

a. Universal (open, anything goes)
   Example: Revenue generation
b. General (specific area)
   Example: Billing and collections
c. Focused (explicit issues or problem)
   Example: Reducing accounts receivable days

The generating phase is fluid in nature. As ideas and solutions are proposed, you can start your brainstorming session off from a universal approach, quickly adopting a more general approach, and finally, ending up in a highly focused session.

2. Prioritizing Phase—Prioritizing is a critical phase, but usually forgotten or passed over by most people in their effort to quickly introduce a new idea, a methodology, or a solution. The prioritizing phase is used to put your ideas and solutions in the right "doable" perspective regarding three influential considerations:

a. Customer Needs—Share your ideas and solutions with your customers, patients, and employees, soliciting their comments, revisions, and approval.
b. Resources—Failing to determine the required and available resources to undertake your solution can only lead to failure. Consider your resources, such as people, capital, space, tools, materials, and product before plowing ahead to harvest the benefits your solution offers.
c. Time Period—Time is also a valuable resource to consider, such as your time, their time, planning time, delivery time, start time, required time, and completion time. Time is a fleeing, intangible asset. However, the consequences of running out of time are always tangible. Timing is everything, so plan yours well.

3. Executing Phase—Now comes the opportunity to venture forth with your new idea or your solution. The executing phase consists of the planning, tracking, and revising elements of brainstorming necessary in bringing the reality of your brainstorming efforts to fulfillment.

- **a.** Planning and Executing—Create and carry out an action plan based on your prioritizing phase results.
- **b.** Tracking and Feedback—As with any plan implementation, tracking your efforts and reporting the achieved results is important. Depending on the magnitude of your project, the tracking vehicle can be as simple as pen and paper, or it may require a computerized tracking program.
- **c.** Analyzing and Revising—Analyzing your efforts and revising the same as necessary to achieve the end goal is also a key part of the overall brainstorming process. When a revision is warranted and made, ensure that everyone involved and affected is kept well informed, especially before making the changes.

Brainstorming Process

If you use my seven-step brainstorming process, I guarantee you will increase the effectiveness of your brainstorming session and have better end results. Here is my seven-step brainstorming process.

1. Meet Off-Site—Never engage in serious brainstorming in your office, or in the conference room. Leave your office or facility behind and go find an open, spacious place, such as a park, large hotel lobby, or nature reserve to meet. Open space tends to open your mind. You will also have fewer business interruptions off-site.

2. Comfortable Attire—Wear loose, comfortably fitting clothing, no suits, ties, high heels, or makeup. All right, makeup is permitted. I was just seeing if you were skim reading.

3. Quantity of Ideas—Focus on generating a large quantity of ideas and possible solutions, not the quality. With quantity, you will experience a sprinkling of quality. Be patient and string along. Before you realize it, a few worthy pearls will eventually be strung before your eyes.

4. Never Discuss an Idea—Most important, and under no circumstances are you to engage in discussing any of the ideas or solutions presented during the session. If for any reason, intentionally or by accident, you put down or make fun of a person's idea or suggestion, that person will be very reluctant to share another idea or solution. Embarrassing, challenging, and ignoring another person is guaranteed to seal their lips for the rest of the brainstorming session. Not only their lips are sealed, but everyone else will clam up, fearing the same ridicule, and abruptly closing down all participation. The worse side effect is that a great idea or solution that was on someone's lips, but because of your non-supportive verbal and body language, that someone quickly swallowed their idea for eternity. Encourage people to participate in your brainstorming sessions with encouraging remarks, or mark my words, it is over.

5. Customize and Prioritize Ideas—Create a list of all the ideas and solutions brought forth during the brainstorming session. Now send the list to those who were participants, and ask each to prioritize the items from their own perspective. Send the same list to other people whose opinions you value, asking them to prioritize the list as well. Finally, remember to send the list to a select few of your customers, as well as your customer advisory board, soliciting their inputs. You do have a customer advisory board, don't you? Tell each person prioritizing the list to feel free to add any additional personal ideas and solutions they believe are important. Now compile one master list from the many prioritized lists.

6. Create Tiger Teams—Regardless of their position, identify individuals within your organization who are known for getting the job done, regardless of the circumstances and challenges. Bring the selected individuals together, forming a Tiger Team to undertake the carrying out of your top priority idea or solution. Empower your Tiger Team for success, let them go, and stand back and listen to the roar, in more ways than one. Remember, do not send a pussycat out to do a tiger's job, or you will really have a tiger by the tail, as the saying goes.

7. Take Action—Simply put, if you do not do something, nothing will change. And if you are afraid of making a mistake, don't be, but be afraid of not learning from your mistakes. To get perfect, one must make mistakes. I made a few I would like to forget.

GOALS, OBJECTIVES, AND THINGS

Successful people, healthcare providers included, succeed because they know what they want to achieve and how to go about accomplishing the same. To enhance your chances for success, you must do the same. Zero in on a target. Achieving Ultimate Patient Satisfaction is no different. You must identify your primary target or goal. The goal-setting process I am going to share with you now has been working well for me over the years. Here is how it works.

Your first step is to be able to distinguish between and define goals and objectives. To my way of thinking, a goal is a long-range target, six months or longer in time. A goal represents a significant personal or business achievement. Goals are few in number, but strategic in nature and consequences. Goals comprise objectives. An objective is a short-range ambition or action, supportive of a specific goal, and usually achievable within 60 to 90 days. Typically, to achieve a goal, you have to achieve several related objectives. Objectives are more numerous than goals and tactical in nature, as are the consequences. Objectives are achieved by doing things. I am sure you have things to do, probably, as you read this book. A thing is defined as an action or task that commands a considerably smaller amount of our time than an objective. That thing you want to do may take a few minutes of your time or consume several days of intensive labor, depending on things, of course. I always looked at goal setting as a dynamics triad of events. Simply put, it infers that you first do things, then complete objectives, and finally achieve goals, all of which enable you to grow and prosper.

Success Takes Planning

Another way to distinguish the relationship between goals, objectives, and things is to project a military perspective as depicted in Figure 10–2, Military Analogy Table. As with most things in life, love, and war, it is the accumulation of little things that usually results in bigger things

FIGURE 10–2

Military Analogy

War	Strategies	Goals	Healthcare Industry
Battle	Tactics	Objectives	Market share
Skirmish	Actions	Things	Customer service

happening. The reason for planning is to gain bigger things by executing little things well.

"When your strategy is deep and far reaching, then what you gain by your calculations is much, so you can win before you even fight"

The Art of War - Sun Tzu

Success seldom comes easily, especially to those unwilling to step outside of their comfort zone. And you will quickly learn that significant goals will more than likely wind up forcing your team or organization outside of their comfort zones. Moving people and organizations outside of their comfort zones always results in expected and natural resistance. But you have to resist the easy and stretch for success.

Setting Goals

By setting an UPS goal without planning on how you are going to achieve the same, you are setting yourself up for failure. Determining goals, planning, aggressive execution, and analyzing one's progress adds to success. It is a package deal, held together by commitment. You can start setting and achieving your UPS goals by adhering to the following 10 easy steps:

1. Analyzing your current patients' satisfaction level and service delivery methodologies by determining the basic who, what, where, when, how, and why about your services.

2. Determining what UPS means to you financially, operationally, and strategically and how you will achieve it.

3. Writing individual, departmental, and organizational UPS goals down and posting them for all to see.

4. Making UPS goals specific and measurable, the more specific and measurable, the better.

5. Prioritizing your UPS goals and focusing your resources on those priorities.

6. Monitoring the individuals', department's, and organization's progress in achieving each of their established UPS goals and objectives.

7. Self-managing your time and actions to achieve those UPS goals.

8. Making and communicating all necessary revisions and adjustments in a timely fashion and in an appropriate manner.

9. Believing that you can achieve established UPS goals, and creating and maintaining a positive attitude and working environment to that end.

10. Rewarding the individuals, departments, and organization when an established UPS goal is achieved. Reward the smallest improvements to gain the biggest improvements.

   Note: As an example, an organization rewards itself by being able to afford a new piece of capital equipment as a direct cost-savings result attributed to achieving an UPS goal.

Five Key UPS Goal Setting Opportunities

The road to success will be less of a challenge and more achievable if you focus on setting your UPS goals in one or more of the five and interrelated areas in Figure 10–3. Setting UPS goals needs to be from a patient's perspective, not yours.

FIGURE 10–3

Goal Setting Opportunities

Types	Area
Encounters	Employees, physicians, volunteers: pre-on-site, on-site, post-on-site
Expectations	Patients, family members, visitors
Environment	Admitting, department areas, waiting areas, patient-rooms, meals, etc.
Education	In-service, self-care, procedures, surgery, medication, home care, etc.
Employees	Behaviors, attire, encounter training, team building, dealing with upset patients, telephone etiquette, problem solving, technical, etc.

FIGURE 10–4

UPS Goals List

Person:		
Department:		
Encounters	1	
	2	
	3	
Expectations	1	
	2	
	3	
Environment	1	
	2	
	3	
Education	1	
	2	
	3	
Employees	1	
	2	
	3	
Other	1	
	2	
	3	

Listing UPS Goals

As an example, you may want to consider using a formal means of list-ing individual, department, and organization UPS goals, such as those shown in Figure 10–4.

UPS Goal Worksheet

You will find that using a goal worksheet will enable appropriate recording and tracking of progress in achieving established UPS goals. A basic example of such a worksheet is shown in Figure 10–5. Your spreadsheet program will work well as a worksheet, as will any of the many project-management software programs available to computer-ize such processes.

FIGURE 10-5

Ultimate Patient Satisfaction Goal Worksheet

Responsible Party:	Priority	PCD	ACD
Goal			
Objectives	**Priority**	**PCD**	**ACD**
1			
2			
3			
Things to Do	**Priority**	**PCD**	**ACD**
1			
2			
3			
4			
5			
6			
7			

Projected Completion Date = PCD
Actual Completion Date = ACD

11
CHAPTER

Employees, the Crucible for Caring

If you love your job, you will never have to go to work again . . .

Ultimate Patient Satisfaction (UPS) depends on, and is deeply rooted in, employee satisfaction. However, many fail to realize that critical rooting starts at the top with management. In any organization, the senior executives are charged with setting the tone for employee satisfaction. In doing so, an employee satisfaction culture is being established for all others to emulate. Without a total and consistent commitment to employee satisfaction from within your organization's executive ranks, you cannot realistically believe that patient satisfaction will ever be achieved, especially Ultimate Patient Satisfaction, with any competitive consistency. Failure at the executive level to actively and dependably demonstrate the right attitude and accepted behavior quickly sends compromising and confusing messages to employees. These mixed messages, or signals, more often than not lead to poor employee and customer satisfaction. However, when it comes to satisfying employees, you must also remember that management cannot please all of its employees all of the time, but with a little effort, management can please most of its employees most of the time.

SMART HIRING

Though it may be odd-sounding, the basic ingredient for achieving employee satisfaction is in hiring the right employees from the start. Any great chef knows and will tell you the importance of starting off with the best ingredients. How important blending and mixing them with care and creating the proper cooking conditions are necessary to bring forth a culinary masterpiece of scrumptious perfection. So, employ the advice of a gourmet chef the next time you are thinking about employing new people, start off with the right stuff. Any persons responsible for hiring people for your organization, especially human resource managers, need to make a special effort in hiring interpersonal skills before technical expertise. Exceptional people have great people skills. You want people who are committed to cooking up and delivering patient satisfaction from their hearts, not a book. To hire the kind of person who will best enable you to deliver Ultimate Patient Satisfaction, consider developing a basic Ultimate Patient Satisfaction characteristic set, similar to a cook's secret recipe or ingredients. Every candidate for employment, including physicians, must possess and demonstrate those characteristics or you pass on hiring them. To help you from jumping out of the frying pan and into the fire, consider hiring not only your support personnel, but only technically qualified people who exhibit the following 22 yummy characteristics:

1. Presents a good first impression;
2. Optimistic lifestyle;
3. Constructive attitude;
4. Enthusiastic about helping people;
5. Self-improvement driven;
6. Aptitude to quickly learn new things;
7. Assertive and competitive nature;
8. Friendly and outgoing;
9. Patient orientation;
10. Receives intrinsic rewards from caring for patients;
11. Proactive mind-set;
12. High performance consistency;
13. Organized with logical thought processing;
14. Good decision-making skills;

15. Follow-through orientation;
16. Team participant and player;
17. Mature demeanor;
18. Good interpersonal skills;
19. Good verbal, written, and communications skills;
20. Possesses a sense of humor;
21. Requires minimal supervision, low maintenance employee (LME); and
22. Strong belief in your corporate philosophies.

By hiring the right people to start with, you are increasing your chances for success, because you will have the right kind of employee necessary for delivering Ultimate Patient Satisfaction. You may not be able to find people with all the Ultimate Patient Satisfaction characteristics all the time. However, do not compromise your efforts by settling for less because you are in a hurry. In the long run, time is on your side, so take some and start making the best of it. Consider hiring those individuals who possess the greatest number of desired traits. You may find it beneficial to establish a minimum cutoff number, such as 18 out of 22 traits. Another option is to identify those traits that can be taught to someone and do so as warranted. I think of the 22 Ultimate Patient Satisfaction characteristics listed, you could teach six. I will help you with the first one. You could put all employees through a program to improve their verbal, written, and communications skills. Which do you think are the other five teachables? The chances are also greatly in your favor that employees demonstrating the above 22 Ultimate Patient Satisfaction characteristics will make better organizational fits, require minimal supervision, and be more productive. I am guilty of making this mistake in the past and learned the hard way. Many of us have interpersonal skeletons in our closest waiting to come out in unsuspecting organizations. So remember, foregoing the above 22 Ultimate Patient Satisfaction characteristics in lieu of hiring a person with just a strong technical background will often come back to haunt you and your organization.

TECHIES

It seems every organization has its fair share of techies who are not service-oriented. You know the kind of person I am referring to, those individuals who have superior technical, administrative, or operational skills coupled with inferior interpersonal skills. The person can be at the front desk or reading an x-ray in the back room. Techies tend to be scattered through an organization, from top to bottom, and show a tendency for migrating into critical service positions. Hiring people with poor interpersonal skills is like buying a cake with no icing, you still have a cake and can eat it, however, the best part is missing, the part making the sweet difference. You will find that hiring and promoting people on their technical merits alone is another avoidable mistake we keep making. Doing so is equivalent to a chef cooking with stale ingredients, it may look like a cake, but it tastes like soap. So wash your hands of bad habits and old ways, and start hiring and firing attitude. If you want to deliver Ultimate Patient Satisfaction, your guiding rule for hiring people is, attitude before technical skills. It is difficult, if not impossible, to teach a pessimistic person to have a positive, caring attitude toward others and life in general. Besides, have you ever met a successful pessimist? And do you have the time?

ORGANIZATIONAL FITABILITY

An employee's ability to excel and reach their fullest potential in your organization depends on many things. Together I refer to these "things" as an employee's Organizational Fitability Factor, OFF. If you want to increase the likelihood that a new employee, especially a senior manager, will fit well within your organization and its culture, remember that when hiring a person, considering their OFF is a critical component to your overall decision-making process. To help ensure a new employee's ability to succeed in your organization, start hiring people with the highest OFFs. You can determine a person's Organizational Fitability Factor during the interviewing process by asking specific open-ended questions that are revealing in nature. For the interviewing session to be effective, the interviewer needs to uncover and see the total individual, and in the process be gaining insight into how adaptable the candidate will be to your organizational demands and culture, and especially whether or not the pressures of the job will eventually lead to poor performance and stress-induced failure. To help you in determining someone's Organizational Fitability Factor, try evaluating the total situation the next time you are interviewing a potential employee, a potenial company asset. Consider the following:

1. The Total Individual—Determine the "Total Individual" based on the following six criteria:
   a. Academic preparation
   b. Professional experience
   c. Technical skills
   d. Personal and spiritual values
   e. Personality type
   f. Interpersonal skills

2. The Organization's Demands and Culture—Determining to what extent the organization's demands such as customer orientation, service orientation, lean and mean, compensation, minimal supervision, high performance standards, corporate vision, mission, philosophies, management style, teammanship, and the overall working environment will affect their OFF.

3. The Job Pressures and Marketplace Demands—Determining if the pressures associated with the job and position such as coworkers, fast pace, overtime, deadlines, travel, responsibilities, constant change, empowerment, work station, and competitive threats will affect their OFF.

Delivering Ultimate Patient Satisfaction is directly linked to each employee's OFF. The higher the employee's OFF, the greater is the chance that the person will be on when it comes to excelling at delivering Ultimate Patient Satisfaction. Employees hired with low OFFs seldom work out, and it is only a matter of time before they are off seeking new employment elsewhere.

ROW, ROW, ROW YOUR BOAT

To be successful in achieving employee satisfaction and hence, Ultimate Patient Satisfaction, it is imperative for healthcare organizations to have all their O.A.R.S. in the water at the same time, and rowing in the same direction. Converted into a landlubber's vernacular, this means you must hire managers, supervisors, and lead employees who have the interpersonal skills, professional attitude, and expertise to consistently demonstrate on a daily basis, four critical make-or-break-you characteristics, O.A.R.S.

Those characteristics or traits are: an **O**ptimistic Nature, an **A**ttitude of Allegiance, an excellent **R**ole Model presence, and an effective Service Orientation. To start rowing in the same direction, you first have to get all your O.A.R.S. in the water. And by that I mean hiring people who possess an optimistic nature that is encouraging rather than discouraging; hiring people with an attitude of allegiance to the company, its philosophies, and its management team; hiring people who are excellent role models for others to watch, learn from, and emulate; and hiring people with an effective service orientation. Your organization's long-term success is directly dependent on the O.A.R.S. characteristics being effectively communicated and demonstrated by those who influence your employees. Managers, supervisors, and key employees must lead, coach, and show their O.A.R.S. in every thought they think, in every word they use, and in every deed they do, if you want everyone rowing in the same direction. Hopefully, you can see how the daily actions of these key people directly affect your employees' perception about your company, its mission, and philosophies regarding patient satisfaction. We all know a person's actions speak louder than their words, a tenet manager often forgets, but employees never do.

Another important point about rowing in the same direction is that managers and employees must all adhere to the same rules in order to stay on course, minimize unnecessary delays, and arrive at their planned destination physically and mentally prepared to work together. With management, team leaders, and employees' oars all in the water at the same time, you will find little difficulty having everyone rowing in the same direction once you define the direction and evenly share the rowing chores. And it is just as important to remember that once an organization has all its OARS in the water, pulling harmoniously, and rowing in the same direction, its competition will be left in its wake every time. Achieving Ultimate Patient Satisfaction is a team effort, a team journey, and team adventure.

ATTITUDE IS EVERYTHING

What do the words, having a "bad attitude," mean to you? If asked to define "bad attitude" most of us would have little trouble doing so. More than likely, your individual definition would be slightly different from mine and others. But each definition would still convey some commonly descriptive negative adjectives, attributes, and behaviors. However, like quality, attitude is based on one's own perception. You will find that telling an employee they have a bad attitude is an ineffective approach to behavior modification. When you tell a person that their attitude is inappropriate, the offended person may very well think, how could this be? I think my attitude is good. After all, I have been acting this way for most of my adult life and no one confronted me about my attitude before now. Remember, you are who you are because of when, when you were a child. Informing a person they have a less than desirable attitude is worthless at best, especially if it is a subjective conclusion on your part. Unless you have established written attitude and accepted behavior standards, you nor your employees have a realistic reference point upon which to judge another's attitude or behavior. Without creating and using employee attitude and behavior standards, you missed the boat. The first step on your journey toward Ultimate Patient Satisfaction is to stop and take the necessary time for creating attitude and accepted behavior standards. Start by qualifying and quantifying the desired employee's attitude and behavior you want. Consider the viewpoints of management, coworkers, and your customers, especially the patient. If helping fellow coworkers and patients without being asked demonstrates the right attitude, define the word helping. Consider providing several examples of employees helping coworkers and patients without being asked. If being rude is unacceptable behavior, then define the word "rude" for your employees, along with providing three examples of rudeness. If you cannot accurately define it, you cannot accurately measure it, and only things measured are monitored. Attitude is subjective at best, unless it is defined.

Your attitude is perceived by others as an aura, comprising your body language, facial expressions, tones of voice, spoken words, dress, grooming, and your general outlook on life itself. Our attitudes determine how we will react to people, events, and changes in our lives. We can change neither the past nor the inevitable fact that things will not always go our way. However, we can change our attitude to encourage the best in ourselves, in others, and in situations. A strong positive attitude is the foundation for success. You have a choice regarding your attitude, so embrace positive thoughts and deeds, shunning the ugly things in life. To help you better understand attitude, refer to page 168 and read *Your Attitude* by the author.

Attitudinal Consequences

The concept of Ultimate Patient Satisfaction is simple, but delivering it with consistency is not easy. Ultimate Patient Satisfaction is a way of life, a culture founded on explicit expectations and corresponding consequences. Hence, the underlying success for achieving Ultimate Patient Satisfaction is establishing non-negotiable attitude and behavior standards that all employees must adhere to on a daily basis, regardless of their position, and without exception. You must be committed to ensuring that any employee and physician who do not comply with your organization's established attitude and behavior standards pay the consequences. There must be no exceptions when it comes to attitudinal consequences. You can start the Ultimate Patient Satisfaction process by forming an UPS expectations team consisting of a group of high attitude, low maintenance employees. You know the kind, your best all-around employees, your role models for other employees, the employees with the right stuff. For maximum insight and results, consider placing a few patient or customer representatives on the team as well. Empower the team to cross all barriers, break all taboos, and kill the sacred cows along the way. Let them revolutionize the way your organization and its employees encounter, interact, and deliver patient service. Assign them the task of creating a list of acceptable attitudes and behaviors, what I call "great expectations." Though by no means inclusive, here are 19 areas worth considering as you create your own list of great expectations.

1. Answering the telephone;
2. Disconnecting from a telephone conversation;
3. Greeting patients and their family members;
4. Handling complaints;
5. Defusing upset patients and their family members;
6. Interacting with fellow coworkers;
7. Working with other departments;
8. Providing directions;
9. Answering questions;
10. Unacceptable language, be specific and list offensive words;
11. Destructive gossiping;
12. Performance requirements;
13. Solving customer problems;
14. Accepted attire, grooming, and hygiene;
15. Safety procedures and precautions;
16. Cleaning work area(s);

17. Using elevators;

18. Handling confidential information; and

19. Parking.

Once your Ultimate Patient Satisfaction team has identified, qualified, and quantified acceptable employee attitude and behavior, you are ready for the next step. The second step is to introduce and educate all employees to the acceptable and non-negotiable attitude and behavior guidelines and the consequences for failing to consistently follow those guidelines. As an example, consider number 19 from the previous list. Here is a short list of seven accepted behaviors regarding employee parking:

- Employees must have a valid driver's license to drive and park a motor vehicle on premises;
- Employees must park their vehicle in designated parking area or space;
- Employees' vehicles must meet all federal, state, and local safety inspection regulations;
- Employees' vehicles must appropriately display their issued identification sticker;
- Employees must respect other parked vehicles, avoid causing physical damage;
- Employees must not dispose of trash or foreign material on parking grounds; and
- Employees must possess active bodily injury and property damage liability insurance for the motor vehicle they are driving and parking on premises with a minimal coverage of $_____.

As a daily reminder, post your attitude and behavioral guidelines in common employee areas, such as work areas, break areas, cafeteria, locker room, personal work station, and beside the time clock. A point in passing, mounting a video surveillance camera overseeing the time-clock area can significantly reduce checking in and out fraud.

PRUNING THE DEAD, THE DYING, AND THE DISEASED

The most difficult part in achieving Ultimate Patient Satisfaction for most managers is organizational gardening. Keeping employees on the payroll who fail to achieve the established attitude and behavior standards, team spirit, and service orientation required to deliver Ultimate Patient Satisfaction is detrimental to the health of your organization. Negative people drain your corporate strength, resources, and life's blood like leeches by placing an invisible, yet noticeable, hardship on the organization and its employees. When someone says, "it cannot be done," they are usually right. They cannot do it. Stop and think. If you had to terminate an employee who constantly exhibited a poor attitude, where would you want that person to be employed after leaving your facility? If you said "the competition" pat yourself on the back. You would be right from my point of view though leaving the industry is a better solution. I would even volunteer to subsidize the ex-employee's salary to ensure their continued employment with my competition. Why the competition? Because that person's poor attitude will resurface in time, polluting your competitor's company by lowering its employees' morale and productivity, just as it did yours. Research shows that in any industry, low employee morale adversely affects productivity and eventually customer satisfaction. Therefore when you keep a marginal attitude employee for subjective emotional, technical, or personal reasons, you are not only hurting your organization but helping the competition. Yes, you are helping the competition and employing subjective reasoning at its worst. You have heard it all before: Joan came with the building, we just cannot let her go; John is the only person who knows what the Esc key is for on the keyboard; Jill is married to the son of the owner's daughter and the only person who knows how to file a claim; and Jim is the only person who knows where that blue pipe goes, and why. Keep in mind that an employee with a non-constructive or bad attitude is like the proverbial rotten apple in a barrel (your organization); in time all apples (your employees) that come in contact with the rotten apple (the negative employee) become rotten and spoiled. Read your job description, does it include a statement to the effect that, "you are required to help the competition?" I doubt it seriously. However, that is the perceived message you are conveying to your other employees when you fail to realize a negative person in the organization and take appropriate action. By allowing negative people to stay (fester) within your organization, for whatever unjustifiable reasons, you are only helping the competition. When was the last time you cleared your barrel of spoiled apples? Maybe it is time, if you want to deliver Ultimate Patient

Satisfaction. At the moment of truth, when it is time to prune dead and diseased performers from organizational branches, many managers are totally ill prepared to mentally snip and administratively cut. Any gardener worth their tea roses knows that pruning is fundamental to improving a garden. Pruning is important to a garden, especially if you want your plants and trees growing to their fullest potential and beauty. Is an organization not a garden of sorts, where leaders are always planting ideas, growing people and revenues, nurturing products, fertilizing with capital, new people, and concepts? To help you in establishing your own pruning policies and procedures, you may want to consider using the Ultimate Patient Satisfaction Termination Protocol Guide to augment current policies (see Pg. 139). It goes without saying, but just to be on the safe side, make sure you consult an attorney experienced in labor law before implementing any policy or procedure that effects employees, their employment, and rights under existing laws.

It should be noted that people are creatures of habit and resist change. Hence, and because of this often hindering human trait, studies show that 90-day probation periods seldom work in reality. Most people are firmly set in their ways by the time you employ them. Further, one's attitude, being a core behavior, is not easily changed in adults. Once an employee's mind is made up, it rarely can be changed. You can teach old dogs new tricks, but they never forget the old ones. Most people insist on reverting to past habits, their comfort zone.

Another key step toward achieving Ultimate Patient Satisfaction is for all company personnel, executives, managers, and employees to aggressively work together and start pruning dead and diseased performers from the corporate tree. Underperformers consume resources, seldom blossom, and bear little, if any, significant fruit. If you fail to effectively prune, your future will be limited, if not destined, to a me-too provider's life in a highly contested healthcare market. Research also tells us that poor attitudes are the root cause of morale problems in any organization, and if left to germinate within, the consequences may not be to your liking. However, it is also important to realize that a poor attitude is not the exclusive domain of the lower organization tiers, but is often found in the highest and most isolated ivory towers and boardrooms. The higher up in the organizational structure that poor attitude prevails, the more difficult it will be achieving Ultimate Patient Satisfaction. When executive attitudinal differences are affecting an organization's ability to change for the better, and in doing so, achieving Ultimate Patient Satisfaction, you need to search your heart and decide if this is the kind of company or person you want to work and associate with. If the soul-searching answer is no, then explore new employment opportunities. Trust me, you will be much happier in an organization whose philosophies coincide with your personal beliefs. That was another lesson I personally learned the hard way. One last point on terminating underperformers and poor attitude people; let an underperformer go without malice in your heart or checkbook. You are not out to destroy their life, nor do you want to. Instead, provide the level of severance you would want under the same circumstances. Usually, I recommend a 90-day severance, including full pay and healthcare benefits for employees who were acting in good faith and had not intentionally conducted themselves in any adverse manner. Remember. An employee's best performance may not be adequate for meeting your minimum requirements. Nothing personal, it is just the way it turned out. When possible, always assume the position of helping people to help themselves, the best you can. Even if you have to let an employee go, let them go without losing face and on a positive note. What goes around comes around.

THE POWER OF OPEN-BOOK MANAGEMENT

One of the most powerful things a company can do to achieve employee satisfaction is to embrace Open-Book Management (OBM) concepts. OBM goes a long way toward maximizing overall employee satisfaction. As more employees actually become involved with your organization's daily operations, two important things happen: employees' morale improves and their productivity increases, a dream most managers would deem worth dreaming. Open-Book Management is a methodology that turns every employee within an organization into what I call an Employee Business Unit (EBU). The EBU's primary focus and responsibility are reducing costs and maximizing profitability within their areas of responsibilities, and outside if possible. As an EBU, each employee, with no exception, takes on a new role in making the company more profitable at what it does. In order for Open-Book Management to work properly, you must be providing each EBU (employee) the information and the empowerment required to solve problems, cut costs, and increase company

TERMINATION PROTOCOL GUIDE

1. Establish expectations

Establish Ultimate Patient Satisfaction performance, attitude, and behavior expectations. Ensure each employee receives a copy. Post the same in strategic locations for daily reinforcement. Include expectations in every job description and place a signed copy in each employee's personnel record.

2. Review performance

An employee's performance is reviewed bimonthly against Ultimate Patient Satisfaction expectations and policies. An objective evaluation is taken to ensure fairness. Those employees functioning below Ultimate Patient Satisfaction expectations are properly informed.

3. Informed feedback

An employee is informed of their unacceptable behavior. The manager has three options available:

(a) A corrective warning and educational session

(b) Ninety-day probation period

    (1) Termination results if the employee fails to achieve the desired Ultimate Patient Satisfaction behavior expectations and maintain the same on a consistent basis.

(c) Termination

4. Execute termination

An employee is terminated for failure to meet and consistently perform established Ultimate Patient Satisfaction expectations. Termination is executed, when not voluntary.

5. Severance package

An employee is offered a short-term severance package, usually 90 days, as an incentive for their immediate and voluntary termination.

profits. This is accomplished by providing every employee in the company with the necessary basic training to understand the fundamental terminology and principles of running and monitoring your business. Each of your employees needs to know about your products and services, your market, your customers, your competition, and how you get paid or reimbursed for your services. Do your employees understand the impact, good or bad, that Medicare and Medicaid patients and reimbursement are having on your business, hospital, or practice?

Employee Business Units

The next step in OBM is creating an environment in which management feels comfortable to openly and willingly start sharing operational and financial information with each employee. Did he say, financial information? Yes I did. The success of an OBM style depends on the free flow of information. Every EBU needs to be receiving the following three types of operational information:

1. Financial Data: Each EBU needs to have access to individual, departmental, and corporate information regarding costs, operating expenses, revenues, profits, and profit margins. How else can your employees truly feel part of the organization and actively be helping you reduce your operating costs and becoming more profitable?

2. Corporate Planning: Each EBU needs to read the corporate or strategic plan (hopefully you have one) so the employee knows where the company is going. Employees need to know and understand not only where the company's going, but what is in it for them getting you there. They want to also know their future role and stake for actively participating in getting you where you want to go.

3. Marketing Plan: Each EBU needs to read the company's marketing action plan (hopefully you have one) so they know who, what, when, where, how, and why about where the organization is going and how it's going to get there. And just as important, to what extent will their role and overall level of participation be in the process, along with your expectations of their performance. Every employee

(EBU) needs to have an assigned role, responsibilities, and accountability in moving the company forward. It is a team effort. Remember.

I have often marveled at how most companies reserve their corporate and marketing plans for a privileged few, such as the president, chief executive officer, board members, senior managers, and selected individuals and then turn around and wonder why their employees do not know where the organization is going, how it will get there, and what roles they can play to make it happen. Communication problems are the number one reason for divorces in America and I believe employee dissatisfaction too. By not openly communicating with your employees in good faith, your employees will have the tendency to divorce themselves from your goals and their productivity. An important job becomes a mundane exercise in passing the time or a necessary evil. Maryrose, a special friend, often refers to this process as the "Wonder Syndrome," I wonder "What I am doing, and doing here." In healthcare, it appears that many senior managers not only have neglected pruning their organizational gardens, but unknowingly (?) have been using the mushroom theory of management, keeping their employees in the dark and feeding them large quantities of a bull-derivative fertilizer. No wonder morale is low. What compounds the problem is that you have been consistently treating your employees like children. Children have a greater fear of the dark. So take one giant enlightening step out of the dark ages and start living by Open-Book Management. You will become their beacon of understanding as they eagerly bask in the rays of operational enlightenment. To this end, every employee needs to know who, what, why, where, and how about their company's operations and expectations. In an effective Open-Book Management environment each EBU knows the following:

1. The overall financial status and position of the company;
2. Who and how the company gets paid for its efforts;
3. The costs to provide a specific product or service;
4. The company's product and service line;
5. The profitability of each product or service;
6. How their performance or lack thereof impacts profitability;

7. Their success is directly connected to the company's success;
8. Where the company is going and the obstacles it must circumvent or neutralize;
9. How the company is expected to get there;
10. The company's competitive threats; and
11. How they can personally generate business or referrals.

Each employee needs to realize that their job security, paycheck, benefits, advancement, and future way of life are directly dependent on how well the company competes in the marketplace. And, each employee must further understand their performance needs to be significant in nature to effectively contribute to their tenure with your company. You must encourage and empower employees to take a proactive part in making your company profitable. In an efficient Open-Book Management environment each EBU desires to:

1. Take an active part in the company's success;
2. Understand basic operational and financial issues and decisions; and
3. Make the company more profitable.

The Way to OBM

The five fundamental steps to Open-Book Management (OBM) are as follows:

1. Teach business basics;
   a. Business 101
   b. Marketing and sales
   c. Operations
2. Provide information;
   a. Financial
   b. Marketing
   c. Operations
3. Empower and entrust employees;
   a. Solve problems
   b. Reduce costs
   c. Change procedures

4. Reward employees based on customer satisfaction and company's success;
   a. Profit sharing
   b. Equity in company
   c. Accountability
5. Tracking, measuring, and posting results against goals;
   a. Company
   b. Department
   c. Individuals

Remember, in any organization, creativity output is directly related to and proportional to information quality and input. So open up, and start sharing data with your employees and watch your profitability climb, if not skyrocket!

Football

Reflect on this football analogy. Open-book management is a football huddle, in which every player learns what is expected of them and the other players to execute the next play. Open-book management is an organizational huddle, in which every employee learns what is expected of them and the other employees in the corporation. If during the huddle, the quarterback decided not to communicate with the other players and not call a play, what would the team do once they returned to the line of scrimmage? I am not sure either. The players might start complaining to one another, milling around, or calling a time out. Regardless of what the players decided to do, their team was at a loss, and did not know who, what, where, when, and how to execute the next play. The same is true for an organization that huddles a lot (holds meetings) and is reluctant to share the critical information its employees need to know to do their job and function as a team. So employees start complaining to one another, milling around as production falls off, and calling in sick (their form of a personal time out). If you are going to play the game of healthcare, play it as a well-informed team.

BEYOND THE SUGGESTION BOX

The United Negro College Fund said it best, "A Mind is a Terrible Thing to Waste." Are you wasting corporate assets because you failed to exploit employees' gray matter to their fullest potential? Not tapping your organization's mental resource is more than a waste, it is corporate self-sabotage. We are all familiar with the suggestion box concept, where customers and employees are given a means of making a recommendation or sharing an idea with upper management. If you are upper management, how can you be down with your customers and employees? When used right, the suggestion box is a valuable management tool for generating ideas, more so when the rewards are proportional to savings. However, the suggestion box remains a non-focused approach for gaining broad input. You may want to consider augmenting or swapping out your suggestion box program with what I call the "problem" box. The problem box concept calls upon your organization's brain trust, its employees. Trust me, every organization has a brain trust, though sometimes it is an arguable position at best. A problem box channels and focuses your brain trust's energies into pondering one significant issue or concern at a time. I tend to believe it is better to have many people thinking, rather than a few individuals pondering, to solve a problem. As an example, an organization employing 500 people has an opportunity for having 500 brains thinking about a specific problem. Or better yet, thousands of brains, if the employees discuss the problem with their family members, relatives, and friends. You never know whom your employees know, are married to, play golf with, or work out with. The problem box concept has the following 11 basic steps:

1. Defining a problem, issue, or concern you want solved;
2. Providing information about the problem and why it is a concern;
3. Giving an example of the problem's impact on operations;
4. Explaining the benefits to solving the problem;
5. Providing a reward that is truly reflective of the problem's magnitude;
6. Establishing an appropriate cutoff date for solution;
7. Evaluating suggested solutions;
8. Implementing the best solution;
9. Rewarding the winner(s) promptly;
10. Distributing information about the winning solution and the winner(s) system-wide; and
11. Posting the next problem.

EMPLOYEE-ENCOUNTER-ENHANCEMENT EXERCISES

Another means for increasing employee satisfaction is training your employees on how to provide Ultimate Patient Satisfaction. Knowing how, and practicing what you know, build self-confidence and reduce stress in people. As you tackle the rewarding challenges of creating an Ultimate Patient Satisfaction environment, you will find that besides being an effective training method, engaging employees in role playing scenarios is fun, helpful in building team spirit, and useful as an employee bonding agent. Your training should encompass identifying and demonstrating accepted Ultimate Patient Satisfaction attitude and behaviors. Employee-Encounter-Enhancement Exercises (E4) are also a great and creative way to structure interactive learning experiences, creating active employee participation, and preparing employees to face the world. E4 is practical, entertaining, and informative as well. One of the true benefits from using E4 programs is that employees have the opportunity to see it, hear it, do it, and discuss it. Recording your E4 sessions allows group discussions and critique at a later date or with a different group or department. If you are interested in establishing an Employee-Encounter-Enhancement Exercise Program, first recruit employees to form an E4 production team. Next, you can use the following eight steps outlined to guide you through the process of creating your E4 program and producing your own employee-patient scenarios. The following eight E4 steps are:

1. Identifying employee-patient encounters and classifying by category or type, such as in the act of admitting, checking in or out, assisting a patient, defusing an upset patient or family member, caring for a patient, giving directions, communicating bad news, and educating the patient. Document all patient-employee encounters and assign each to a category;

2. Creating an E4 depository of defined employee-patient encounters;

3. Assembling the necessary audio-video equipment to record and play back the E4 sessions, such as a video or cam-recorder, a TV monitor, a VCR, a tripod, and an audiotape recorder;

4. Developing the E4 format to be used in scenario enactments such as identifying the:
   a. Setting
   b. Situation
   c. Encounter type
   d. Responsive-interaction
      1. Wrong way
      2. Accepted Ultimate Patient Satisfaction way
5. Writing the E4 scripts;
6. Producing the scenarios on tape, using employee/actors;
7. Distributing E4 scenario recordings for in-service training; and
8. Analyzing E4 scenarios individually and as a group.

You have the option of using the actual employees responsible for specific patient satisfaction encounters or a pool of employee actors when recording E4 skits. Consider using audiotape recorders to simulate telephone conversations. After recording the E4 skits, analyze each E4 for appropriate response and handling, body language, word selection, tone of voice, and interpersonal skills. By making several copies from the master recording, you and others will be able to use the E4 training tapes over and over. To reinforce everyone's employee-encounter-enhancement skill, consider starting every meeting with a 5 to 10-minute Ultimate Patient Satisfaction E4 training video. If done with some creative thought, a few props, and a few hams (employees with self-proclaimed movie star potential), your efforts will be instrumental in converting good patient satisfaction into Ultimate Patient Satisfaction. Move over Alfred Hitchcock!

VALUE-ADDED EMPLOYEE

Your organization cannot be expected to be totally responsible and accountable for employee satisfaction on their own. Each employee must also be responsible and stand accountable for overall employee satisfaction, their personal actions, and even those of their coworkers. Employees must start taking personal responsibility for improving their employability, and in the process, start significantly contributing to their employer's success. The more-for-less reality that is sweeping the healthcare industry is causing, no forcing, providers to be constantly searching for high-impact performing, low maintenance employees (LME). While the search is taking place both inside and outside the organization and healthcare industry, providers will show a preference for hiring a value-added employee, an employee who increases the organization's value, an asset, not excess. You can start increasing your value to the company and your coworkers by becoming a value-added employee (VAE). If you are a high-impact performing, low maintenance employee, the chances are you are capable of becoming a value-added employee with a little work. A value-added employee is a special breed of person who brings an attractive array of related and relative knowledge, skills, and desire, all of which significantly contribute to making that person more employable and valuable to their organization, their department, and their team. The value-added employee focuses on constantly reinventing their job value, day in and day out. When your organization is being forced to do more with fewer people, the most valuable people (the keepers) are those who have significantly increased their value since joining the company. Are you significantly more valuable than when you were hired? Really? How would you justify hiring yourself again? Really?

On the yellow-brick road to becoming a value-added employee, you cannot always rely on your company to provide the heart, the courage, and the brains required to be self-motivated. Nor can you realistically expect your company to be providing all your training. You must stand accountable, taking it upon yourself to ensure that you are still employable, and worth your corporate contribution, now and in the future. If you are interested in increasing your employability and becoming a value-added employee, you better start the following:

1. **Demonstrating the right attitude;**
   Constantly exhibit and demonstrate your loyalty to the company, its customers, and fellow coworkers.
2. **Getting cross-trained;**
   Focus on gaining new knowledge and learning new job skills related to your company's needs and long-term success.
3. **Becoming computer literate;**
   Endeavor to become computer literate by learning how to use the three basic business software programs: word processing, spreadsheet, and a relational database.
4. **Building alliances and networks;**
   Start building personal, customer, coworker, and corporate

alliances and networks with leading employers, managed care plans, referral sources, local chambers of commerce, universities, and community leaders, etc.

5. **Improving Your Selling Skills;**
   If you do not know how to sell, learn, and learn quickly, attend multiple sales training programs, master the basics, and remember, in every organization, every employee sells, every day, in many different ways. Every patient-employee encounter is a sales call, you are selling yourself, your company, and your patient satisfaction. There are no exceptions.

6. **Developing a Strong Customer Service Orientation;**
   Read up on the subject, eat, drink, and breathe customer service, especially patient satisfaction, and live to provide Ultimate Patient Satisfaction.

7. **Developing a Business Mentality;**
   At a minimum, start developing a basic understanding and working knowledge of basic business principles and terminology, take a few courses, read a few books, and ask others, start becoming a disciple of good business practices. Learn about your company's business, products, services, and customers. Knowledge is power. Start getting stronger when it comes to your company's business, become an EBU.

8. **Being Accountable for Your Actions;** and
   Stand up and start demonstrating that you believe in every spoken word and every deed. Learn how you can be tactfully rocking the boat while still rowing in the same direction, especially when you know it is off course. But always be careful, rockers and messengers are often the targets of frustration and deposed of in some form or fashion.

9. **Functioning as a Significantly Contributing Team Player.**
   To be successful and thrive in a managed care environment, the future dictates that your organization needs to be building teams of value-added employees who are significantly contributing team players. Start doing things without being asked or told, go the extra mile when no one will pay the toll or ever know, smile, even if it hurts, and make personal sacrifices for the betterment of your organization, your department, and your team. By the way, if you do not have a team, start one.

Along with becoming a value-added employee come greater self-confidence, self-esteem, and self-reliance, all three contributions to on-the-job satisfaction leading to personal satisfaction, which in essence is the core building block of employee satisfaction that Ultimate Patient Satisfaction is built. When you love your job, you will never have to work again.

BEYOND THE COMPETITIVE EDGE, THE COMPETITIVE LEDGE™

Senior management can do many things to improve overall employee satisfaction. One thing, however, is critical, and that is creating a Competitive Ledge™, assuming a position beyond a competitive edge. Because we are creatures of habit, creating a Competitive Ledge™ is easier said than done. I define a Competitive Ledge™ as a proactive marketing position obtained that best enables an entity to respond to customer perceptions, needs, and desires within an extended window of opportunity, outside the short-term response capabilities of its competition. Creating a Competitive Ledge™ magnifies your strategic ability to allocate and maneuver your organization's people, its resources, and its services to exploit business opportunities unimpeded by the competition. Gaining the sometimes elusive Competitive Ledge™ requires you and your organization to take a quantum leap in revolutionizing your industry, delivering your services, and to lead, where others will hesitate to venture! Remember, Competitive Ledge™ is a step in the right direction and a step beyond your competition's competitive edge. To help you step out in establishing your Competitive Ledge™, consider the following three-point strategy:

1. Identify your core area of competence;
2. Consolidate your assets in developing your primary core area of competence; and
3. Focus all efforts on delivering your primary core area of competence better than the competition, and in the process providing as well as the competition in all other areas, but in none, worse.

There are three strategic resources common to all organizations and leaders: assets, enablers, and motivators. However, each organization's strategic resources are never equal, nor will they be because of the constantly changing business and market variables. The magnitude by which an organization's strategic resources vary, however, determines its strengths and weaknesses related to a specific market and time. Each strategic resource is further divided into three key sub-resources. A sub-resource is either tangible or intangible in nature and in and of itself, critical to an organization's overall success. Refer to Figure 11–1 the Strategic Resources Success Table. You will discover that the triad grouping of strategic resources listed in Figure 11–1 are interrelated, and can be read up and down, left to right, and diagonally.

FIGURE 11-1

Strategic Resources Success Table

Assets	Enablers	Motivators
People	Communications	Attitude
Partnerships	Commitment	Aptitude
Profits	Capital	Aspirations

Assets

People: The ability to have the *right* person, in the *right* job, with the *right* skills, with the *right* training, using the *right* tools, receiving the *right* management support, and demonstrating the *right* attitude is a company's *greatest* asset.

Partnerships: The ability to create and effectively manage strategic relationships with your employees, customers, competitors and suppliers.

Profits: The ability to manage your business in such a manner to ethically generate a fair return for services provided others without compromising quality

Enablers

Communications: Establishing an open-book-management environment and exploiting enabling technologies to enhance internal and external communications

	with employees, customers, and suppliers to maximize overall efficiencies and end user satisfaction.
Commitment:	Establishing system-wide team responsibility and accountability, top-to-bottom, management and employee commitment to specific goals and objectives.
Capital:	Establishing and maintaining access to growth capital.

Motivators

Attitude:	Rewarding people who are demonstrating desired attitudes.
Aptitude:	Rewarding people who are also high performers in their areas of responsibilities.
Aspirations:	Rewarding people who are creating the vision and leading the way.

When it is all said and done, employee satisfaction is the keystone to achieving Ultimate Patient Satisfaction, and everyone's unwritten responsibility for which we all share in the accountability.

CONTINUUM OF CARE STRATEGY

The continuum of care strategy is important to achieving Ultimate Patient Satisfaction; however, the continuum of care has five parts. You need to bring the five parts together, creating a strategic synergy and value greater than the parts. The five parts are as follows:

1. Continuum of caring—UPS;
2. Continuum of care—medical intervention;
3. Continuum of the caregiver—same caregivers throughout treatment, such as, home care nurse;
4. Continuum of communications—proactive, open, and complete awareness among all parties; and
5. Continuum of continuity—treatable within one healthcare system, one source provider.

12

Changing Mind-Sets, Behaviors, and Habits

Bringing out the best in people, the organizational challenge . . .

CREATING A WINNING MIND-SET

I define mind-set as the way people think, based on what people know, and what people believe. A winning mind-set is a self-motivating and empowering way of thinking that enables an individual and organization to achieve their goals in a chaotic, changing, and challenging environment. In essence, you are what you think. We all know healthcare is changing, and so you, your organization, and its people must too. In today's world, creating a winning mind-set starts by unlearning the past. You begin unlearning the past by proactively opening your mind to change, not solely for the sake of changing, but for the benefit. You need to actively seek new ways and means for revolutionizing your industry and in the process, delivering your services better than the masses of me-too providers. To unlearn the past, you begin focusing your resources and energies on the future; after all, that is where you will be spending the rest of your life. Typically, as your mind-set is being shaped, you remember the past, you live in the present, and you dream of the future. However, now you need to be unlearning the past, living in reality, and preparing for the future because there is no other way if you want to survive and thrive in healthcare. Though you must unlearn the past, you must never forget the important lessons learned from the past. The past is your gateway and insight into the future. You need to realize that unlearning the past calls for changing not only your mind-set, but your behavior and habits as well. You have to start changing the way you think, especially the way your organization is going to be delivering its services in a changing healthcare industry, whose future is unknown. However, there are things one can do to speed up the mind-set changing process. You can aggressively be creating a winning mind-set by:

1. Becoming more proactive, challenging status quo mentalities;
2. Thinking delivery revolution, separating yourself from me-too providers;
3. Building long-term partnerships, creating profitable relationships;
4. Seeking enabling technologies, increasing your speed and accuracy;
5. Championing your customers, delivering Ultimate Patient Satisfaction; and
6. Believing in yourself, staying focused and committed.

To be truly effective, your winning mind-set must be anchored in a vision, a strategic vision of the future. And a vision needs a supporting plan, a strategic plan. With this in mind, however, I know many people and organizations that have a vision, but no plan, or have a plan and no vision. As with a horse and carriage, visioning and planning are most effective together. Creating a plan without a vision is like placing the cart before the horse, doable but hard to steer. Unequivocally, if your organization has no vision, nor plan, on which to build winning mind-sets, its opportunities will be like a mirage, appearing on the horizon as a fleeing aberration of a perceived reality, wasting your previous resources in the chase. You are always in touch with reality with a winning mind-set. Giving in and giving up are all but impossible with a winning mind-set. A point worth remembering is that a person's own ego is often their biggest obstacle to a winning mind-set, especially when fighting to hold onto the past.

THE PAIN OF CHANGE

Where there is contentment, there is no progress. People resist change. It is human nature. We only change to the degree necessary to reduce the pain of not changing. Refer to Figure 12–1. How quickly people change is relevant to the degree of pain they suffer in not changing. Pain and changing, the two are inseparably linked. People live and organizations operate within a comfort zone, an area built on habits, tradition, and past knowledge. You have a comfort zone as well. Your patients each have a comfort zone too. It is that secure world we come to know and to cherish. So why leave our comfort zone for the unknown and insecurity of change? Pain! The fear of pain starts people thinking about changing. Real pain brings real change. The greater the pain, the faster people change. Pain is the instrument of change. It is that simple. One of my

FIGURE 12-1

Forces of Change/Benefit to Change

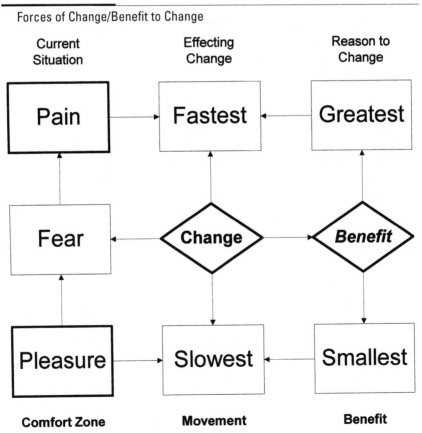

Comfort Zone   Movement   Benefit

personal quotations is, "Change is the reason for changing." Because the world around people is constantly changing, people have to constantly change to survive. You know, economic-evolution.

THE ENDLESS CYCLE OF CHANGE

Change is an endless cycle. Years ago I wrote the following descriptive verse to convey my thoughts on the endless cycle of change:

"The Endless Cycle of Change"

People are creatures of habit, and
creatures of habit resist change; but
things have to change to remain the same, and
being proactive forces change; but
opportunities are born of change, and
open minds are open to opportunities; but
opportunity is the beginning of success, and
success brings rewards; but
rewarded people embrace change, and
change creates new habits; but
people are creatures of habit, once again.

CONQUERING CHANGE

The fear of change is strong in most people. Conquering one's fear takes knowledge. Effecting change is in effect conquering change. Effective communication spreads knowledge, quelling people's fears. If you want to effect change without destroying people's morale, consider following the seven-Cs to conquering change:

1. Courage—Having the courage to determine when change is necessary and beneficial, even if it means challenging a coworker's or corporate culture.
2. Commitment—Remaining committed to effecting positive change, even under adverse circumstances, obstacles, and difficulties.
3. Communicate—Communicating and discussing openly the benefit and consequence of both changing and not changing.
4. Consensus—Making every effort to gain a consensus among all concerned parties that change is necessary and who, what, when, where, how, and why you are changing.

5. Concentration—Concentrating the people, the effort, and the resources to effect change. Focus your time and efforts on those goals that effect change.

6. Confirmation—Tracking your progress in effecting change, and consistently and effectively communicating the same to all concerned parties.

7. Congratulations—Rewarding quickly those effectively making the desired change, no matter how small a change may be. The aggregate of small changes results in a large change.

Always remember that the "pain of change can feel good." A noted business guru, Peter F. Drucker, said it a different way. He said, "Systematic innovation requires a willingness to look on change as an opportunity." But no matter how you say it, change is here to stay. Change is the engine of growth, rooted in the past, blooming in the present, and giving fruit in the future.

THE EFFECTIVE COACHING-MANAGER

You manage resources and lead people. All great leaders are also great coaches. Today's healthcare manager needs to become a coaching-manager, managing today's business, while at the same time coaching to effect change for the future and the betterment of people and the organization. The effective coaching-manager surpasses other managers by finding and developing the hidden potential to excel that exists in each person. To be effective at coaching people and effecting change mandates a coaching-manager mastering and employing the following seven related skills and actions:

1. Listening
   (a) Make and keep eye contact
   (b) Stop talking
   (c) Do not interrupt
   (d) Do not think about what you are going to say
   (e) Indicating attention by nodding or saying "Uh-huh"
   (f) Looking for nonverbal communication signals
   (g) Assuming open body language
   (h) Minimizing distractions

2. Observing
    (a) Watching for clues a person needs help
    (b) Can take on additional responsibility
    (c) Increased autonomy
    (d) Changes in performance, good and bad
    (e) Under varying performance situations and patient-encounters
    (f) Reaction to change
    (g) Response to stressful circumstances
3. Analyzing
    (a) Determining root causes for specific behaviors
    (b) Changes in performance, good and bad
    (c) Learning a person's best learning style
    (d) Determining most effective motivational and behavior reinforcement
4. Interviewing
    (a) Forming and asking various types of questions
    (b) Probing for strengths and weaknesses, both physical and mental
    (c) Determining a person's skills and proficiencies
    (d) Identifying a person's core values
    (e) Gathering relevant and objective information
5. Agreeing
    (a) Creating agreement among all concerned parties
    (b) Consummating performance contracts, put it in writing
    (c) Establishing a person's individual responsibilities and accountabilities
    (d) Knowing a person's individual authority
    (e) Establishing consequence for noncompliance
6. Feeding
    (a) Knowing when to provide feedback
    (b) Knowing most effective type of feedback to use
    (c) Providing clear, specific, and timely feedback
7. Rewarding
    (a) Establishing rewarding performance incentives
    (b) Knowing when to use tangible, as opposed to, intangible rewards
    (c) Knowing the most effective reward approaches to use
    (d) Looking for every little reason to praise a person

Holding a Coaching-Manager Session

To maximize your effectiveness as a coaching-manager, consider using the following seven-step coaching-manager approach during your next coaching session. You start by:

> **Step 1**—Defining the specific areas of concern or problem you want to bring to the person's attention. Typically, concerns and problems center on three root issues, a person's attendance, performance, and conduct.
>
> **Step 2**—Presenting specific dates and time periods that the person's behavior or problem (violation) occurred.
>
> **Step 3**—Comparing a person's expected performance to their actual performance.
>
> **Step 4**—Providing good business reasons why the person's behavior or problem needs to be corrected for the betterment of all parties.
>
> **Step 5**—Listing specific consequences the person can expect if their behavior is not changed or the problem is not corrected.
>
> **Step 6**—Determining how you plan to monitor the person's behavior or corrective action and explain the same to the person.
>
> **Step 7**—Using appropriate positive reinforcement and feedback techniques to achieve desired results.

The Coaching-Manager

Being a good coaching-manager takes practice and time. However, there are certain common habits that are shared by all great coaching-managers. You will find that by practicing what "I" preach, and adhering to the following nine key habits, before you know it (though others will know before you), you will have become an effective coaching-manager. To be an effective coaching-manager, you need to start as follows:

> **1.** Offer exact, defined, written standards of performance;
>
> **2.** Assume an objective, rather than a subjective, approach;
>
> **3.** Be sincere and unselfish in helping people grow professionally and personally;

4. Look for gradual improvements in people and reward accordingly;
5. Establish an urgent business rapport with each person;
6. Provide constructive criticism as an explanation, not a complaint;
7. Develop a winning strategy for achieving positive change;
8. Create a self-motivating working environment for people; and
9. Provide the necessary job training and tools people need for succeeding.

And if I were to pass along just one more step, it would be to start being humble in all you say and do. Step back and let others step forward for recognition, praise, and reward. You have done your job, bringing out the best in people. What in life is worth pursuing more than helping others help themselves?

What Employees Think About and Want Answered

Employees are people too, and they have many questions needing answers before they can physically and mentally commit 100% to their job. As their coaching-manager, an important part of your job is answering their often burning, difficult, and tricky questions to their fullest understanding and satisfaction. Generally speaking, most people have the same list of questions needing answers. The following are 13 of the most common questions employees ask their supervisor:

1. How well am I doing?
2. How do you see me?
3. What is expected of me?
4. How can I best perform my current job?
5. What kind of support and training will I receive?
6. What is the corporate culture like?
7. Do I fit into that corporate culture?
8. How can I get where I want to go from my current position?
9. Who will be my mentor in getting there?
10. Can I take risks?
11. Am I being paid to think, or just work?

12. What are the rewards for working effectively, efficiently, and delivering high performance?

13. How will you, as my manager, help me realize job satisfaction and achieve my career goals?

A coaching-manager does not wait to be asked. They answer the above questions before being asked.

MANAGEMENT SELF-ANALYSIS

Read the following five management self-analysis statements. Answer yes or no to those statements that you currently experience as a manager. Remember. Be honest with yourself. After all, if you cannot trust yourself, whom can you trust?

Yes No

☐ ☐ Does your people's performance rise just before a deadline?

☐ ☐ Have you ever said the following to another person?
  a. "I love my job, but it is the paperwork I hate."
  b. "I am under lots of pressure to reduce costs and increase revenues."
  c. "I always get the dirty projects, the projects nobody wants."

☐ ☐ Does your people's performance drop off once the department goals are met?

☐ ☐ Do you seldom celebrate your people reaching a professional or personal goal?

☐ ☐ Does your people's performance drop off after removing a performance requirement?

An effective coaching-manager would answer "no" to all the above questions. The lesser your coaching orientation, the more "yes" boxes you have checked.

Performance Coaching

A person's performance is directly related to their attitude and working habits. These working habits are repeated behaviors. All levels of performance within an organization are the direct reflection of the behaviors the organization chooses to reinforce, or not to reinforce. Poor performance from an individual, a team, a department, or an organization itself, is indisputably an indication that the organization (management) is reinforcing the wrong behaviors. You get what you reinforce. It is that simple. You do not break a habit, you mend behavior. Ultimate Patient Satisfaction requires changing behaviors throughout the organization, top to bottom. Here is how you can start changing behavior.

Changing Behavior

You change a person's performance by changing behavior. You change behavior by changing its consequences. You can change a person's performance by rewarding desired behavior and penalizing unwanted behavior. You can gain valuable insight into how positive reinforcement works in changing people's behavior and performance by spending a little time reviewing Figure 12–2, Behavior Consequences Table.

Creating and Using Positive Reinforcers

By now you have a good understanding of how positive reinforcement helps change behaviors. When engaging in behavior modification, you need to keep in mind the following five things.

FIGURE 12–2

Behavior Consequences

Reinforcement Type	Effect	Outcome	Performance
Positive	Behavior repeated because of pleasant result	People work harder than before	Maximum (proactive strategy)
Neutral	Behavior may or may not be repeated	People's unappreciated behavior vanishes	Seesaws (no strategy)
Negative	Behavior repeated to escape the unpleasant result	People do only what's necessary to escape punishment	Minimum (reactive strategy)

Criticism should be objective, to the point, and short, or not at all;

Avoid blaming and shaming;

Reinforce the punishment;

Employ personal reinforcers; and

Separate positive reinforcement from punishment.

Specific Behavior Criteria

Creating an UPS behavior criteria list, including all behavior changes necessary to achieve your desired results, will go a long way in making change easier.

Be Patient, Behavior Reversal Takes Time

To change a person and organization's behavior is time-consuming, usually taking a minimum of 20 to 30 days. However, reversed behavior can reverse itself back for lack of consistent positive reinforcement until it becomes a habit again. Figure 12–3, Behavior Reversal Table, shows the four components for behavior reversing. This chapter discusses all four in detail. Behavior reversal is an extended process, not a quick happening.

THE EIGHT PARADIGMS OF EFFECTIVE POSITIVE REINFORCEMENT

Using positive reinforcement effectively requires you to employ the following eight strategic paradigms:

    1. Honesty—Ensuring your people understand why you are asking them for certain behaviors or performances. Explain why change is imperative for their personal and the organization's success.

FIGURE 12–3

Behavior Reversal

Event	Behavior	Consequence	Commitment
Reason	Response	Reinforcer	20 to 30 days

2. **Integrity**—Making sure that what you say actually happens once people have achieved the desired behavior or performance. Nobody likes or trusts a welsher.

3. **Equality**—Treating all people equally in all that you say and do, regardless of their position in the organization. Actions speak louder than words.

4. **Respect**—Treating all people with personal and professional respect in all that you say and do, regardless of their position in the organization.

5. **Justice**—Rewarding those people best that perform best. Hold all others to the consequence of not changing as needed.

6. **Self-esteem**—Providing reinforcement and rewards that give people tangible proof that they are adding value to the organization. People add more value when they are valued.

7. **Growth**—Encouraging people to grow personally and professionally using positive reinforcement coaching. As people grow, their value to the organization grows.

8. **Security**—Determining the desired UPS behaviors you want and making sure that both you and the person you are coaching know exactly what those behaviors are, and what the corresponding consequences will be. Security comes from knowing where one stands.

You will discover that managers who embrace the coaching-management style based on positive reinforcement as a way of life, find working with people becomes a pleasant win/win experience and a cause for daily celebration.

Coaching-Manager Worksheet

Achieving Ultimate Patient Satisfaction will more than likely require effecting behavior change throughout your organization. You have been shown how to effect change. Figure 12–4, UPS Behavior Change Worksheet, will enable you to track your progress and the progress of others. The worksheet is self-explanatory in nature. Tracking each person's, each department's, and the organization's behavior changes separately provides you an effective control and feedback system for effecting change.

FIGURE 12-4

UPS Behavior Change Worksheet

| Goal # | Completion Date | | P R | Comments |
	Target	Actual		
Objectives				
1				
2				
3				
Things				
1				
2				
3				
UPS Action Team/Responsible Person	Telephone #			Comments
Leader				
Team member				
Team member				
Team member				

PR = Priority Rating

GETTING AHEAD USING FEEDBACK

If you are like me, the chances are you discovered criticism is a bad form of feedback the hard way, you criticized someone. Over time I learned the four basic types of feedback. The four types of feedback are shown in Figure 12–5, along with their purpose, result, and effect. I believe of the four types of feedback, coaching is the most effective. As you can see from reviewing Figure 12–5, silence is a form of feedback, the worst. If you have something to say, you better say it, or things will get worse.

Effective coaching-managers focus on using the coaching approach for providing feedback. You will find the coaching approach is also very effective in building up a person's self-confidence, self-esteem, and self-motivation. So the next time you have to criticize a person, don't, begin coaching instead.

FIGURE 12-5

Types of Feedback

Type	Purpose	Result	Effect
Silence	No response provided	Maintains status quo or behavior becomes extinct	Decreases confidence Reduces performance Creates paranoia Causes undue surprises Generates confusion
Criticism	Identifies undesirable behaviors	May stop undesirable behaviors	Decreases confidence Fosters excuses Generates blaming Leads to avoidance Hurts relationship Produces stress
Counseling	Defines desired behaviors and how to effect change	May change undesirable behaviors to desirable behaviors	May improve confidence May increase performance Strengthens relationship
Coaching	Explain desired behaviors and associated consequences while reinforcing positive efforts toward desired change	Changes undesirable behaviors and increases performance	Maximizes self-confidence Increases self-esteem Enhances performance Boosts self-motivation

Feedback Secrets

Finally, a few secrets to providing effective feedback are as follows:

1. Responding quickly to a person with coaching feedback;
2. Providing a person specific feedback on a regular and effective basis;

3. Rating a person's or organization's actual change against specific behavior criteria;

4. Graphing a person's or organization's progress against expectations;

5. Being honest with feedback;

6. Being respectful in giving feedback; and

7. Providing examples for improvement.

Give and Take

Receiving feedback is also a very important skill all coaching-managers need to master. The following are a few tips that will serve you well:

1. Start accepting feedback as a personal opportunity for improving, learning, and growing;

2. Start listening more and talking less, give your fullest attention;

3. Start asking for specific examples of cause and for improvement;

4. Start opening up, be receptive and not defensive;

5. Stop rationalizing in an effort to defend your actions;

6. Stop being uptight, relax;

7. Stop wandering around, stay focused on the issues at hand; and

8. Stop challenging and resisting feedback and the feedback giver.

"If you want to survive and thrive, start aligning your employees' behavior with the long-term goals and interests of your organization."

John F. O'Malley

13

Rewarding the Right Attitude

Hiring, rewarding, and firing attitude, the secret to success . . .

WHAT IS ATTITUDE?

Hiring, rewarding, and firing attitude is the secret to success in any business, including healthcare. So what is this thing called attitude? Well to start with, attitude is subjective. Your attitude is perceived by others as an aura, comprising your body language, facial expressions, tones of voice, spoken words, dress, grooming, and your general outlook on life itself. Your attitude determines how you will react to people, events, and changes in your life. You can change neither the past nor the inevitable fact that things will not always go your way. However, you can change your attitude to encourage the best in you, in others, and in situations. A strong positive attitude is the foundation for success. You have a choice regarding your attitude, so embrace positive thoughts and deeds, shunning the ugly things in life. Take some time to read and reflect on "Your Attitude."

"YOUR ATTITUDE"

by John F. O'Malley

Your attitude is your "Mood for Life" barometer. Your attitude is a mirror of your beliefs, biases, and thoughts. Your attitude influences your every action and encounter with others. Your attitude reflects your feelings and temperament toward yourself and others. Your attitude dictates your way of life, your happiness, and sadness. Your attitude is contagious. Your attitude can inspire greatness in others. Your attitude can also breed defeatism in others. Your attitude can enable you and others to accomplish the impossible. Your attitude is a self-prophesy of your future. Your attitude is the most important asset you own. Your attitude, guard it well and let no one or event change it for worse. Your attitude, you have a choice. Your attitude, take charge of it. Your attitude, it's UP to you.

UPS EVALUATION ELEMENTS

There are numerous methodologies or approaches used to reward managers and employees. However, I favor any system that is based on rewarding individuals, teams, and departments for significant improvements in the areas of their responsibilities, and not for delivering and maintaining status quo performance. Remember, an organization's status quo performance can be good, or even excellent, but never good enough if you want to be competing in the future. To flourish and thrive in healthcare, you and your company cannot afford to accept status quo performance from your managers, employees, and fellow coworkers. So keep in mind that with status quo you will never grow. Speaking of status quo, you will still find many healthcare providers using generic-group or category-compensation programs. This type of annual compensation plan is designed to give all employees who fall within some predetermined performance criteria or range the same incentive. As an example, employees receiving a satisfactory evaluation would be eligible for a 3% salary adjustment, whereas an employee having an excellent evaluation might receive a 4% increase. I believe, generic, across the board salary increases or bonuses are more harmful than good. The average-performance employees are happy, but the high-end performers, the ones who really make a difference in you and your organization being successful, become increasingly frustrated. All employees were not created equally when it comes to significantly improving the company's competitive position. Receiving a marginally higher incentive for superior performance irritates most high-end performers. Employees have their own evaluation grapevine (gripevine) and know better than anyone else how well another employee is performing, or better yet, a manager. Consider that even if an employee receives an excellent performance rating, their performance may or may not have made a significant improvement in one or more of the following four strategic corporate growth factors:

1. Employee satisfaction;
2. Customer-patient satisfaction;
3. Revenue generation; and
4. Cost management.

Most of us know that to a great extent, performance evaluations are subjective in nature because of human nature. My point is this, it is all too common to be subjective rather than objective in evaluating employees. In being subjective, you can and often do end up with two people who have received an excellent performance rating at their annual review. However, while one employee excelled at achieving status quo results, the other was making significant improvements in one or more of the strategic evaluation elements. Which would you rather be paying for, excellence in status quo execution or excellence in improving performance? If your answer is status quo, put this book away for a rainy day or use it as a doorstop.

I take it that if you are reading on, you choose excellence in improving performance. Great. Growing your organization depends not on achieving excellence at maintaining status quo, but excelling at improving overall performance. Deming, the quality guru, said that only excellence counts, all else is for naught. I like to say only excellence counts in those areas that improve the performance of the individual, department, and organization, and all else is status quo! To this end, you will find that by creating a compensation plan based on achieving significant improvements in employee satisfaction, customer-patient satisfaction, revenue generation, and cost management, your chances for surviving and thriving as a healthcare provider have been stacked in your favor. When creating or reengineering your current performance and incentive pay programs, consider basing those programs on the four strategic corporate growth factors detailed in Figure 13–1, the UPS Rewarding System Table.

EXCELLENT PERFORMANCE

To me, an employee who performs well in executing their assigned responsibilities and achieving their goals and objectives has performed satisfactorily. The employee has done just what they were hired to do, and does it well. You should expect every employee to excel at their job. Employees who do not excel are in the wrong job, perhaps even

FIGURE 13–1

UPS Rewarding System

Strategic Area	Evaluated	Process
Employee satisfaction	Interpersonal skills, coworker support and development, productive team participation	Combined supervisor and peer evaluation for salary adjustments, promotions, and incentives
Patient satisfaction	Reducing the number of patient complaints, moving satisfied patients to very satisfied patients, and contributing to organization becoming the provider of choice	Surveys and third-party confirmation on organization's overall patient satisfaction rating to include departments, units, and individuals as warranted
Revenue generation	Creating new business, keeping existing customers, and reimbursement-cash flow management	Determining the gross revenue generation from existing and new customers (referral sources), and conducting coding, billing, and collections audits by a third party
Cost management	Cost reduction strategies, implementation tactics, and ongoing maintenance of cost reduction activities.	Determining the effective cost savings related to performance improvement or service per implemented strategy, and monitor for consistency

the wrong department or company. However, many managers rate an employee's satisfactory performance as excellent, saying they do their job well. But that is what the employee is being paid to do, is it not? Only those employees who are proactively exceeding their current job responsibilities by assuming significant responsibilities in one or more of the four strategic corporate growth factors are candidates for receiving an excellent rating. As a gung-ho private in the U.S. Marines, I was told, if you want to be a sergeant, start acting like a sergeant, before long people will think you are a sergeant, and promote you to sergeant. I did and I was.

EMPOWERING PERFORMANCE

Empowering your employee to excel is a great way to maximize corporate assets. However, empowering your employees can be tricky, especially if done in a vacuum. To work, you need to be bringing together three essential entities, you, them, and us, to work as one. You will find Figure 13–2, Empowering Employees to Excel Table, outlines the necessary mind-sets for succeeding. One last point, find the time to create what I call an employee empowerment statement or guide. The guide is used for identifying each employee's empowerment level, hence, defining and quantifying their frontline decision-making

FIGURE 13–2

Empowering Employees to Excel

You—Employer	Them—Employee	Us—Team
Provide information, training, and feedback	Focus on delivering benchmark quality and customer service, reducing costs, and increasing profits	Always searching for cost-effective ways for improving our quality, service, and corporate performance
Demonstrate employee and service orientation	Act for the betterment of coworkers, customers, and organization	Resolve internal and external conflict, while focusing on employee and customer satisfaction
Acknowledge and reward desired behavior	Reward desired behavior in coworkers and customers	Proactively trimming the organization of resource and performance fat

powers. As an example, hospital operators are informed that they are able to make the following decisions without seeking authorization.

1. Provide transportation to or from the hospital for patients living within a 10-mile radius, not to exceed $20.00;
2. Provide a complementary hospital meal for family members visiting a patient, not to exceed $5.00; and
3. Send flowers to an upset patient not to exceed $15.00.

ANNUAL REVIEW

Time-consuming annual employee reviews are one of the dredges of being a manager, or so it seems to most of the managers I have talked with over the years. And in reality, such reviews tend to be, more often than not, subjective and superficial in nature. Most are insignificant in effecting change and rewarding results. Many managers are still ill-prepared to conduct truly objective employee reviews, and almost always revert to a subjective evaluation and a non-confronting approach or alternative. Besides, good managers are coaches who coach employees on a daily basis, not annually. However, I guess the annual review system, and the employee's perceived salary adjustment associated with the same, has evolved as a necessary habit (evil) based on archaic employer-employee philosophies. But there is a better way to reward your employees.

Those Who Know Best Review

What better way is there to judge my performance as a healthcare consultant then by asking the people I am currently working with, and those whom I have served in the past, as to their overall satisfaction and achieved results? You may even want to ask other consultants and associations. Why not incorporate the same concept in your employee's evaluation protocols? Consider revising your annual performance evaluation program so that every employee, including managers, receives their evaluation by an array of peers and coworkers. Known as ACE, Array of Coworker Evaluators, an employee receives a performance evaluation from their coworkers, instead of just their immediate supervisor. The ACE methodology allows firsthand performance information by the people who know best, one's coworkers, to be instrumental in evaluating an employee's interpersonal skills and significant contribution in the four strategic corporate growth factors. It is so simple, it scares us, but it shouldn't. The concept of having employees evaluating their fellow coworker's performance causes all employees to take stock of their own responsibilities and how well they execute supportive actions. However, you can expect that there will always be some degree of subjectiveness in any evaluating process, including ACE. But I believe that employees will be more objective than most think, and managers can be. Once the evaluation is completed for a specific employee, a manager would review the results with the employee and develop an agreement on any corrective actions or self-improvement needed.

Consider creating an ACE form and having a selected group of employees evaluate each of their coworkers as their performance pertains to the four strategic corporate growth factors discussed earlier. Do this quarterly or semi-annually, not annually. You will find that reviewing each employee's strategic performance on a more frequent basis enables you to make timely adjustments and quickly identify areas of concern. A manager is responsible for overseeing the frequency, evaluation, and actions required to gain individual employee performance improvement. To be effective, ACE evaluators' anonymity must be ensured by the process and management. Whatever your evaluation approach is and no matter how effective, performance reviewing does not guarantee people will change the way they work. So remember, the world consists of only the quick and the dead. If you are not quick to respond to customer demands, you are dead in the water; the same holds true for improving your employee's performance.

PROFIT SHARING

Study after study shows that companies that have an equitable employee profit-sharing program in place experience increased productivity, increased employee morale, and low turnover. Stop to think, if you adopted a profit-sharing plan, perhaps your annual evaluations and salary adjustments might be a thing of the past. Developing compensation and profit-sharing plans is not the scope of this chapter or book, however, enough information is readily available for someone wishing to explore that option further. Not-for-profit entities need to explore performance-based pay methodologies more aggressively.

PSYCHOLOGICAL COMPENSATION

Cash is not always king when it comes to motivating employees. However, the positive reward that is gained from the activity itself, rather than from what the employee ultimately derives from undertaking and completing an activity, is often perceived by the employee to be of greater value than cash itself. These non-cash benefits are referred to as intrinsic rewards by psychologists. When you feel ownership, intrinsic rewards tend to take on greater value than extrinsic benefits, like dollar incentives. An intrinsic reward can be just as simple as enjoying what you are doing, or taking special pride in the accomplishment or outcome. The extrinsic reward, in time, often loses its luster as a motivator, giving way to intrinsic benefits that ownership fosters. Not everyone can own the company, but employees can gain ownership by buying into a project, a program, and a corporate goal or philosophy. Employees are more likely to excel for a cause or philosophy than they are psychologically committed to (intrinsic) than a task they are just getting paid (extrinsic) to carry out. Mercenaries seldom, if ever, fight for a cause, and thus rarely win a war on their own fighting skills. Do you think mercenary mind-set employees are any different? Because extrinsic rewards tend to quickly lose their employee-motivating properties, you need to create the opportunities for employees to gain ownership in whatever they are doing. The following are 12 opportunities for providing employee ownership:

1. Let your employees create their individual tasks and performance responsibilities based on set goals, going even as far as permitting each employee to create their own job description;
2. Offer employee stock options;
3. Start using performance pay and profit sharing;
4. Offer a fully vested retirement program upon hire, or 90 days thereafter, and not the typical five years to fully vested approach;
5. Provide company-wide executive and peer recognition;
6. Demonstrate your trust by offering a high-profile project or assignment;
7. Consider a promotion or title name change;

8. Permit the employee to go to a sweet offsite seminar (SOS);
9. Attend a high-level meeting, board meetings are not off-limits;
10. Go on a special business trip with top executives;
11. Receive a "day off for appreciation" for consistently demonstrating a great attitude; and
12. Participate in hiring new employees for their department.

Every employee has value to offer the company, or they should not have been hired in the first place, so let your employees buy in. Try giving each employee an intrinsic reason for wanting to make you and the organization successful. Your employees need to believe in the organization's purpose for existing and its mission. Consider providing opportunities for each employee to share your dreams and create one or two of their own.

ENHANCED EMPLOYEE ENVIRONMENT

Another way to reward your employees is by eradicating anti-motivators from their work area, their department, and the organization. You can start enhancing your employees' environment by eliminating the following:

1. Office politics, racism, and sexual harassment;
2. Childish policies and rules;
3. Habitual, insignificant, and endless meetings;
4. Rewarding the mediocrity;
5. Incompetent employees and supervisors;
6. People with negative attitudes, system-wide, top-to-bottom;
7. Favoritism and subjective reviews;
8. Unsafe, noisy, and dirty working areas;
9. Useless paperwork, record keeping, and reports; and
10. Archaic equipment, processes, and systems.

MOTIVATING TOP PERFORMERS

According to research conducted by Hewitt and Associates, the following are the five top plans for motivating top performers:

1. Spot bonus for specific event—51%;
2. Personal goal performance awards—44%;
3. Company–department goal awards—43%;
4. Cash profit sharing—29%; and
5. Stock option-purchase awards—13%.

WHAT IS IMPORTANT IN A JOB

David Michaelson & Associate-ICR research shows that for workers 25 to 49 years old, the important aspects of their current job are the following:

1. Money—40%;
2. Like coworkers—30%;
3. Independence—26%;
4. Gratifying work—26%;
5. Nice workplace—23%;
6. Does public good—16%; and
7. Good for career—11%.

Looking closely at the above information, suggests that money, though rated number one in importance at 40%, leaves 60% of the people saying money is not everything. Also note that most employers and organizations can readily provide six out of the seven with little, if any, capital expenditure but heaps of empowerment and entrusting.

TOTAL QUALITY MANAGEMENT (TQM) COMPENSATION

What good is it for you and your organization to be TQM-focused on and committed to delivering customer and patient satisfaction by successfully meeting their needs more efficiently and profitably (TQM?), if your compensation and reward systems do not appropriately reflect the importance of that commitment? Start linking employee, department, and organizational TQM goals with Total Expected Compensation (TEC). For my two-cents, you cannot overlook the importance TEC plays in modifying behavior and effecting change, so converting your company's salary and benefit program(s) into a dynamic and effective TQM modifier is a critical management responsibility with great payback potential.

You can start using one or more of the following three patient satisfaction measurement opportunities to better leverage TQM to TEC:

1. Patient satisfaction rating;
2. Patient movement from satisfied to very satisfied; and
3. Patient satisfaction factors, such as waiting time, infections, and mistakes.

Remember, where there is a strong, determined will to reward for excellence in customer service, there is always a reliable way to measure customer satisfaction and compensate employees accordingly. After all, as the saying goes, "you get what you pay for." So do not leave TQM to chance.

LEGAL NOTE

I am not an attorney. The compensation, performance pay, and incentive concepts presented previously are my personal thoughts on the subject and may or may not be viable options depending on your particular situation. Therefore, I highly recommend that before you start reengineering your salary program, you review all relevant federal, state, and local laws and regulations. I am also sure that employee unions may find paying for significant improvements a little threatening. However, employers have known for decades the secret to keeping their company a non-union operation: you have to create and maintain employee satisfaction to the level where the benefits to joining a union are insignificant and not worth the benefit of changing.

REWARDING OPTIONS

The following three books will provide you additional information on rewarding people:

1001 Ways to Reward Employees, Bob Nelson, Workman Publishing, 800-722-7202

People, Performance, and Pay: Dynamic Compensation for Changing Organizations, David Hofrichter, Thomas Flannery, Paul Platten, Free Press, 1996, 800-223-2348

Super Motivation, Dean R. Spitzer, AMACOM, 800-262-9699

CHAPTER

Very Important Volunteers

Viva volunteers, healthcare's unsung heroes and heroines ...

Day in and day out, volunteers across America are the unsung heroes and heroines of the healthcare delivery system. Over the years, volunteers have been channeled into performing many seemingly petty tasks that other healthcare professionals and technologists feel reluctant to carry out on their own. The volunteer pool was treated as a pseudo employee base that was used to fill minimal-wage marketing (MWM) positions in an effort to reduce costs. We use volunteers to plug the gaps, to process undesirable paperwork, to undertake mundane tasks, to help out here and there, to run errands, and to shuttle patients between departments and out the door. In return, we stuffed volunteers in small waiting or holding rooms, sparsely and poorly furnished, and for the most part, left them to their own doing. Once a year we held an annual award party. Management saw the volunteer as an instrument for offsetting operating costs. Used effectively, volunteers enabled management to reduce the organization's full-time equivalent (FTE) demands. With this in mind, volunteers were dispersed throughout the healthcare provider's organization. However, as many healthcare organizations became accustomed to using volunteers to augment their existing employee base and thus, reducing their overall costs, especially hospitals, most senior managers failed at seeing and developing this strategic and valuable corporate resource beyond their myopic financial concerns and immediate needs. I venture to say that most hospital administrators do not fully grasp the strategic importance volunteers are playing in the scheme of things. It is seen as just one of those time-draining nuisances, no real importance, jobs somebody has to do, hopefully not senior management. "Oh, yeah?" I say. Surely, there are greater contributions volunteers can make than just offsetting costs? Have you ever considered turning your volunteers into a proactive patient satisfaction force, an army of goodwill ambassadors, or perhaps a battalion of image-enhancement and referral-building disciples? The chances are that your volunteers are well distributed throughout the community you serve, and for the asking, providing living testimony that you care. When was the last time you spent quality time analyzing your volunteer program? Too busy, you say. I hope not for your sake and the sake of Ultimate Patient Satisfaction.

If you have a corps of volunteers, whether it is two or 200, stop and consider the strategic impact those individuals have on your organization's well-being. Once you explore and fully understand the significant effect patient-volunteer encounters have on your ability to achieve Ultimate Patient Satisfaction, only then will you make the necessary commitment to developing your volunteers to their fullest contributing potential. You can get started by turning your corps of volunteers into an army of ambassadors, that is, ambassadors of goodwill and patient satisfaction gurus.

VOLUNTEER VIVA PROGRAM

VIVA is an acronym for Very Important Volunteer Asset. If you already have a volunteer program in place, take the time and conduct a detailed evaluation and analysis from a strategic viewpoint. That is to say, treat and analyze your volunteer group as a product, a delivered service. Consider approaching your analysis from a marketing perspective and at a minimum, thoroughly determine the volunteer group's true cost-saving value to the organization, its impact on overall patient and employee satisfaction, and its strengths and weaknesses. Once you have determined these key factors, quantify your volunteer group's strategic importance to the organization. If upon conclusion of your evaluation you determine that the volunteer group has no strategic importance, get started creating one. In the event your not-for-profit or for-profit organization does not have a volunteer group, you will still benefit from undertaking the same type of evaluation and analysis. You will find that by conducting such a proactive analysis, or market research approach, there does exist a truly strategic organizational value to a well-conceived and a well-run volunteer group.

Regardless of the number of people in your volunteer program, you cannot afford to take your volunteer program lightly. In designing a new, or upgrading an existing volunteer program, start by establishing up-front accountability by appointing a senior manager to oversee and develop this corporate asset. Quite often, as the case may be, a hospital will pass this critical responsibility to a junior person in the organization, such as patient advocates, marketing representatives, or other persons empowered to do little, if anything, to effect change. As within any industry and business, strategic corporate assets are receiving appropriate attention from top management. Only seasoned and proven managers are entrusted, or honored, with the responsibility of protecting, developing, and exploiting strategic assets for the organization's prosperity. Healthcare providers cannot afford to be any different. Once accountability has been assigned at the most effective management level, organize a three-person team to create or update your volunteer program. You may want to consider some or all of the following when creating your formal volunteer program.

MISSION STATEMENT

In conjunction with several influential volunteers, create a mission statement that strengthens the volunteer group's strategic value, that reflects corporate philosophies, and that helps achieve organizational goals.

VOLUNTEER SERVICES

Identify and list the areas within your organization by position, tasks, and department where volunteers can be assigned to support the staff and assist patients. This list becomes your "Chart of Volunteer Services." Similar to an employee job description, develop a formal and written volunteer performance requirement for each task and position. Working together, human resource personnel, risk management, and department heads should be able to identify appropriate and safe tasks and positions for volunteers. Use a standardized format in writing performance requirements.

ASSIGNMENT ALLOCATION

Create an objective, means, or protocol for assigning volunteers to specific tasks and positions as defined in the Chart of Volunteer Services. As an example, before a volunteer can staff the information desk, they must have one year of general volunteering, completed appropriate training, and demonstrate the ability to remain calm in crisis situations. People are creatures of habit, and so are your volunteers. Make an effort to eliminate the process where volunteers go where they want and do what they want, insensitive to your organization's needs. Instead of permitting your volunteers to hang around to earn their 15 years of service pin, consider focusing your VIVA to support corporate objectives.

APPEARANCE AND ATTIRE

Establish appropriate grooming, attire, and hygiene guidelines for all volunteers to follow, especially for those volunteers who come in contact with your patients and their family members. Ask any patient. Many healthcare providers have relaxed or dressed down their dress codes to the point where it is extremely difficult for the patient to distinguish a nurse from the billing clerk, a doctor from some laboratory technologist or vendor. When you fly Delta Airlines, a red-coated representative greets you in the terminal to help you make your next connection, though I have to admit that even Delta has had relapses on wearing their famous red coat, but so has their service. Appropriate dress helps in establishing a corporate image, on the other hand patients often perceive sloppy attire with poor quality. Most organizations readily provide their volunteers a uniform of sorts and some even go as far as making the volunteer pay for their own outfit. Talk about being sick. Why should any volunteer have to pay for giving you free labor? Consider dressing your volunteers well, after all, are they not your front-line image? Do not skimp to save a few dollars up front, if you have to, take the money out of the marketing budget and charge it to advertising and public relations. Choose a color that is cheerful, not conservative. I think yellow is a bright and cheerful color that flatters most people, however, most people like blue. Remember, you are not running a fashion show, but you do want your volunteers to radiate a warm, friendly demeanor.

INFECTION CONTROL

Infection control is serious business for healthcare providers, an estimated 3% to 5% of hospital inpatients contract an infection every year yet many facilities do not have an active program for addressing the less than sterile volunteers. Do not take chances spreading disease, accounting for and eliminating who-knows-what bacteria, viruses, and germs volunteers involuntarily spread from patient to patient, and employee to employee. To be on the safe side, consider having in-service training for your volunteers about preventing the transmitting and spreading of germs by appropriate hand washing and infection control. Do not let a volunteer serve until these classes have been satisfactorily completed.

CODE OF CONDUCT

To ensure a uniform delivery of volunteer services throughout your system, you may want to consider creating a volunteer code of conduct (VCC), which adherence to is mandatory for all volunteers. Consider establishing a team comprising your best volunteers to write a code of conduct, the commandments of volunteering if you please. The code should define acceptable and unacceptable behavior. To help, you may want to consider the following 15 volunteer commandments or codes of conduct, in whole or part. A volunteer is always:

1. Serving where needed with eagerness;
2. Exhibiting a contagious and positive attitude for helping others;
3. Demonstrating a genuine sense of caring in everything said and done;
4. Seeking opportunities to assist others;
5. Thinking like a patient;
6. Smiling, instead of frowning;
7. Praising, not criticizing others;
8. Ensuring patients' rights and confidentiality is never compromised;

9. Showing empathy, not indifference toward patients;
10. Presenting a professional image by always being appropriately attired and groomed;
11. Shunning, not spreading disdainful gossip about patients, employees, and others volunteers;
12. Uttering no vulgarity and displaying no obscene gestures;
13. Being honest and trustworthy;
14. Respecting all people, regardless of their sex, race, religion, and social status; and
15. Being accountable for their actions.

Every volunteer should have a copy of your finalized and official "code of conduct." A laminated pocket card is ideal, but also consider posting the volunteer code of conduct in an area where all your volunteers will see it on a daily basis.

AMBASSADOR RATING

Never let your volunteers go unsupervised and always be monitoring their compliance to establish rules and expected performance. Evaluating each volunteer's performance is a must and no different from monitoring and reviewing employees' performances. Few healthcare organizations have set guidelines for evaluating volunteers. The "If we bug them, they will leave" mind-set has kept management from pressing performance expectations on their volunteer groups. Remember, you are looking for a few good volunteers, not a mass of do-what-you-please individuals. Like employees, volunteers need the control and discipline of a good coach-manager. The actions and lack of action by volunteers are directly reflecting on the organization's image, and because of just that, volunteers need objective supervision and control to ensure Ultimate Patient Satisfaction. Consider establishing an ambassador rating program for grading each volunteer's performance and their strategic value to achieving Ultimate Patient Satisfaction. Such a rating system is simple to administer and might include the following 12 factors:

1. Role model status;
2. Supervisory demands;
3. Delivered performance;

4. Interpersonal skills;

5. Professional appearance;

6. Patient satisfaction and service orientation;

7. Accountability, dependability, and flexibility;

8. Accumulative hours of service;

9. Useable skills;

10. Ability to train others;

11. Team player; and

12. Overall system knowledge.

Upon identifying and defining each element or factor you will use in your rating system, create the ways and means of evaluating each volunteer accordingly on a predetermined time schedule. Semi-annually or annually is best, however, and it is important to remember that each volunteer, just like an employee, needs to be coached daily to get and maintain the image and level of performance you are expecting and need to demand in today's competitive environment.

IDENTIFICATION

With the strange and unfortunate happenings in today's world, I strongly recommend, for security reasons, that every volunteer in your organization be issued a form of personal identification in line with what is given to employees. The best sources of identification will sport a large, color-portrait photograph of the volunteer, clearly indicating that the wearer is a volunteer, and their name will be readable from 10 feet away. Currently, name tags, snap on or necklace type ID badges, colored arm bands, uniforms, or jackets are typically used by facilities to identify volunteers. When making your ID selection, consider one or more of the above combinations, making the act easier for patients and visitors to quickly and passively identify volunteers.

RECOGNITION SYSTEMS

Everyone likes to be recognized for a job well done. And that is double-fold for the people you do not pay. Volunteers are no different. Recognition is very important to them. It is your job to create the necessary programs that efficiently and cost-effectively recognize each individual volunteer's contributions in the manner most appreciated by them. You have many appreciation options to choose from that can be mixed and matched to construct a recognition program that is well accepted by your volunteers. However, do not go about creating a recognition program in a vacuum, asking your volunteers what they feel are the most effective and appropriate ways and means for the organization to show its appreciation. Based on the length of service and volunteer hours, you may want to consider a recognition package consisting of one or more of the following 27 possibilities:

1. Annual recognition dinner;
2. Plaque, certificate, or vase;
3. Pins and jewelry;
4. Ring (superbowl of volunteering) (employees too?);
5. Special arm bands, vests, blazers, jackets, or stripe on pants legs;
6. Front page recognition in the organization's newsletter;
7. Special function or party;
8. Free breakfast and lunch;
9. Preferred assignment;
10. Private room if admitted to your hospital;
11. Prorated medical discounts;
12. Unannounced flowers or a fruit basket delivered to their residence;
13. Signed thank-you card from the board, chief executive officer, administrator, department, and staff;
14. Dedicate a room or building in their name;
15. Dedicated parking space;
16. Dedicated stone, brick, bronze, or cement memorial;
17. Enhanced benefits;
18. Selecting a volunteer of the week (52 opportunities);
19. Volunteers of the year (chosen from volunteers of the week winners);
20. VIVA wall, a wall in the volunteer room to display recognition awards;
21. Place a recognition article in the volunteer's local newspaper;

22. Offer uniform upgrade or distinctive color of honor;
23. Prepaid dinner and trips;
24. Prepaid shopping spree or gift certificates;
25. Institute a hug-a-volunteer contest once a year;
26. Executive and department head luncheon; and
27. Posted recognition throughout system, such as in waiting areas or on food tray placemat.

HOURS VERSUS YEARS

Consider tracking and reporting a volunteer's service longevity in hours instead of years. There are two good reasons for doing so; the first deals with actuality and the second deals with competitiveness. As an example, suppose an individual being recognized for 22 years of volunteering has accumulated a total of 3168 service hours in the process, while another person with 11 years of volunteering has amassed 6336 service hours in half the time. We agree that each volunteer needs to be recognized for their efforts and service hours. However, if volunteer seniority recognition is based solely on the number of years served, a person serving fewer years but accumulating more service hours is done an injustice. Furthermore, to drive the more competitive volunteers, recognizing hours is more effective. Here is why. A volunteer may not be able to catch up in the number of years served with a senior volunteer, but they certainly can be increasing their number of service hours to gain the lead in time. Consider posting and updating each volunteer's service hours on a monthly basis. This approach will passively fire up competitiveness within the group to increase individual volunteer service hours. In the end, the competitiveness will be providing your organization with more service hours, a win-win situation.

WRITTEN GUIDELINES

Before starting, every volunteer should be given a volunteer guidebook explaining your volunteer program. Such a document enables a volunteer to be reviewing the program's guidelines, rules, and the terms and conditions at their own leisurely pace. So, once you have finished defining your volunteer program, consider putting it in writing. Creating a well-written, four-color, photo-packed volunteer guide or brochure is critical in establishing uniformity in people usually set in their ways. While creating your volunteer guide, keep in mind that this document needs to be supporting three key functions: recruiting, educating, and setting standards of excellence. When designing the guide or brochure, remember to keep those three points in mind. The brochure will be a great marketing and selling tool for recruiting volunteers, especially since only 15% of all adult volunteers give their time to hospitals/healthcare organizations according to a recent survey by Princeton Survey Research associates. Remember, you have to inform and then sell people on volunteering their valuable time to help you and your patients. As a teaching aid, the brochure needs to outline your volunteer program in detail, including expectations. And last, but most important, the brochure will help you establish a volunteer service image and through that, a system-wide standard of excellence delivered with purpose and consistency.

KEY ENCOUNTER ASSESSMENT

Part of your volunteer needs and service assessment should be identifying each and every patient-volunteer encounter opportunity; do this system-wide. This needs to be done, position by position, department by department, and facility by facility. An important part of patient-volunteer encounter assessing is to identify the skills needed in specific volunteer positions to ensure quality patient-volunteer encounters. I call this process PAVE, proactively analyzing volunteer encounters. It's a process for paving the road to enhance patient-volunteer encounters. Too often volunteers are seen just as a warm body for stuffing into any vacant position, disregarding the impact that person will have on patient satisfaction. Hopefully you realize PAVE's value in helping you better understand the real and diverse impact volunteers have on your overall patient satisfaction. Second, PAVE information is key to creating an effective volunteer training program. And third, you will start becoming more effective in matching the right volunteer to the right position or job, an important step on your journey to Ultimate Patient Satisfaction.

RECRUITING

Upon establishing that a volunteer group has great strategic importance to your organization's success, you need to start taking the volunteer recruiting process more seriously. It is just as important as hiring an employee, and management needs to be treating it as such.

Assuming you have taken the necessary time for calculating a volunteer's worth to the company annually, hence, how much money saved in FTE costs, determining your recruiting package and commitment becomes much easier. As an example, if each volunteer in effect saves you $8000 annually, surely, you can provide each a free uniform. As an example using the same scenario, 50 active volunteers are saving a hospital $400,000 annually.

Someone needs to be held accountable for recruiting quality volunteers. Once you have assigned recruiting accountability to the appropriate person (not people), the next step is to start developing a best-volunteer profile based on your existing volunteers. The following 18 data bits of information will help you get started down the profiling road:

1. Age;
2. Sex;
3. Ethnic background;
4. Religious affiliation;
5. Retirement status;
6. Geographic proximity to facility (winter and summer migratory?);
7. Mode of transportation;
8. Family status;
9. Living affiliations;
10. Previous patient or related to;
11. Education;
12. How initially recruited;
13. Recruited by;
14. Volunteer hours per week;
15. Reason for volunteering;
16. Volunteering likes and dislikes;
17. Memberships in clubs, hobbies; and
18. Ambassador rating (a rating given to each volunteer).

The profiling methodology presented will help you in determining what your best (preferred) volunteers all have in common. You will find using the analyzed data for each of your best volunteers helpful in constructing a volunteer recruiting profile that best matches your best volunteers. Now you know who, what, where, and when and should be able to identify how to attract more volunteers of the desired quality and caliber you what. Remember, start thinking of your volunteers as an elite group of people who cherish their contributions to mankind. Make becoming a volunteer an honor for people, an honor being based on serving with pride and with the highest level of commitment to excellence. Let it be known that your volunteer program is not for everyone and people wishing (begging) to join must demonstrate their ability and commitment to executing to the highest of standards, Ultimate Patient Satisfaction.

Attracting the right people to volunteer often means addressing the common question, what is in it for me? Many volunteers have self-serving or hidden reasons for volunteering besides unwavering compassion for their fellow man and community service. It may be as simple as loneliness, or as complex as paying back society for previous actions. To that end, however, you will find that most existing volunteer programs contain sundries of benefits, incentives, goodies, and freebies being used for enticing people into becoming a volunteer. The enticing package of goodies is also being used for rewarding a current volunteer's service longevity. You may want to revisit your volunteer benefit package and update its value to be more appealing and competitive. Remember, in determining a value to place on your volunteer benefit package, consider the cost savings the program offers and make the value so reflective. Again, do not skimp, make it a viable and worthy program that attracts and keeps great volunteers. In putting together your volunteer benefits package, you may want to consider including all or some of the following 16 incentives:

1. Pleasant and well-furnished volunteer room;
2. Free or discounted meals based on the number of volunteer hours;
3. Personal on-site locker;
4. Reserved parking;
5. Transportation assistance;
6. Special recognition programs;
7. Gift shop discounts;
8. Free or discounted medical services based on the number of volunteer hours;

9. Free uniforms;
10. Specialized training;
11. Empowerment to solve problems;
12. Group activities outside facility;
13. Buddy system;
14. Volunteer brochure;
15. Photo identification badge; and/or
16. Free discount dining and entertainment coupon books.

VOLUNTEER POOL CLEANING

Those fortunate, or unfortunate, enough to have a backyard swimming pool know the ongoing chore of cleaning the pool of debris. Well, in order to have an outstanding volunteer pool, you need to periodically clean your pool. Easy to say, especially when someone has been volunteering many years and has become part of the establishment by default, but it must be done. Just as you have a plan for recruiting people, you need an objective process for terminating the volunteering services of any individual who has difficulty conforming to your needs, expectations, and guidelines. Remember, not everyone makes a good volunteer just because they volunteered. You have standards, stick to them and the strategic value of your volunteer group will increase.

TRAINING PROGRAM

Sad to say, but most healthcare organizations provide very little, if any, formal volunteer training, and even fewer have a written volunteer training program in place. It is bad enough that operators and receptionists are not receiving appropriate training in healthcare facilities and offices, do not compound the problem by succumbing to the temptation for placing an untrained or poorly trained volunteer into mainstream contact with your patients and their family members. Before doing so, please first consider the ramifications and consequences. I think the consequences are monumental in nature and can adversely affect your patients' satisfaction. By subjecting your patients to inappropriately trained volunteers, you risk the chance of causing an unfavorable patient-volunteer encounter. Why take chances? You will find creating an effective volunteer training program is easy, especially if you consider including the following 20 items.

1. Organization and management structure;
2. Delivery system (department by department);
3. Medical staff (introduction to specialties);
4. Service orientation (patient-encounter protocols);
5. Telephone usage (answering and transferring calls);
6. Encounter role playing (how to react and respond);
7. Team dynamics (working as a team player);
8. Review expectations (accepted behavior);
9. Establish performance requirements (service assignments available and qualifications);
10. Facility layout and navigation (finding their way);
11. Cardiopulmonary resuscitation (CPR) certification (you never know);
12. Most commonly asked questions and the appropriate response (review and drill);
13. Providing driving directions to facility (review and drill);
14. Dealing with upset patients and family members (how to and drill);
15. Dealing with upset employees and doctors (how to and drill);
16. Advancing testimonials (how to and drill);
17. Reporting patient issues, concerns, and complaints (review);
18. Patient rights and confidentiality issues (review);
19. Transporting patients (how to and drill); and
20. Emergency safety guidelines and regulations (review and drill).

Only individuals satisfactorily completing the basic training program are granted the honor of being an accredited volunteer, and perhaps someday, a possible marketing advantage over your competition. And from a risk management standpoint, I can envision the day, to reduce possible legal risks or altercations, only accredited volunteers will be allowed to work in hospitals and interface with patients. Who knows, you may be the first to pioneer the worthy concept. Make a big deal about people completing your volunteer training program by having a graduation ceremony. Under no circumstances assign an untrained volunteer to a task or position that might result in a patient-volunteer encounter. To this end, identify service activities to which untrained volunteers can be assigned while completing their basic training. This may seem like a lot of effort, but remember that a well-trained volunteer group will greatly enhance the organization's ability to differentiate itself and services from the competition. In many instances a volunteer is the first and last encounter and impression your patient and their family members experience. Start being more perceptive and realize that your volunteers' actions are a direct reflection of your true commitment to quality and Ultimate Patient Satisfaction. A strong volunteer corps is an asset warranting development and nurturing.

BUDDY MENTOR

In maximizing your training effectiveness, you might want to consider assigning each new volunteer a buddy, or mentor. Volunteer buddies spend their time introducing new trainees to the system, by on-the-job, get-to-know-you-better talks and walks. When assigning a new person a volunteer buddy, ensure the selected mentor is one of your best volunteers. Selecting the best sets the best example from which the new volunteer will learn, further ensuring that only the best habits are passed along during the break-in period.

VOLUNTEER DIRECTORY

To help in facilitating a better informed and friendly environment for your volunteers, you may want to consider creating a volunteer directory, similar to a medical staff directory, to pass out to employees and departments. The directory could be in either, or both, an electronic (a computer database) or printed format and would present useful information about each volunteer. Access to such information expedites and enhances employee-volunteer relationships by enabling employees, physicians, and managers to learn more about the volunteers they see or work with on a daily basis. At minimum, your volunteer directory might contain the 17 volunteer approved information as follows:

1. Name (Mary Smith);
2. Volunteer's start date (11-22-93);

3. Title (senior volunteer);
4. Assignment (a pediatric reception desk);
5. Areas of volunteering interests (pediatrics, surgery, marketing);
6. Areas of support expertise (clerical);
7. Volunteering awards (8000 hours, 25 years);
8. Volunteer office or position (president);
9. Volunteer committees (gift shop, annual ball);
10. Birthday: (February 3rd);
11. Spouse's name (Ross);
12. Education (B.S. in education);
13. Hobbies (gardening, reading, painting, and skydiving);
14. Pets (a white dog named Spot);
15. Reason for volunteering (to personalize each patient's hospital stay);
16. Employment status (retired); and
17. Previous occupation (domestic engineer).

Creating a volunteer directory in the form of a database is easy and cost-effective. The computerized volunteer directory can be quickly updated (real-time) to reflect individual and current changes within the volunteer group. A printed directory, if kept simple, can be updated periodically and provide a useful function. Only volunteers with a predetermined number of volunteer service hours are included in the directory. Chances are your patients will find a volunteer directory of interest in building friendly relationships, especially those patients required to spend more than one day as your guest. Volunteers can learn about their fellow volunteers, especially about the new volunteer who only works a couple of hours a month or in a typically out of the way place. If you have an internal employee newsletter, start featuring a short bio on a new volunteer every month. With exposure, employees will start getting to know the volunteers better.

EARLY WARNING SYSTEM

Depending on the size and needs of an organization, volunteers are dispersed throughout the system. As moles, volunteers silently are burrowing into the everyday delivery landscape. Each volunteer is inadvertently becoming the testimonial eyes and ears of an unrecognized patient advocate. However, because of unassuming, non-threatening positions, volunteers are always in a position for observing, listening, and analyzing employee-patient encounters in the daily struggle to deliver healthcare. And because few volunteers like to rock the boat, or feel it is not their job or responsibility to do so, many questionable staff deeds and patient-volunteer encounters drift out of short-term memory, never to be addressed, especially by those concerned. In an effort to curtail such happenings from going unreported, you may want to consider implementing a program that encourages employees and volunteers to openly, but tactfully, draw attention to any adverse employee, volunteer, or patient situations they witness. Because of its sensitive nature, the program needs to be friendly to both employees and volunteers, while at the same time maintaining the anonymity of the offending and disclosing party. Not unlike Santa Claus, volunteers know who is naughty and nice in your organization. I just wish they would turn over their list periodically. It is also fact that volunteers often talk among themselves about your organization's operational and personnel shortcomings. Soon, if uncorrected, these issues and concerns spread into their private lives, often engulfing their families and friends, who in turn may become overly informed, if not caught up in the ongoing soap opera. To avert such happenings, you may want to consider providing volunteers an instrument for reporting their concerns, an early warning system for management. If incidents become concerns, and concerns become issues, you can expect your volunteers to turn into town criers, spreading the word in the community you serve. This destructive word is passed along to your current and prospective patients, your referral sources, and your competition.

15

Visitors, Your Forgotten Customer

The ever-vigilant horde of family members, relatives, and friends . . .

Each year, companies spend hundreds of millions of dollars in exposing, informing, and selling the general public on the merits of their services in hopes that those targeted individuals will in turn become paying customers. Any business concern, such as fast food chains, retail stores, and manufacturers relying on repeat customers, needs to identify the ways and means for enticing as many people as possible into their place of business and healthcare providers are no different. What better place or environment to demonstrate the services offered by a hospital than on its own premise and under its direct control? There is no advertising professional who does not desire a captive audience situation, where his or her company's services can be exalted. Yet, more often than not, healthcare providers and their marketing efforts have been completely ignoring one of their greatest captive audiences and potential pool of future patients. Your patients' ever-vigilant hordes of family members, relatives, and friends visiting your hospital or facility are the forgotten customers.

THE OPPORTUNITY

Maximizing a business's advertising dollars means cost-effective advertising, which equates to effective advertising enhancing earnings, and enhanced earnings means making the bottom line top priority. Business is business, and healthcare is big business. However, many people and associations are starting to question if healthcare's top priority is its bottom line as well. And justly so, especially if you are sick and requiring medical intervention. That being as it may, a healthcare provider failing to include its total customer base as part of its overall communication plans is forfeiting a tremendous marketing opportunity. An opportunity exists for the healthcare provider to communicate its organization's mission, services, and image to potential customers. Who then is this horde of forgotten customers? The forgotten customer is that spouse, family member, relative, neighbor, business associate, or friend escorting, accompanying, or visiting a patient. The horde is the public, the people who are going to form a personal, and often long-lasting opinion, positive or negative, about your facility or hospital. An often underestimated or overlooked moment of truth in delivering service are the people who, not needing medical intervention, are observing your every effort and lack thereof to service patients. And more often than not, these eyewitnesses openly start sharing their thoughts and opinions with others in the community. Visitors, your guests, the steady stream of potential customers, day in and day out, congregating in waiting areas, sipping coffee in the cafeteria, wandering the corridors, using restrooms, making purchases in the gift shop, searching for a parking space, and being ignored. Visitors, their comings and goings hardly noticed by staff, the faceless people, the quiet shadows wandering and left alone, developing impressions and perceptions about your facility, and the way your staff and doctors are delivering care. Your guests are not qualified for the most part to base their impressions on your professional medical skills or your high technology. Instead, guests' perceptions of care will be forming in more earthy terms, such as your friendly environment, your facility aesthetics, and your staff's orientation toward service. Just another visitor today to you, but perhaps your visitor is tomorrow's decision maker for medical intervention or healthcare service contracting. Many health maintenance organizations and companies are starting to employ third party mystery patients and observers for determining your service orientation and contracting potential.

DETERMINING YOUR ANNUAL VISITOR BASE (AVB)

Though seldom thought as such, patient escorts and visitors constitute the largest group of traffic flow in and around a hospital. A hospital's management team, medical staff, and employees need to quickly realize the importance of meeting the needs of this special group of people. This fluid visitor base is constantly utilizing hospital resources and facilities. To illustrate the magnitude of a visitor base, consider a hospital with 18,000 inpatient admissions annually. With the typical inpatient receiving four visitors per day on average, and considering the national average of 6.2 days per hospital inpatient stay, the annual number of visits totals 446,400. Each visit is a service encounter between the hospital's staff and the visitor, providing the opportunity to demonstrate your service orientation to a potential patient. Ever wonder how many patients you are losing as a result of dissatisfied visitors? Do you know what your hospital or facility's expected annual visitor base (AVB) is? However, it does not stop there, you will find by estimating and adding the number of clergy, salespeople, inspectors, doctors, maintenance, deliveries, and emergency service personnel visits to your AVB, you will have a more accurate AVB number. The larger the hospital, the greater its AVB. In some larger hospitals and medical centers, their AVB may actually exceed 1 million visitor encounters or service events. The numbers expressed do not include outpatient or emergency medical treatment visitors (those who transport and assist others seeking treatment at the hospital), which would more than likely double or triple your AVB. When was the last time a visitor survey was conducted? Such a survey might include the number of visitors per day, sex and age of visitors, relationship to patient, busiest visiting hours and day, and visitors per patient. These data can readily be converted to useful information and prove invaluable in creating an effective visitor satisfaction program, a key aspect in obtaining Ultimate Patient Satisfaction.

Hospital and healthcare executives are coming around to realizing theirs is a service industry for the most part, servicing the public, not unlike the transportation, banking, retail, hotel, and travel industries. And it will appear even more so with the shift toward outpatient and home care services. Healthcare providers are quickly learning what it is taking to become successful at service, that is, quality service, the driving force behind all prosperous industry leaders today and will be remaining so in our service-oriented future. There is no substitute for good service. Good service can often transform a lackluster "me-too" product or service into a more desirable one. Consider the fact that the overwhelming majority of people who frequent your place of business, and hospitals today are also considered places of business, are not in need of medical attention. The necessity for a more meaningful visitor service orientation is becoming more self-evident to the progressive healthcare providers.

ENHANCING THE VISITOR'S VISIT

Since going to a hospital nowadays is often a group participation activity, a hospital's strategic marketing plan calls for including a Visitor Satisfaction Program (VSP). In designing your visitor satisfaction program, you must be paying close attention to accommodating your visitors' needs, to communicating your image and message, and to soliciting feedback from your visitors. A visitor satisfaction program needs to be an integral part of any public relations activity and proactively coordinated for maximizing existing market opportunities. The depth and scope of any such program directly reflect management's commitment and creativity. You may find the following seven elements worth considering for inclusion in your visitor satisfaction program:

1. Welcome, tours, and education activities;
2. Visitor feedback system;
3. Self-referral programs;
4. Services, promotional and advertising opportunities;
5. Market research activities;
6. Visitor-employee encounter training; and
7. Visitor eating and entertainment options.

The remainder of this chapter will deal with identifying some obvious, and not so obvious, areas to pursue in developing your visitor satisfaction program.

PARKING

Parking, the nemesis of most large hospitals and university medical centers; there never seems to be enough convenient parking for everyone, including the employees, the medical staff, the patients, let alone the visitors. That may be the case, but there are alternatives you can start using to offset the parking hassle, for instance, offer a reduced parking pass for those visitors who expect to frequently use the parking facilities over an extended period of time. Make such passes convenient to purchase in the gift shop, during the admission process, or from the cashier. Offer valet parking, if not for all visitors, then make it available for the physically challenged, people using your emergency services, and for visitors who are requiring some degree of special assistance. Arrange discounted fares with local public transportation companies, such as bus and taxi companies. Start making parking less of an effort.

SIGNAGE

Invest in simple, clear and easy to decipher signage for both the inside and outside of your facility or hospital and keep the signage current, at eye level and in large letters. Determining your patients' and visitors' cultural mix will help in using the signage that best reflects their needs. Consider employing focus groups consisting of community residents to review your signage from the patients' and visitors' points of view. Do not rely on input from seasoned employees who, over the years, have mastered the maze of hallways and doors. Start checking exterior signage as part of your quality control efforts for visibility, fading, lighting, graffiti, and state of repair. Deteriorating signage is very distracting and will often be adversely compromising your total image.

FOOD

Consider issuing discounted food and beverage selections in the cafeteria, providing your patients with coupons to pass out to their visitors for a small coffee or other beverage. Retailers have always known that discounted products, especially large margin products, more than likely will be generating additional purchases. Start offering meals at reduced prices for those family members you are expecting to be spending considerable time with a seriously ill patient. Empowering staff to hand them out to selected visitors generates considerable good will. Try promoting specialty and event sales in the gift shop in accordance with local and national traditions, surveying your patients and visitors in an effort to identify what merchandise the gift shop needs to carry, and at what price points. Generating revenue by providing opportunities for visitors to be purchasing various food, beverages, and gifts also has its merits if ethically optimized through creative retail marketing and sales efforts. Consider outsourcing the gift shop to professionals, freeing your volunteers for more important patient support services.

MARKET RESEARCH

An easy and convenient way to collect data on community healthcare needs, wants, and expectations is on-site market research. Start using the opportunity for surveying visitors. Consider conducting market research with questionnaires, visitor focus groups, and one-on-one encounters between accommodating visitors and designated marketing and/or management personnel. To achieve useable results, questionnaires, focus group guidelines, and roving ambassador inquiries must be properly constructed, tested, and administered by competent individuals. You can even start training and using your volunteers to constantly be surveying visitors (and patients) as opportunities are presented. The familiar "suggestion box" is still a valuable tool for collecting information, especially if conveniently located, distributed, and maintained. Be sure that the process for collecting and following up with suggestions is strictly enforced. Posting accepted visitors' suggestions and the reward each received will drastically spur participation by others. Ensure someone contacts each person submitting a suggestion, thanking them and explaining the status of their suggestion, letting them know management is receptive to sound ideas.

CLEANLINESS

"Cleanliness is next to godliness" as the saying goes and so goeth the visitor washrooms. Priority should be given to ensure that all such facilities are regularly checked for consumables and cleanliness, especially during peak visitor hours. A simple thing like an unkept, unsightly washroom can leave a negative impression with a visitor. Does your facility or hospital have enough washrooms to quickly and effectively accommodate its female visitors? Many municipalities are replacing their archaic restroom standards with new standards, calling for increasing the number of female facilities in public buildings.

WAITING AREAS

Your waiting areas need to be clean, open, and user-friendly. Visitors need ample opportunities to relax and reflect. Consider turning waiting time into a learning experience by providing visitors opportunities to learn more about your organization, its mission, and its services. Create a wall of learning, displaying photographs, items, charts, and other informative information and curiosities for visitors to while away their boredom. Always be searching for creative communicating tools and media to get your message across or educate the public. Several things come to mind; depict an operation, new technologies, MRI scan, how a pacemaker works, show the various joint replacement options and parts, people using your product, or receiving care. Try securing vendor support in putting on educational displays. Consider letting community artists display their wares, hanging schoolchildren's paintings, having contests and letting visitors vote, and showing special healthcare educational movies in your auditorium, promote a renovation program or new service. Ensure all your waiting areas are well stocked with promotional point-of-purchase displays. Do not allow your promotional material to turn into an eyesore through neglect, assign a volunteer to routinely inspect such areas and replenish the materials as necessary. Some visitors will want privacy during the time they are waiting. Ensure privacy areas are available in major waiting areas, such as the lobby. An outside garden or sanctuary is ideal for quiet moments. If you have a chapel on the premises, keep it in a good state of repair, too many are left in ungodly conditions. Start evaluating visitor traffic flow patterns for any signs of congestion, making visitors' ease of movement throughout your facility a reality, and not drudgery, especially for the physically impaired visitor.

INTERNAL ADVERTISING

In addition to the standard print and electronic advertising mediums available, consider implementing an internal advertising program utilizing high visibility and accessibility, they are free! As an example, most hospital visitors must endure an elevator ride to and from a patient's room. Installing encased message boards in elevators will quickly transform the elevator into an effective advertising and educational instrument. Visitors, your momentarily captive audiences, are exposed to selected product and service messages. Your employees may also learn on-the-job, but they should be using the steps more than the elevator. Wherever people are found, advertising, in one form or another, will soon follow. The time is forthcoming when building owners will be selling wall space in high-traffic corridors and elevators to advertisers. Just about all facilities provide a television in the lobby area for patient and visitor entertainment. So why not take control with your own channel, offering information about your products and services? The initial investment needed for customizing a hospital television system to facilitate the interjection of custom programming and advertising is worth the expense. Places where large numbers of visitors congregate or frequent are prime candidates for accommodating some form of advertising. For example, an emergency department's decor featuring physician referral information, chemical dependency program, battered woman assistance, and child abuse hotlines are but a few examples. Whereas, you will find, the cafeteria is a good place to be promoting eating disorders and weight control programs. The main lobby and waiting areas might emphasize assisted living, day care, home care, and mental health services. Let us not forget restroom opportunities for providing information on more personal issues, such as breast self-examination, mammograms, incontinence, and perhaps impotency and prostate screening. Displaying your various affiliations with managed care plans and alternative healthcare systems can be very effective in promoting community enrollment. As a slight detour, if you own and operate one or more vehicles that are driven throughout the community, consider turning the said vehicle into a tasteful mobile advertising platform. Just as buses and taxis carry advertising, there is no reason why your vehicles should not carry appropriate advertising or community service messages. The benefits from implementing a comprehensive internal advertising program as part of the overall advertising plan is worth pursuing, no matter how you look at it.

REFERRAL SERVICES

There are various referral programs you can be promoting to visitors via strategically placed advertisements throughout your facility, hospital, and satellite centers and subsidiaries. A hospital's physician referral service is one important example. Such information needs to be conspicuously displayed in your main lobby and emergency department with supportive referral materials and a hotline. More healthcare providers are investing in interactive video-voice response systems for providing local and remote physician referral service. These technology-driven physician referral systems are great for displaying physicians' profiles and providing a direct audiovisual link to the selected physician's office. Installing such systems in strategic locations throughout a service area, possibly in shopping malls, would increase market penetration. Another useful application is informing people about your emergency medical services, and at the same time encouraging advance enrollment in your pre-emergency registration program. Promoting sports medicine, rehabilitation, as well as maternity programs is also a possibility for encouraging visitors to self-refer to your facilities. As an example, maternity services have the ability for attracting young female patients into your healthcare system, which often results in spinoff care and services for the entire family over the years. Hopefully, you can see the opportunities and benefits for generating repeat business. Using effective referral programs has great potential and is extremely important to any healthcare provider. Furthermore, the mere fact that one was born at a particular hospital often fosters a certain loyalty toward that hospital, and if the experience was a positive one for all concerned, the hospital can expect repeat business over the years to come. The same kind of referral system can be used as part of an aggressive volunteer recruiting effort wherever visitors are to be found.

PROMOTIONAL TOURS

Hospital and facility tours are often restricted to dignitaries or groups of schoolchildren. However, consider giving tours to visitors as an educational and information exchange. By offering facility tours to visitors, you have the best opportunity to convey your form of healthcare. An educated visitor will leave with more to pass along to family, friends, and associates about your facility. Those long waiting periods are now becoming channeled learning experiences about healthcare, hospitals, procedures, and much more. Consider creating a list of tours, establishing a tour schedule, and posting the same in conspicuous places for all to read, such as your main lobby or waiting areas. Every person taking a tour needs to be given an informative brochure about your facility and services. You will discover that tours provide another captive audience opportunity. Every tour needs to be used for presenting specific facts and information, promoting selected services, and building your image as "the provider of choice." Try scheduling hospital tours to coincide with low-staff demand and traffic days and your traditionally non-peak hours. Also, start including weekend and evening tours during visiting hours. Most tours are conducted haphazardly, relying on whoever is available and presenting what I refer to as the "whatever the guide likes or can remember" syndrome. To be successful at touring, you need to be spending the time and energy necessary for creating standard tours, each with its own "How to" tour guidebooks. Consider providing employees and volunteers tour training. Those who complete the tour guide training program successfully are awarded a certificate of achievement. Training is an effective means of ensuring that all tour guides are conducting tours in a professional and consistent manner. After all, the image of your facility is "on the line." Would you want an amateur showing off your facilities?

The self-serving mentality of healthcare providers, especially hospital administrators, must give way to the future, and the future is bright for those who are embracing a service orientation philosophy. Your visitors expect it, your patients demand it, your business dictates it, and your competition is doing it.

Question: Why did your patient cross the street?

Answer: To seek out better service from your competition!

16

Turning Testimonials into Referrals

Start to let those who are satisfied sell your services . . .

There are two types of testimonials, favorable and nonfavorable. Testimonials can also be delivered using one or more of the four following techniques: (1) verbal, the patient or family member verbalizes their appreciation, acceptance, and accolades regarding their care and the service they experienced, (2) nonverbal, where body language is used to convey a favorable, or nonfavorable feeling, from a simple but radiating smile, to a face-contorting frown, (3) physically, as when an individual becomes so upset that they resort to physical displays, sometimes violently, and (4) written, such as completing a satisfaction questionnaire, or in the form of an unsolicited letter. You may also experience a testimonial that is a combination of two or more of the above. However, in this chapter we will be focusing on capitalizing on the image-building and referral-generating powers of favorable testimonials.

COLLECTING TESTIMONIALS

You will quickly discover that aggressively collecting patients' testimonials will be a very rewarding enterprise. If you are not already aggressively doing it, get in the habit of actively requesting testimonials from your patients and their family members that express their satisfaction. Though seldom thought of or attempted, organizations should also concentrate on soliciting testimonials from the managed care plans, employers, and referral sources that they serve. Pause a moment. Can you think back to the last time a patient really benefited from your services? I mean, really benefited. Your care and service were magnificent. The patient's medical outcome rivaled the best. World class providers like Mayo and Cleveland Clinics could do no better. If you can, start tracking that patient down and solicit a favorable testimonial. Think back again. Are their other patients or family members you can contact for testimonials? When soliciting testimonials remember to give prospective testimonialists a reason to submit to your request. Explain that their testimonial will help influence another person to seek out your facility and services, thus experiencing the same high quality and excellence in caring the prospect did. You need to be making every effort to ensure they understand and can visualize how their inspiring testimonial will help someone else needing medical intervention. Honest and favorable testimonials are a community service in a world where finding out information regarding healthcare providers is difficult, if not totally impossible.

Another point for you to remember when collecting testimonials is to ask for a photograph to go along with the testimonial. A photographic testimonial is worth a thousand words, more if the patient is smiling. Usually, patients do not send you a testimonial with an 8×10, black and white glossy attached, however, you need to make a serious effort to get a photograph with each and every testimonial, even if you have to take the picture yourself. To this end, you will need a loaded, functional camera available on-site and ready to use at a moment's notice. Many major hospitals have a photographer on staff and if you do, seek out their help in this area. Consider buying a scanner and digital camera, so your testimonial pictures can be easily transposed into newsletters and marketing collateral.

Book'em Dano

Once you have collected a good sampling of great testimonials, place them in a quality, three-ring binder, protecting each in a clear plastic sheet cover. Depending on the number of testimonials, you may want to consider grouping the testimonials by procedure. As an example, here are six testimonials on rehabilitated knees with the patients sporting a smile and painlessly engaged in a rigorous activity. Make several copies of your testimonial binder, placing one or more copies in your reception area, patient atrium, or guest lounge. I hope you do not have a waiting room, and label it so, if so, naughty on you. Now when your patients, their family members, or escorts are waiting, they have the opportunity to read great things about you, your staff, and your quality of care. The same type of book can be used as a sales tool in marketing (selling) your services to managed care plans, employers, and other referral sources.

When soliciting testimonials from current referral sources and employers, take the time to write the testimonial for them, including pertinent information that will influence others. See the following example:

Dear Ms. Smith:

I want to share with you our excitement and gratitude for the outstanding job your home health agency has done in reducing our overall healthcare costs. My finance officer estimates the savings are approaching $350,000 for the last eight months. We are also very pleased with the quality care our employees have been receiving in your hands. A recent internal satisfaction survey indicated 98% of our employees to be satisfied or very satisfied with your services and their encounters with your staff. Again, thank you for caring so much about the well-being of our employees and their families. I also want to stress how much your cost-effective and service-oriented healthcare is contributing to a healthy bottom line for St. John's Industries. I cannot thank you enough for caring so much.

Sincerly,

A very happy CEO

In the preceding example, the estimated $350,000 during the last eight months was arrived at jointly by the employer and the provider and was included in the testimonial letter along with the satisfaction rating at the request of the provider. In other words, when you know things are going well with a referral source or employer, suggest and request a testimonial letter, helping them in writing the same. Remember to include important information to quantify your services, qualify your successes, and point out their favorable satisfaction.

Posting Testimonials

Whomever the testimonial may be from, such as patients, their family members, escorts, referral sources, employers, and managed care plans, your most favorable testimonials need posting in conspicuous locations for patients, visitors, and employees to read. We all know how difficult it is sometimes to read our own handwriting, let alone another person's script. To overcome this communications obstacle, you may want to consider typing the testimonial text on a card and placing it beside the testimonial letter. Such action will make it easier for more people to quickly read the testimonial letter. In considering where to post your testimonials, several locations come to mind, such as admission areas, guest lounges, cafeterias, atriums, reception areas, hallways, elevators, active stairwells, chapel, volunteer lounge, and any other place that people visit or use. Restrooms, changing booths, patient holding areas, and procedure rooms are still more areas where testimonials can be appropriately displayed, especially those testimonials with an expressive photograph.

Posting Unfavorable Comments

Yet another opportunity for posting is viable if you feel comfortable with the idea, and that is to post that occasional negative comment. Next to the negative comment describe how the concern or situation was addressed. And if possible, request a response letter from the formerly dissatisfied patient, indicating their satisfaction with how the issue was resolved, corrected, or eliminated. Post the response letter next to your explanation of how the issue was resolved. Such a dissatisfaction reversal tactic can be very powerful if done correctly. We all make mistakes but only a very few are ever admitted, especially in healthcare.

Reenforcing Negativity

Mr. Brown, the patient in Room 22, informs the volunteer delivering the morning newspaper that the tuna fish he had for lunch yesterday looked like cat food. He is use to eating chunky tuna fish, the way his wife makes at home. Quickly the volunteer replies, "Yeah, I know what you mean, it looks like cat food to me, too." This seemingly harmless exchange of words was in reality your volunteer reinforcing negativity, fueling dissatisfaction if you will. The patient's dissatisfaction with the tuna fish was reconfirmed by the volunteer, who was just helping out by delivering the newspaper. A better and more appropriate response would have been, "I know what you mean, I like chunky tuna fish myself. The dietitian told me the reason our tuna fish is made less chunky is so it is easier to chew and digest. This is important because many patients have difficulty eating chunky foods when they are not feeling good. I am sure you understand and can appreciate why the tuna fish is not as chunky as we make it ourselves at home. Besides, regardless of the texture, I find the taste most delicious." Can you see the difference in the response? Of the two examples provided, the first fanned the fuse, the other defused the situation. Quite a difference, do you not think? Usually, however, responses like the latter do not come naturally. You have to train your people to give the appropriate responses to negative statements and challenging questions. Here is another example of what I mean by reinforcing negativity. "Where have you been?" the patient shouted as the nurse was entering the room, "I pushed my call button 10 minutes ago!" "I am sorry it took so long in responding to your summons, Ms. Murray, but we are short-staffed. With all the cutbacks going on in the hospital, we are unable to respond any quicker. Please try being a little more patient with us." Wow. How is that for reinforcing negativity? The nurse should have replied something to the effect, "Good evening, (patients' first name), what can I do for you?" The patient quipped back, "How about responding faster to my call button, a person could die waiting for a nurse around here." "I can understand why you might feel neglected, so let me reassure you that we have no intentions of forgetting you are here, (patients' first name). You are very important to me and the rest of the staff and I am sure you will feel just the opposite when you learn I was with another patient whose condition required me to spend a little extra time with them. I came as soon as possible. And under similar circumstances, I know you would want me to do the same for you, if you were receiving care when another patient summoned me. Let me help you now and I will come back a little later to check on you, OK?" These are but two examples of how a technically superior person was ill trained in defusing potential problems. Usually without knowing it, staff can easily find themselves reinforcing negativity, which only escalates patients to a higher degree of dissatisfaction. To effectively address this potential communications problem area, you may want to consider creating a patient-employee encounter situation guide. Such a guide is required for providing your employees with the most appropriate and authorized response to adverse situations, negative statements, and challenging questions involving patients and visitors. The guide can also function as a training manual for teaching employees how to respond under pressure.

Advancing Testimonials

A patient just gave a verbal compliment to one of your employees, perhaps a nurse, technologist, or office manager, "Thank you for making my hospital stay so pleasant. I really appreciated the special and personalized care shown me." The nurse responds, "Why thank you, I appreciate you saying so." Where has the testimonial gone? The testimonial went nowhere fast. The testimonial has died on the provider vine. By advancing the testimonial, I mean, having the testimonial recipient showing their appreciation and requesting that the giver of the testimonial tell someone else what they just told the recipient. In other words, the testimonial is advanced, leaving your facility, and goes back to the patient's doctor, managed-care plan, and employer. Getting your employees conditioned to be always advancing the testimonial takes training. Each staff member must be taught, if not drilled, how to advance a testimonial beyond the hospital, the practice, or facility. Whenever a verbal testimonial is advanced back to the referral source, managed care plan, and employer, your image and competitive position as a healthcare provider is enhanced and enhanced. So get busy advancing those testimonials. Remember, you have to learn how to toot your own horn, the competition will not do it for you.

Distribution Dynamics

Each healthcare provider needs to assign accountability for collecting, organizing, and processing testimonials to an individual, usually someone in marketing or the patient advocate. The testimonial accountant, for lack of a better name, is responsible for forwarding high-impact testimonials to the appropriate referral source, managed care plan, employer, business and community leaders, clergy, school officials, and political leaders to promote your image. Testimonials also need to be circulated to all employees. This can be accomplished via a company newsletter, bulletin board, and employee slicks. In advertising, a glossy, high-impact, one-page (8½ × 11) advertisement is often referred to as a slick. I use the term employee slick to identify a special, one-page write-up about an employee or department that has done something of significant value which is worth sharing with their fellow coworkers and management, short of an internal brag sheet. Your e-mail network is another vehicle for communicating received testimonials system-wide.

Newsletter

If you send out a newsletter to patients, referral sources, and the community at large, always include three testimonials, not two, not four, but three. Three is a magic number. People remember more information presented in groups of three, so give your readers three testimonials and do not forget the pictures.

Advertising and Marketing Collateral

You may want to consider using testimonials in your advertising and marketing collateral material. Secure written permission beforehand from the appropriate person or guardian to use a given testimonial. Whole advertising campaigns can be built around testimonials that have significant influential value.

In-Room Television

Another often overlooked communication instrument is the in-room television. Consider a separate channel to run your testimonials, interviewing style, or you could be spot-dropping testimonials like infomercials within your self-generated programming.

Discharge Communications

Your volunteers often play a very important, if not pivotal, role in advancing favorable testimonials and flaming nonfavorable statements and events. As an example, in many hospitals, during the discharge process, the last hospital representative with whom a patient has contact is a volunteer. As the volunteer is wheeling a patient to waiting transportation, your last on-site opportunity to leave and reinforce a positive impression is slipping away. This is not the time to throw one last log on the fire of dissatisfaction. The same holds true for nurses and anyone else engaged in the discharge, the checkout, or the exiting process. To capitalize on this last opportunity to leave a patient and their family members with a positive feeling about you and your organization, you may want to consider establishing discharge or exiting communication guidelines. Every staff person, whether a physician, nurse, or volunteer should be instructed on how to verbally and physically (body language) engage in discharging or exiting a patient. Creating a standard discharge and exiting dialog is easy, just start thinking like a patient. How would you like to be treated when leaving a hospital, physician's office, or other healthcare facility? To help you start creating your own discharge dialog, review the following seven-statement approach presented, feeling free to customize the process to your own liking. The set of verbal discharge and exiting communications consists of the following seven-statement approach:

1. Thank-you statement;
2. Enjoyment statement;
3. Reassuring statement;
4. Confirmation statement;
5. Follow-up statement;
6. Warm parting statement, and
7. Provider of choice statement.

Review the example of the following seven-statement approach in action. Upon discharging and exiting the patient from the hospital, the nurse engaged in the following communications with the patient:

Ms. Smith, I want to thank you for choosing St. John's Hospital for your medical care.

The staff and I enjoyed having you as our guest, we enjoyed caring for you.

Do you have any last minute questions or concerns we need to address before you go home?

Is it fair to say that you are very satisfied with the service and care provided during your stay with us?

We (I) will be checking in on you during the next few days to see how you are doing. Also, you may be contacted by one or more people regarding your satisfaction with our service and caring, such as your managed care plan, our hospital, or even a third-party surveyor.

Ms. Smith, you take it easy and get plenty of rest, we all care about your well-being. Good-bye and please do not hesitate to call me personally if we can be of any further service.

Please remember St John's is always here to serve you and wants to be your hospital of choice.

You will find that the key to creating your organization's last good impression with a patient is to have a consistent, yet flexible, positive approach to terminating official contact with each patient and their family members. Having a patient disconnect protocol is an important part of total patient care and Ultimate Patient Satisfaction.

There will be times when a patient is thinking positive things about their experience at your facility, but forgets or neglects to openly communicate those feelings to anyone. And patient satisfaction surveys often do not encourage open-ended responses from the patient. However, when such a question is asked, the answer is often brief and difficult to interpret, hence, every healthcare provider needs its staff and volunteers properly trained in the art of soliciting testimonials from patients and their family members.

Audiotape

An audiotape describing a given procedure can be laced with related testimonials to reduce any prospect or patient anxiety. Hearing reassuring words of testimony from former patients is a great way to put new patients at ease. Another use for audiotapes is providing discharge instructions and other useful information for the patient and family to review, and reference at home.

17

CHAPTER

Surveying Those Who Know Best

Let your patients be your guiding light . . .

Because 9 out of 10 people will not tell you they have problems, effectively measuring patient satisfaction is one of the critical components or steps in achieving Ultimate Patient Satisfaction. Without reliable and frequent feedback regarding your services and your delivery style, you can only hope your organization is performing at the level necessary for achieving Ultimate Patient Satisfaction. Reliable feedback is only forthcoming from the people who are being exposed to and are experiencing your healthcare delivery system firsthand, either actively as patients or passively as nonpatients. In both cases, patients and nonpatients are capable of providing you and your organization a wealth of information, knowledge, and insight regarding your caring, care, and service orientation. The patient is the end user, and in some incidences the guinea pig, for your being and the delivery of medical intervention. They are the behind the service facade experts. Patients really do know best, even if they seldom openly tell you how they truly feel about you, your services, and the manner in which the same was delivered. On the other hand, nonpatients, such as patients' escorts, family members, visitors, and third-party evaluators are the second best, though on certain occasions are the best as well. The nonpatients, constantly present and observing patient shadows cast upon your facility and into its midst, are forming their own opinions about how well your organization cares about caring. You will find that nonpatients are often more critical about your service than the patients themselves.

SO WHAT AND WHO CARES

What is all the fuss about, you have great patient satisfaction? Your patients have been giving you high marks, rating their satisfaction in the high 90's. Guess what? The vast majority of healthcare providers have patient satisfaction ratings in the high 90's. Many healthcare providers appear to be kidding themselves regarding how great their customer and patient satisfaction really is by relying on less than appropriate (scientific) surveying and analyzing methodologies. I dare say it is the truth in many cases, however. But the fact still remains, your patients' level of satisfaction is important to many individuals and entities. Patient satisfaction is quickly becoming one of the three primary factors for choosing a healthcare provider. The other two are costs and quality. However, I predict that in time patient satisfaction will become the dominating decision denominator in choosing a doctor, hospital, and any other healthcare provider or service. There are more than a few people and organizations interested in knowing your patients' level of satisfaction scores, such as the following:

1. Patients;
2. Family members and friends;
3. Managed care organizations;
4. Employers;
5. Coworkers;
6. Accreditation agencies;
7. Consumer advocacy groups; and
8. Patient support groups.

Besides, your organization will never succeed in achieving Ultimate Patient Satisfaction unless you are always remembering that Ultimate Patient Satisfaction is not just a score, it is a way of life. Your patients need to be seeing, feeling, and experiencing Ultimate Patient Satisfaction in every employee-patient encounter, in every physician-patient encounter, and in every service encounter. Apples for apples,

Ultimate Patient Satisfaction outshines all attempts at maximizing patient satisfaction because it is a way of life, not just a way of doing business.

SATISFACTION PERCEPTION FACTORS

What makes you happy might have been upsetting to another person and vice versa. Patients are no different when it comes to quality and service. At best, patient satisfaction is a subjective thing. Just like quality, patient satisfaction is a personal perception held by each patient independent of other patients about your caring, care, and service. What you believe is quality and when your patients are satisfied is of little or no value in the mind of the end user, the patient. The patient will form their own short-term opinion based on the following four personal factors:

1. Previous knowledge—Your soon-to-be patient's information about their medical condition, its treatment, its cure, your organization, its medical staff, its outcomes, its service orientation, and secondhand, third-party inputs about the same.

2. Past experience—Your soon-to-be patient's personal experiences, both active and passive, regarding your organization and that of other healthcare providers, including any experienced spectator participation concerning a third party, such as a sick or injured family member or friend.

3. Expectations—Your soon-to-be patient's perception of what to expect while in your charge based in part on many things, such as previous knowledge, past experience, your advertising, consumer group articles, shared support group scenarios, and third-party testimonials.

4. Reality—Your patient's firsthand service and staff encounters, the perceived value for an outcome achieved, treatment of family and friends, open and honest communications, the total healthcare delivery system experience. Your organization in a nutshell, TQM.

Your patient's expectations must become your reality, or in reality you are not delivering Ultimate Patient Satisfaction.

LONG-TERM PATIENT SATISFACTION

However, your patient's long-term satisfaction, the most important, is also based on the previous four perception factors plus one additional factor. Long-term patient satisfaction (LPS) is defined as the resulting level of satisfaction retained or gained by a patient, after the said patient has left the healthcare provider's charge and care, and after having adequate time for personally reflecting and analyzing the total healthcare experience, especially after receiving third-party influence. Once in their own secure environment, usually home with family members and friends, your patients will have the opportunity for rethinking their experience and their actual level of satisfaction. A patient's long-term level of satisfaction will take one of three courses: it decreases, it remains the same, or it increases. Based on many factors, such as the medical outcome, maximum medical improvement, quality of life, unexpected costs, out-of-pocket expenses, input from family and friends, and any medical malpractice issues, your patient's satisfaction will be influenced and converted to long-term satisfaction. Most influencing factors are out of your control. Consider following up on long-term satisfaction by conducting another survey four to six weeks after your patients go home. Patients experiencing an Ultimate Patient Satisfaction environment are less likely to change from a favorable satisfaction level to a less favorable level.

SURVEY PATIENT ENCOUNTERS AND EXPERIENCES

Knowing what to survey is more important than conducting a survey. Most healthcare provider-patient encounter opportunities can be broken down into three major categories: pre office/facility/home visits, actual office/facility/home visits, and post office/facility/home visits. For simplicity, a physician office visit will be used as an example, however, I am confident you can easily extrapolate the following information as it relates to other entities, such as hospitals, centers, clinics, nursing homes, and home care environments. To help you begin determining the various patient encounters a typical healthcare provider is likely to present to their patients, I have identified and listed 24 generic encounter points related to visiting a doctor's office. The 24 encounter opportunities are divided into the three major provider-patient categories. As you review the following list, keep in mind that I used only a few descriptive words to identify a process encounter point, but try visualizing the total patient encounter experience in as minute detail as possible.

Pre office visits	Office visits	Post office visits
Schedule an office visit	Staff greeting	Diagnostic test results
Personal information	Verifying information	Schedule another visit
Medical history	Educating	Check patients' progress
Healthcare coverage	Reflective time (waiting)	Check patients' compliance
Payment method	Meet the physician	Refer to a specialist
Pre office visit information	Medical intervention	Payment and collections
Procedure information	Instructions	Satisfaction surveys
Directions to office	Checkout	Thank you

You need to be actively surveying your patients regarding all of the previous encounter opportunities if you want to excel at delivering Ultimate Patient Satisfaction. The survey is used for identifying service deficiencies and determining the best corrective course of action from the patient's point of view. A total or macro patient satisfaction survey may very well include three mini or micro surveys each covering 8 of the 24 encounter opportunities.

THIRD-PARTY INFLUENCES

When truly trying to establish your staff's ability for delivering the highest level of patient satisfaction possible, you need to be aware of and accounting for the adverse effects that may be caused by third-party influences. As an example, consider some of the typical third-party influences associated with a hospital that could very well upset a physician's patients, and possibly cause the same patients to be upset with their doctor:

1. A patient's status, inpatient or outpatient;

2. Admissions and discharge processes;

3. Patient-staff encounters;

4. Patient-physician encounters;

5. Billing and collection methodology;

6. Amenities and food; and

7. Facility, parking, and safety.

SURVEY OPTIONS

Surveying activities come in three methodologies or flavors, vanilla, chocolate, and swirl. After determining your organization's information and surveying needs and available resources, you need to decide who will carry out the task. You are basically held to the following three choices: vanilla, validating your patient satisfaction using only in-house personnel and resources, chocolate, contracting with an outside agency specializing in patient satisfaction surveys, and swirl, seeking the best both approaches to surveying, in-house and third-party, has to offer. I prefer swirls, since you have the opportunity to receive less biased feedback using a third party to validate your own results. Third-party surveys are also offering more credibility, because the survey was conducted by outsiders looking in. Regardless of your approach, you now have five instruments for collecting patient satisfaction information.

Survey Instruments

Aside from the occasional in-your-face dissatisfied patient encounter, which in and of itself is a form of survey, the patient is measuring your willingness to resolve an issue. There are five basic instruments available for collecting patient satisfaction information. The five survey instrument types are outlined in Figure 17–1, Types of Survey Instruments Table. Upon reading the table you will discover that three of the five instruments are passive, reactive in nature and after the fact. The other two instruments are active, proactive in nature and on-the-spot encounters. You will find the table also provides key points for you to consider in creating and conducting your own surveys.

MYSTERY PATIENTS SERVICES

Just as the retail industry is using third-party people for mystery shopping their stores, restaurants, and service centers to provide a wide spectrum of unbiased and valuable feedback on service, employee

FIGURE 17–1

Types of Survey Instruments

Survey Instrument	Considerations and Comments	Dynamics
Written	Upon checkout	Passive-reactive
	Follow up in four to six weeks	
	Open-ended questions	
	Include return and recommend factors	
	Enhance response with offering	
	Periodically used a third-party agency	
	Option for patients to keep their anonymity	
Telephone	Third-party caller	Passive-reactive
	Caller's personality	
	Personality of caller's voice	
	Next day's follow-up call	
	Use a script	
	Call between 9:00 a.m. & 9:00 p.m.	
	Five-minute maximum	
Focus group	Dissatisfied patients	Passive-reactive
	Use a script	
	Facilitator's personality	
	Neutral location	
	Participation offering	
	Third-party facilitator	
	Keeping group participants' anonymity	
Point-of-service	Pre office visit telephone call	Active-proactive
	Check-in	
	Waiting	
	Procedure	
	Checkout	
	Patient advocates	
	Hotlines	
Mystery-patient	Experienced third party	Active-proactive
	Employee-friendly process	
	Confidentiality	
	Pre office arrangements	
	Written reports	
	Suggested improvements	
	Knowledgeable mystery patients	

encounters, and facilities, mystery patients afford healthcare providers and managed care plans to do the same. Strategic Visions Inc., 205-995-8495, has been providing reliable and customized mystery patient services to progressive healthcare providers for some time. By the way, that's my consulting company, and our mystery patient program is called, PASS™, an acronym for Patient Awareness and Service Satisfaction. All mystery patient surveys need to be employee-friendly and focusing on processes.

WANTED: DISSATISFIED PATIENTS

One of the secrets to achieving Ultimate Patient Satisfaction is to, as quickly as possible, identify unhappy patients before they have a chance of becoming dissatisfied patients. I refer to this approach as bounty hunting, the process of searching for dissatisfied patients before they start searching for you. There are two approaches to bounty hunting. The first thing a good bounty hunter does is display wanted posters in high patient and visitor traffic areas. That's right. Consider using wanted posters calling for all dissatisfied patients and visitors to turn themselves in. Such a poster might look like the following:

WANTED

Dissatisfied Patients & Visitors

Please let the nearest staff member know if you are not
Totally *very* Satisfied
with our service for any reason. Without your honest feedback, we cannot make real and significant improvement in our level of service necessary to ensure your *total* personal satisfaction.

Sincerely, Dr. Goodstitch

The second action a good bounty hunter takes is to start profiling their dissatisfied patients under the premise, how can you find that which you do not know what you are looking for? With this in mind, you need to begin identifying the common characteristics and traits shared by your dissatisfied patients and visitors. Once you have completed determining this valuable information, your organization can take the necessary steps to begin identifying those people who fix your dissatisfied patient profile as soon as they come through the door, maybe even before. If your profile indicates that male patients, 50 years of age or older, ending up with exploratory endoscopy tend to be grumpy, dissatisfied, and complain a lot, consider heading them off at the pass. Do not wait until the procedure is over, set the stage early for delivering great staff-encounters and service. In the end, you will both feel better about the whole telltale incident. Here are 15 characteristics or traits you may want to consider using in profiling your dissatisfied patients:

1. Age;
2. Sex;
3. Marital status;
4. Education;
5. Procedure;
6. Referral source;
7. Demographics;
8. Healthcare coverage;
9. Payment method;
10. Staff encounters;
11. Time of day;
12. Occupation;
13. Employer;
14. Religious affiliation; and/or
15. Ethnicity.

RESPONSE RATING SYSTEMS

Creating an appropriate question response rating system can sometimes be challenging, especially if you have limited experience in developing surveys. Based on my past experience and research, I recommend that you consider using a five-point response range for each multiple choice question. The following are several five-point response rating approaches you can use depending on the multiple choice question and the nature of information you are interested in collecting:

A. Agreement
1 = Strongly agree
2 = Agree
3 = Somewhat agree
4 = Disagree
5 = Strongly disagree

B. Perception
1 = Exceeded my expectations
2 = Somewhat met my expectations
3 = Met my expectations
4 = Barely met my expectations
5 = Didn't meet my expectations

C. Rating
1 = Very good
2 = Good
3 = Fair
4 = Poor
5 = Very poor

D. Satisfaction
1 = Very satisfied
2 = Satisfied
3 = Somewhat satisfied
4 = Barely satisfied
5 = Not satisfied

E. Percentage
1 = 90%-100%
2 = 60%-89%
3 = 40%-59%
4 = 20%-39%
5 = 0%-19%

SAMPLE SURVEY QUESTIONS

The following are typical examples of questions you can start asking or using as a reference in helping you create your own set of questions.

You will find that creating focused and specific question sets for various patient encounters, provided services, and the delivery of those services enable you to be developing and using survey shells to quickly customize your surveying efforts. The following are two question sets along with two response rating approaches for getting you started:

Inpatient Nursing Services
Patient satisfaction

Specific Rating
Do you:
- 1 = Strongly agree
- 2 = Agree
- 3 = Somewhat agree
- 4 = Disagree
- 5 = Strongly disagree

Overall Rating
The nursing care I received:
- 1 = Exceeded my expectations
- 2 = Met my expectations
- 3 = Somewhat met my expectations
- 4 = Barely met my expectations
- 5 = Did not meet my expectations

Typical Questions to Ask:
The nurses who cared for me:
- Were genuinely friendly toward me?
- Were genuinely concerned about my well-being?
- Appeared to be skilled at what they did?
- Appeared to work well with other staff nurses?
- Appeared to work well with the other hospital employees?
- Appeared to work well with my doctor?
- Took my concerns and problems seriously?
- Responded timely to the call button?
- Appeared well informed about me and my treatment plan?
- Kept me well informed about my treatment plan?
- Genuinely went out of their way in making me feel special and wanted?

Treated my family members and guest courteously?

Made every effort to make my stay pleasant and comfortable?

When called, appeared eager, willing, and happy to help me?

Were well groomed and dressed at all times?

Washed their hands every time they came into my room prior to administering care?

Answered all my questions about my care and what to expect?

Answered all my questions about scheduled tests and what to expect?

Answered all my questions regarding the medication I was asked to take?

Answered all my general questions about the hospital and what to expect?

Smiled more than frowned?

Were quiet at night so I could sleep?

Were patient with me?

Were very good at anticipating my needs?

Were skilled at giving near painless injections?

Respected my dignity at all times?

Using the above questions as a reference, how would you rate each of the following nursing shifts:

Morning shift (time);

Afternoon shift (time); and

Evening shift (time).

Overall, how would your rate your experience with our nurses? Did you find it easy to distinguish nurses from other staff members entering your room?

Inpatient Accommodations and Services

Patient satisfaction

Specific Rating

Do you:

1 = Strongly agree

2 = Agree

3 = Somewhat agree

4 = Disagree

5 = Strongly disagree

Overall Rating

The accommodations and services:

1 = Exceeded my expectations

2 = Met my expectations

3 = Somewhat met my expectations

4 = Barely met my expectations

5 = Did not meet my expectations

Typical Questions to Ask:

The accommodations and services during my hospital stay:

I found my room was warm and inviting?

I found my room was clean upon my arrival?

I found my room was adequately furnished?

I found the bathroom to be clean upon my arrival?

I found my room to be kept at a comfortable temperature?

I found my floor to be quiet at night?

The cleaning personnel were genuinely friendly toward me?

I found my room was cleaned regularly and with minimal disturbance?

I did not experience any problems receiving and making telephone calls from my room?

I did not experience any problems with the television in my room?

I found my nurse call button in working order?

I found there was adequate food selection and variety?

I received the food items that were ordered for my meal?

I found the food to be of good quality?

I found the food's presentation to my liking?

I found the meals were served on time?

I found the food consistently served at the appropriate temperature?

I found the eating utensils and service were clean?

I found my diet requirements were adequately explained
to me?

I found the volunteers very friendly?

I found the volunteers very helpful?

I found the volunteers to be very knowledgeable about
hospital services?

I found that everyone smiled more than they frowned?

I found my roommate respectful of my needs, privacy, and
visitors?

I found my roommate's visitors respectful of my needs,
privacy, and visitors?

Overall, how would your rate your accommodations and non medical
services during your stay at the hospital?

SURVEY ANALYSIS

In an effort to maximize the information you are deriving from your
patient satisfaction surveys, consider looking at the data from a few
different perspectives. You may find valuable insight by analyzing your
survey responses by referral source, by managed care plan, and by procedure. You may also find it beneficial to compare the differences
among similar functions, multi-facilities, and your delivery systems.
The following tables are examples of how you might approach analyzing patient satisfaction information to identify areas of concern.

In Figure 17–2, patient satisfaction is being analyzed by the referring physician. Looking at the information, you can conclude several things. First, the vast majority, 89% of surveyed patients, are satisfied or very satisfied. However, Dr. Peters' referrals account for 86%
of all dissatisfied and very dissatisfied patients. You would definitely
want to explore further why Dr. Peters' patients account for such an
overwhelming percentage of dissatisfied patients. On the contrary, Dr.
Ross appears to have a very high number of very satisfied patients and
your job is to find out why. In both instances, you have an opportunity
to convert reasons to solutions, and in doing so improve overall patient satisfaction.

In Figure 17–3, patient satisfaction ratings are being analyzed by
managed care plans. By studying the information presented, you
should have realized and started determining why:

FIGURE 17-2

Patient Satisfaction Ratings by Referring Physician

Physician	Very Satisfied	Satisfied	Dissatisfied	Very Dissatisfied	Total Surveyed	Percent of Total Referrals
Lees	9	12	1	0	22	12
Peters	0	2	4	8	14	66
Ross	20	4	0	0	24	8
Shaka	3	16	0	0	19	55
Susanna	2	7	0	0	9	17
Wimmer	12	32	0	1	45	31
Totals	46	73	5	9	133	189

1. Plans #1 and #4 account for 94% of all very satisfied patients;

2. Plans #2 and #3 account for 98% of all dissatisfied patients; and

3. Plan #4 has a 7:1 ratio in favor of very satisfied over satisfied.

Perhaps plan #4 is providing its members better coverage, better service, and better information regarding what to expect from your healthcare delivery system. Finding out is very important to your patients' satisfaction.

While Figure 17–4 compares diagnostic imaging procedures, the data clearly show that more people are rating their MRI experience at a dissatisfied or very dissatisfied level, compared to those patients who had a CT scan (97% to 3%). This major difference between MRI and CT services needs to be identified and corrected quickly. Perhaps a radiology technologist is the reason, regardless, you need to find out.

SURVEY MAPPING

When analyzing your patient satisfaction data, I suggest you plot where dissatisfied patients live. Using a map of your service area, pinpoint the locations satisfied and dissatisfied patients live. Now look for patterns. You may discover that a high percentage of your dissatisfied patients have a significantly longer drive to your facility than satisfied patients. This information suggests that the longer drive may be the patient's real issue. However, the stage is being set, one mile at a time, for complaints yet to come. Spending more quality time with the patient will often offset the time they spent driving. Or perhaps, your patient satisfaction

FIGURE 17-3

Patient Satisfaction Ratings by Managed Care Plan

Managed Care Plan	Very Satisfied	Satisfied	Dissatisfied	Very Dissatisfied	Total Surveyed	Percent of Total Referrals
Plan #1	350	796	3	0	1149	79
Plan #2	85	1334	23	44	1486	93
Plan #3	0	350	99	12	461	52
Plan #4	980	150	0	0	1130	98
Totals	1415	2630	125	56	4226	81

drops off gradually in proportion to the distance patients live from the point of service. Analyzing further, you may discover that patients from a specific geographical area show a higher than expected dissatisfaction. The key here is to identify patterns that will help you in determining and addressing any related or associated group dissatisfaction within your service area. Group dissatisfaction could be the result of many things, such as cultural differences, race, and neighborhood preferences.

You will find the following reference book and resources useful in your surveying efforts.

Satisfaction Survey Software Programs
Survey Pro 2.0, Apain Software, 800-237-4565
Complaints Desk, Spectrum Computer Technology, 800-879-3225

Books
The Survey Kit Series, Sage Publications, American Demographics, 800-828-1133
Measuring Customer Satisfaction, Bob E. Hayes, ASQC Quality Press, 800-248-1946
Help Desk Institute, many titles, 800-248-5667

FIGURE 17-4

Patient Satisfaction Ratings by Procedure

Procedure	Very Satisfied	Satisfied	Dissatisfied	Very Dissatisfied	Total Surveyed	Percent of Total Referrals
MRI	12	380	112	29	533	59
CT	145	227	4	0	376	41
Totals	157	607	116	29	909	100

18
CHAPTER

Patient Database Marketing

"A little knowledge that *acts* is worth infinitely more than much knowledge that is idle."

Kahlil Gibran

Healthcare systems and providers are often data-rich and information-poor! Like most healthcare providers, you too are inundated daily with patient data, but are you collecting it, analyzing it, and reporting it in an effective manner and useful format? Unfortunately, though there are exceptions, most healthcare providers have an abundance of financial information (costs?). And providers also have only marginal information about their customers, especially about their patients. Outside the healthcare industry, database marketing has been around quite some time. Progressive retailers have been using computerized database marketing methodologies for well over several decades or more. The advanced and progressive healthcare providers are just now starting to catch on and catch up with the retail industry. Never forget that marketing is a battle for the mind and information about your customers is your ammunition. Run out of ammunition, and you are destined to lose your marketing battle due to status quo data and tactics. Patient information is critical to your ability to wage a decisive campaign for achieving Ultimate Patient Satisfaction, so you better start loading up.

THE BASIC DATABASE

Before you charge into database marketing, you will first want to consider creating a patient database. Now do not surrender to hostile appearing terminology and technology, and start giving up because you fear the unknown. On the contrary, after our basic database boot camp, you will be well armed with the basic knowledge required for feeling confident and secure in setting up a database marketing program. Starting off on the right foot is very important. So remember, you will find that creating a database is not difficult, but actually fun. A database is a collection of data, stored as records (macro data) and fields (micro data), similar to a filing cabinet's drawers and files (see Figure 18-1). A safe assumption on my part, I hope, is that you can recognize the basic run of the office filing cabinet on sight. If you have filed a piece of paper, a report, or other document within a file folder, understanding databases is well within your mental acuity. But to be on the safe side we will start out slow, all right? Now, in your mind visualize a vertical, four-drawer, filing cabinet. The filing cabinet itself is the database, and each file folder within the filing cabinet is a record. All the bits and pieces of information within each file folder or record make up the record's fields. A field is a location within a record for a specific bit of information, such as a name, address, zip code, date, time, or any other piece of information you want to store.

There are several types of databases, you are only interested in relational databases, which means that all the database's records (data) within the database are interconnected with each other. You are able

FIGURE 18-1

Basic Database

Filing Cabinet		Database	
File Folder	Record 001	Record 002	Record 999
Information	Field (name)	Field	Field
Information	Field (address)	Field	Field
Information	Field (etc.)	Field	Field

to search, sort, and report all the individual records as one, within a database of similar data. All major word processing software companies are offering a complementing relational database you can purchase, for example, Corel Wordperfect's complementing database is called Paradox. However, in the end, regardless of the database used, your database is only as valuable as your ability for converting its data into useful information. Benjamin Franklin and Adam Smith might have said it best, if they jointly stated that "a penny earned is a penny saved, but an unspent penny not wisely invested loses its value in time." In today's ever-changing healthcare environment, your unused data and information are no exception.

Key Databases

From a healthcare marketeer's perspective, you will find the following 10 databases presented here are key to your continued success and worthy of creating and maintaining. The 10 databases you need are:

1. Patient (end user);
2. Medical referral sources (physicians);
3. Non medical referral sources;
4. Employers;
5. Managed care organizations and plans;
6. Competitors;
7. Service area;
8. Services and outcomes;
9. Vendors; and
10. Dissatisfied customers.

You may want to prioritize the 10 databases depending on your strategic information needs. Ultimate Patient Satisfaction requires, at minimum, databases numbered 1 and 10 in the previous list.

Database Options

There are basically three, reasonable, and cost-effective approaches you can pursue in creating a database. Your first option is to use, as mentioned earlier, one of the many inexpensive relational databases offered by word processing software companies. Some of the more common relational databases are Paradox, Approach, Access, and Alpha-Five. You can purchase any of the aforementioned databases separately or as part of an office productivity package. At this writing, each of the mentioned databases was available for less than $300, a small price to pay for gaining make-or-break knowledge. Second, you can use any of the major spreadsheet software programs as mini databases. Using the rows as records and columns as fields, or vica versa, you will discover a person can do a lot with a spreadsheet and a little ambition. Three of the more popular spreadsheets on the market are Corel Quattro Pro, Lotus 1-2-3, and Microsoft's Excel. Like the relational database, spreadsheet software can be purchased separately or as part of an office productivity package. I highly recommend you consider purchasing one of the major office productivity software packages. Personally, I use Corel Office Professional and find it meets all my business' demanding word processing, spreadsheet, database, presentation, desktop publishing, and marketing needs. And last, but not forgotten, are the various contact management software programs such as Maximizer, Telemagic, and Acts. Contact management programs function as mini databases and are usually limited in their true relational database capabilities, but in a pinch, you can do a lot with the more sophisticated programs. Regardless of your approach to creating and building your databases, a little due diligence, a little price shopping, and a little effort on your part will return big dividends and will keep you from making and becoming sick over an ill-thought-out decision.

Creating a Stand-Alone Database

Before you zip out and buy a database, I suggest you spend the appropriate amount of time planning for this key marketing decision and undertaking. To help you in determining your needs and organizing your planning, I have outlined a 15-step process for creating your own database. To start making your journey into the world of databases easier and less painful, do not forget or detour from the following 15 guiding steps:

1. Determine the type of information you want;
2. Identify your raw data requirements;
3. Determine the type of report you want;

4. Determine your current computer's capabilities and capacity (operating system);
5. Select the type and size database you will use;
6. Upgrade your computer accordingly or buy a new system;
7. Assign data collection responsibilities;
8. Assign data input responsibilities;
9. Identify and resolve access and security issues;
10. Build a small beta database, 20 to 50 records, for training and debugging;
11. Back up program and data;
12. Back up system's electrical power;
13. Verify computer, database, and staff performance and proficiency;
14. Bring the system online; and
15. Fine-tune database and operating system.

And do not forget, you and your staff will need ample time to receive training. Do not take training shortcuts, or you will more than likely, in short order, short-circuit the system.

Data, Data Everywhere

Once you have completed determining the kind of data you need for producing the kinds of information and reports you want, consider creating and using a database information collection planning sheet for defining and monitoring your collecting efforts. A database information collection planning sheet will contain the following:

Data:	Specific data.
Source:	Location or source of data.
Access:	Who is authorized to be collecting data?
Responsibility:	Who is assigned to collecting data?
Format:	Medium and format for submitting data.
Delivery:	Who is to receive the collected data?
Date:	The deadline for submitting data.

You need to be identifying your data needs, determining where the data are to be found, determining how to gain access to the data, assigning a person the responsibility for collecting the data, formatting the data for submittal, identifying to whom the data are to be delivered, and by what date the data need to be submitted. Many people and operating systems within your organization contain the kinds of information you need but getting it can be another issue. However, start calling upon people and accessing operating systems to collect your data. You will discover that an abundance of data and information is available for the asking, copying, and taking and you only have to seek to notice its intimidating and often deforesting abundance. Depending on your informational needs, consider exploring your collection opportunities with the following 21 depositories.

1. Yellow pages;
2. Medical, professional, and business directories;
3. Federal and state professional and business licenses;
4. Personal contacts-network;
5. Patients, employees, and vendors;
6. Public documents, Freedom of Information Act;
7. Research, surveys, and industry reports;
8. Medical, professional, and business associations and societies;
9. Newspapers, trade journals, and publications;
10. Managed care organizations, third-party administrators, and case managers;
11. The Joint Commission Accreditation Reports;
12. Medicare cost reports;
13. Self-insured employers;
14. Federal government statistical and census reports;
15. Lists, marketing companies, and consultants;
16. Trade shows and seminars;
17. Certificates-of-need;
18. Advertising and classified ads;
19. National healthcare databases;
20. Better Business Bureau and consumer groups; and
21. Congressional reports.

And do not forget your own databases, reports, documents, records, and the like as valuable sources of information. If you are serious about reviewing and gathering information, you need to seriously consider having access to the Internet (less than $20 per month), a compact disk (CD) player (less than $200), and an internal computer fax-modem unit (less than $100).

Patient Database Marketing

How you use your patient database is totally up to you, however consider the following five applications:

1. For identifying and profiling common characteristics shared by your best patients;
2. For determining the cause and effect that upset patients have on your business;
3. For identifying and attracting profitable patient groups;
4. For proactively identifying and resolving the causes of patient dissatisfaction; and
5. For tracking patient satisfaction survey results.

Creating a Patient Database

In creating your own patient database you may want to start by collecting the following kinds of information for each patient:

Name	Occupation
Age	Employer
Sex	Work telephone number
Ethnic group	Medical benefits
Religious affiliation	Retirement Status
Residency	Insurance-payor mix
Address	Managed care plan
City	Insurance plan coverage
State	Deductible
Zip code	Copayment
Telephone number	Family Structure
Marital status	Head of Household
Income level	Dependent
Education level	Living alone

Healthcare decision makers
Spouse
   Occupation
   Employer
   Education level
   Retirement status
Family members
   Number
   Sex
   Age
Personal physician status
   Name(s)
   Telephone #
Referral source
   Primary
   Secondary
Allergies and reactions
Procedure(s)
Transportation
   Own
   Public
   Special arrangements
Head of household
Hospital preference
Visit frequency
   Date of first visit
   Date of last visit
   Monthly average

Personal interests
Community interests
Influence level
   Community
   Business
   Political
Preferred media
   Television (program)
   Radio (program)
   Paper (name and edition)
   Magazines (name)
   Outside
Relationship to other patients
Membership(s)
   Organizations
Challenging disabilities
   Sight
   Hearing
   Physical
Special assistance requirements
Registered a complaint
   Nature
   Date
   Action taken
An emergency contact person
   Telephone number

PATIENT PROFILING

If, or when, you have a database similar to the one just described, you have access to the kind of data and information necessary for profiling your patients. A profile is a list of common characteristics or traits shown by select groups of patients. If you were to create a profile of your typical patient, the database might turn up the following information:

Age: 55 plus
Sex: Female
Ethnicity: 62% Hispanic
Medical Insurance: 85%
Employed: 55%
Head of household: 35%
Marital status: 89% married
Residence: Within 12 miles of office
Watches TV: 79%, of which 45% watch the "Today Show"
Transportation: 82% drive their own car
Office visits: 7.9 annually
Employer: 18% Martin Manufacturing

Once you establish a profile for your typical patient, marketing becomes much more definitive as opposed to guessing. If you are happy with your current patient base mix, you now have the needed information to start target marketing to acquire more of the same. Without profiling, you are shotgunning your marketing resources; get focused, get profiling. Use your newly gained knowledge and database to profile your best and typical referral sources, patients (end user, if not a patient), and managed care plans. You can even profile what is profitable business for your organization and what is not, if you collect the right information up front. Consider profiling your profitability by:

Payor mix;
Procedure mix;
Patient mix;
Physician mix; and
Plan mix.

Start putting the power of database marketing to work by investing the time and resources to master the process.

Upset Patient Profiling

Though it has value, collecting and analyzing patient satisfaction data is a benign and passive exercise. You are looking at post service encounter data, which means an upset patient is still upset regardless of your analysis. However, proactively seeking out dissatisfied patients in real-time can be of even greater value to increasing your overall patient satisfaction. Just as you created a profile for your best customers, referral sources, and patients (you have, haven't you?), you may want to consider creating an upset patient profile. And do not forget to create a profile for upset family members and visitors as well. By taking the time for developing a profile of patients who have registered dissatisfaction either verbally, in writing, or through a third person, you are better able to identify, or at least statistically predict, which of your patients are most likely to be dissatisfied with your services. By nipping those dissatisfied patients in the bud, more often than not, you will come out smelling like a rose.

Depending on the size of your organization and the number of patient encounters, an upset patient profile might be desirable for each department or major employee-patient encounter environment, such as diagnostic imaging/radiology, admitting, and outpatient surgery. Once you have developed your upset patient profile, ensure that every employee becomes familiar with it. You and your employees need to start proactively looking for current and new patients who fit the profile best. Post the profile, just as the law enforcement agencies do for ingressing and egressing the country, but at key employee work stations. Knowing beforehand what kind of patient is more prone to perceive poor care and service, hence, also prone to becoming dissatisfied, enables you to be anticipating potential problems early on so you can be working with your patients up front.

Puppies Need Extra Love and Caring

This up-front approach to Ultimate Patient Satisfaction will best position you to ensure your patient's expectations are realistic and that their experience will be the best it can be. By working the patient, I mean, you and your staff spending more personal time communicating with Potential Upset Patients, PUPs, being more patient with your PUPpies, taking the time to inform the PUPpies about things to come, reviewing their options, providing effective PUPpy education, making an effort to develop a rapport with their family members, and whenever possible, going out of your way to show the PUPpies you care. There is also another PUPpy type, a Previously Upset Patient. In this instance, a PUP is a patient who has registered a real-time complaint or negative survey rating regarding a previous experience at your facility. Consider identifying your PUPpies, potential and previously upset patients, up front, before the patient passes through your doorway. Keep your staff well informed about PUPpy profiles, reminding your people that PUPpies require a lot of love, special attention, and lots of care. You especially need to ensure that any negative experience is not repeated. Having a returning PUP experience the same sort of upsetting circumstances or situation that made them upset to begin with makes a clear statement that you really do not care, and your pedigree is showing. There will be no Ultimate Patient Satisfaction blue ribbon for you.

Satisfied Versus Very Satisfied

Another approach to consider is creating two additional patient profiles, one for those patients who claim to be satisfied, and another profile for those patients who are claiming they are very satisfied with your services. The two patient profiles will provide you with valuable information once you compare the satisfied patient group against the profile of those who are very satisfied. As a few examples, you may find that very satisfied patients were closer to the nurse's station on their floor, or that a specific employee or employee shift has a higher incidence of dissatisfaction ratings with patients, or maybe that your satisfied patients had on average shorter stays, or your dissatisfied patients and family members tended to be better educated than the satisfied patients, perhaps a higher percent of dissatisfied patients received care from one or two specific doctors on your medical staff. Armed with this kind of insightful knowledge about satisfied patients, you will find yourself better informed and better prepared for creating an effective plan or process for moving your satisfied patients into the realm of the very satisfied patient category. By learning the differences, you can start making a difference, not before. So stop complaining and start comparing your satisfied and very satisfied patient profiles against each other. Regardless of your healthcare business, organizational function, or size, profiling what your upset or dissatisfied patients have in common with each other will help you better understand their wants and needs, and hopefully, the insight to effectively address those needs. Ultimate Patient Satisfaction is not as distant a goal as you might have initially thought.

Note: Archaic and down computers can be devastating to your chances for achieving Ultimate Patient Satisfaction so start protecting your hardware and software now and not just your data. You are backing up, are you not? I thought so.

P.S. The year 2000 is approaching and bringing in the new century with a major software problem. Starting in the year 2000, all dates will start with 2---, and not 19---. Most computer software is not ready for the switch; is yours? Better have someone start looking into the potential problem.

Reference Book
Strategic Database Marketing, Rob Jackson & Paul Wang—800 828-1133

Mapping Software
Maplink—800 370-8967
Maptitude—888 225-4737

Computer System's Electrical Power Backup
American Power Conversion—800 800-4272

19

CHAPTER

Guess Who is Watching

Telecommunications, the internet, and web-site spies . . .

The cry rang out on February 8, 1996: "The telecommunications companies are coming, the telecommunications companies are coming!" Did you hear it? If you think that healthcare reform is a wake-up call for the industry, then the Telecommunications Act of 1996 should make you jump out of bed. Telecommunication technologies will change the delivery of healthcare and your world forever, and there is no turning back.

TELECOMMUNICATIONS REVOLUTION

The Telecommunications Act (Revolution) of 1996 deregulated the communications industry after 60 years of managed competition. Managed competition, does that term sound familiar? The revolutionaries are many including local and long distance phone companies, cable TV operators, production studios, broadcasting, publishing companies, satellite communications, and wireless services. Microchip technology has melted all communication media together into one, easy to manage format, digital. Digital communication is the future, multimedia (audio, video, graphics, and pictures) the time machine. Every company and every person's future, with few if any exceptions, will be digitized, and healthcare providers will be in the vanguard. Why? Telecommunications companies have targeted two high-growth business segments, the banking/finance and healthcare industries, that exhibit the greatest potential and need for data management, movement, and storage using multimedia communication services. Telecommunications enabling technologies will revolutionize the healthcare industry much the same way that in 1972 the introduction of computed tomography (CT) imaging changed radiology and diagnostic imaging forever, but on a mega scale.

And just as hospitals, physicians, and other providers are scrambling to stake their market dominance during the chaos brought on by healthcare reform, expect no difference from the communications industry. Communication companies like ATT, MCI, Sprint, the seven Baby Bells, GTE, and many yet to be formed entities have been hurled on a collision course of such competitive and technological magnitude that the healthcare industry will be taken along for the ride. And what a ride it will be. Already the players are restructuring, merging, and making deals that will put the Aetna/U.S. Healthcare deal to shame. Like Siamese twins, the telecommunications and the healthcare industries are destined to spend considerable time together. Hopefully, each will realize it is healthier to be joined as they journey into the future than parting to go their own separate ways. As is often the case with Siamese twins, separating is usually at the expense of the other's well-being.

Healthcare cannot afford to go its own separate way, nor does it have the financial resources, technology, and networks to do so. If healthcare providers are to become more efficient at delivering their services and in doing so, reduce their overall operating costs, telecommunication will play a critical role, though often as an unnoticed and unsung hero. For example, experts predict that the rapidly declining price of digital communications will slash tens of billions (yes, billions) of dollars off the country's healthcare bill, as more hospitals buy supplies electronically rather than processing each order by hand. A local example is that a major Birmingham healthcare system has cut 1.5 million dollars from its annual continuing medical educational costs by using TeleVideo conferencing technology. Digital communications may very well be the unexpected heaven-sent silver lining that healthcare providers have been looking for.

Hold onto your rotary phone. Everything is not all that rosy or simple either, and not every telecommunications company is ready to deliver its customers broad-band, multimedia communications networks and the much heralded information superhighway. Many Baby Bells have obsolete, low-band phone networks and lack 100% connection to digital switches necessary to direct multimedia information, and Wall Street analysts feel many are still bloated with unnecessary staff. There are many hurdles telecommunications companies will have to overcome with your patience, input, and help. A few challenging hurdles and concerns are industry data transmission standards, system-wide security, patient confidentiality issues, getting existing and diverse equipment and networks working together, how to replace antiquated technologies and equipment cost-effectively, and the lack of skilled multimedia network building specialists. So relax. Face reality. Your world will not change overnight. However, change will come faster to those providers pursuing enabling technologies than for healthcare couch potatoes. As you can summarize, deregulation will force change, just as many changes and just as much chaos within the telecommunication as healthcare reform have done for the practice of medicine. The battle lines have been drawn, or more appropriately, erased, and the greatest show on earth is about to start, and it is not technology, but a marketing extravaganza, with house receipts expected in the trillions. Out of chaos emerges brilliance, however, and proactive and progressive healthcare providers will benefit from the converging digital communications, enhanced service, lower pricing, and the temporary ensuing confusion.

New Language

But before it can lead the way, the acronyms-plagued telecommunications industry will have to learn a new language, English, if it wants to communicate effectively with its healthcare clients. As a healthcare executive, hospital administrator, or independent provider you do not have to, nor should you be confronted with or expected to understand the telecommunications industry's shorthand jargon like trunk lines, T-1 and ISDN lines, Asymmetric Digital Subscriber Line, routers, digital switches, servers, LANs, HSDL, CAPs, high-speed modems, bandwidth expansion, twisted copper pair, coaxial cables, optical fibers, wireless communications, and asynchronous-transfer-mode switches. We have our own alphabet soup to contend with.

The successful telecommunications companies will make communicating with them painless by disconnecting themselves from their alien tongue and starting to speak the universal language of everyday business people. They will have to start converting telecommunications technology into terms healthcare providers understand, saving time and money. That is right. Their problem-solving efforts need to focus on making their healthcare clients more profitable at what they do, enhance their quality of service, and strengthen their competitiveness. Our telecommunications partners need to find ways to turn networks into time-saving and money-making solutions and not selling technology for the sake of technology. Just as company executives do not want to be in the healthcare business, hospital administrators and physicians are no different and do not want to be in the telecommunications business.

Telemedicine

Converting telecommunications technologies and networks into telemedicine applications that will save the healthcare system billions of dollars is already underway to varying degrees across the country. Usually, but not always, university medical and teaching centers are pioneering the integration of technologies and applications to industry needs. However, major medical systems and entrepreneurial physicians and business people are also making major contributions toward digitized medicine. The following is an insightful, yet small, sampling of promising areas where telecommunications multimedia technologies will change the delivery of healthcare as we know it today:

1. Remote on-site medical evaluations by physicians and nurses.
2. Home healthcare patients being monitored at home and having immediate communications with a nurse.
3. Real-time remote patient monitoring using ambulatory and fixed telemetry units to relay vital signs such as blood pressure, heart rate, and respiratory events for medical evaluation.
4. Remote on-site medical triage services for injured employees and students.

5. Enhanced teleVideo telemetry for emergency service vehicles and crafts.

6. Remote televideo physician referral services using freestanding kiosk units in malls and other high-traffic areas, including worldwide on-line services.

7. Remote healthcare system-wide scheduling, claim processing, and billing and collections.

8. Computerized in-room admission and discharge for hospital patients.

9. System-wide on-demand access to medical records, consultation reports, and test results.

10. Medical triage and intervention for remote military locations, ship board, and battlefield applications.

11. Remote on-site psychiatric intervention screening and consultations.

12. Teleradiology, the transfer of x-ray, MRI, and CT images for diagnostic interpretation, second opinions, training, and storage.

13. Telepathology, the transfer of pathological images for diagnostic interpretation, second opinions, training, and storage.

14. Healthcare and medical data collection, processing, and analysis for various monitoring applications, research, and record keeping.

15. On-demand self-care televideo education programs created for the public.

16. Remote proctor supervision for doctors and medical personnel in training.

17. Quick access medical and clinical information and multimedia-training libraries.

18. Community Healthcare Information Networks (CHINS) for sharing data, outcomes, and cost-efficiencies within a community.

19. Remote televideo conferences and network meetings.

20. Worldwide access to medical expertise, specialists, and diagnostic services.

21. Creating a universal, digital, medical record, and signature capture system and employ and maintain the same within the healthcare industry.

22. Long-term, cost-effective, off-site information storage.

23. Daily system-wide communications using e-mail, pagers, wireless telephones, and voice mail systems.

24. Create international market opportunities through remote medical access points for inquiries, consultations, diagnoses, and second opinions.

25. Marketing and selling end user-oriented medical and health information services on-line, on-demand.

26. Interactive voice response (IVR) and interactive voice-video response (IVVR) systems to answer, direct, and provide specific information to a caller, such as digitized managed care approved provider directories.

27. Telepharmaceuticals management, administering, outcome, and risk analysis for managed care plans, physicians, and patients.

28. Global navigational positioning technologies will be used for monitoring patient and staff location within a facility.

Multimedia telecommunications has the potential to enable responsible healthcare providers to address seven acute issues facing the industry: costs, access, quality, time, medical records, practice standardization, and fraud. The delivery of healthcare is moving away from the provider's independent control and isolationism. Healthcare reform is being swept toward a mainstream of community awareness, provider accountability, and controlled outcomes that benefit the patient, payor, and provider. Telecommunications is permitting, if not forcing, this unavoidable and long overdue journey. So you see, the tide is turning, and healthcare reform is more than the reengineering of delivery systems by managing care, controlling reimbursement, and forging mega-provider networks. Healthcare reform is a team effort that requires enabling technologies, the kind telecommunication companies are turning into cost-reducing, revenue-increasing, and profit-generating solutions.

To reduce their operating costs and to become more efficient at delivering their services, healthcare executives, administrators, and doctors will have to aggressively pursue and openly embrace the strate-

gic alliances, technologies, and business advantages that the telecommunications industry offers. The future delivery of healthcare services
will be drastically shaped by digital and video signals racing back and
forth between two or more points at the near speed of light. Change is
coming, faster to some than others. Now is the time to move forward
with open arms and an open mind. Healthcare, in all its chaos, has en-
tered the dark and twisting tunnel of reform. The chances are that the
light at the end of the tunnel is from an optic fiber. Many telecommunications companies are actively engaged in many aforementioned
telecommunications applications and are forming partnerships with
many local and out-of-state healthcare providers. I strongly encourage
each healthcare provider to actively seek more information about
telecommunications solutions by calling their local telephone company and to learn more about the future. The telecommunications
technology is revolutionizing the healthcare industry. And when it is
all said and done, multimedia telecommunications will emerge as the
backbone of healthcare delivery.

A new piece to the already complex healthcare marketing puzzle
has been added while most healthcare providers are still adjusting to
or reeling from the onslaught of changes brought on by managed care
and industry reform. You may be asking yourself, how could this be
and why? The merger and acquisition feeding frenzy that is reshaping
healthcare has already started to consume telecommunications companies, segments, and independents. Mega networks and vertical integration are not just descriptive words reserved for the healthcare industry. As you read, two giant industries, one just coming out from
under regulation and one entering a more regulated business environment, are converging to change forever the practice of medicine and
the delivery of healthcare.

TELEMARKETING

Marketing healthcare products and services in the age of deregulated
telecommunications will propel you beyond database marketing and
web-site pages. You will find yourself confronted with an array of inte-
grated, IVVR technology options that will create new and exciting approaches to market healthcare to the masses. Those healthcare organizations and marketeers that eagerly embrace and master how to adapt

and capitalize, if not exploit, these emerging enabling technologies will be light years ahead of their competition. Your future dreams and successes will be connected to an optical fiber simultaneously carrying millions of other dreams along an electronic, super-healthcare highway.

To help you better visualize the future impact telecommunications will have on healthcare, consider the following 13 marketing applications and roles technology will play in helping you best position your organization to thrive in a digitized managed care environment:

1. You can expect to see the independent collection, analysis, and dissemination of information about your facility's medical outcomes, patient satisfaction, and annual revenues become public information, with or without your authorization. Community concerns and prying awareness will encourage or discourage patronizing specific physicians, hospitals, or healthcare systems.

2. Referral development activities, especially off-site, will rely more on IVVR technologies. Older, more costly referral development systems will give way to better suited IVVR multimedia platforms. Referral development IVVR kiosks will be located in high ambulatory traffic areas to provide instant access to medical specialists, triaging, and general information. The user will interact using visual and audio interfaces as high-tech, graphic touch screens walk the soon-to-be-patient electronically to your door.

3. Referral sources will be electronically and digitally linked to the host healthcare provider via high-volume, low-noise communication networks and low-cost computer systems. E-mail and computer-generated faxes will enable you to maintain daily contact with your referral base. Newsletters as we know them may become obsolete in time, being replaced with IVVR digital newsletters.

4. Hospitals, managed care plans, and healthcare networks will cash in on digital directories. The more cost-effective digitalized approved provider or medical staff directories will enable real-time updates and revisions. Paper directories will become a thing of the past. Expect future digital directories to use more IVVR formats that permit direct access to a provider's office and human encounter-free appointment scheduling.

5. Occupational healthcare and medical intervention triaging will be offered through IVVR booths, similar to the four photos for a dollar step-in booth commonly seen in malls and amusement centers.

The curtain will be replaced with a security and soundproof door. There will be less need for on-site medical personnel at industrial complexes and remote facilities. Because of the IVVR technologies, the independent or small providers will be able to compete effectively with larger hospitals and healthcare networks, with technology becoming the equalizer.

6. Unassisted appointment scheduling will enable referral sources to quickly access your digital appointment log, select and confirm an appointment, and give and receive information without wasting time speaking to your office staff. Quick in and out scheduling systems will save everyone time and money. There will also be a place for IVVR scheduling systems when medical interaction is complex, when multiple procedure treatment is planned, or when the possibility of complicated surgery exists.

7. Direct access to system-wide patient information will provide a wealth of data that can be quickly converted into customer information, marketing's life blood. Customer and patient satisfaction will start being tracked and reported in real-time using microencounter satisfaction software that enables the monitoring of a patient's satisfaction each step of the treatment process. McHospital saw its 1 billionth satisfied patient today, the electronic scoreboard heralded.

8. On- and off-line IVVR advertising will enable healthcare providers to capture more potential referral sources and patients' time with which to present their products and services. Some examples of online advertising will include IVVR TVs in the patient's room, on- and off-site kiosks, direct referral source links, and the Internet. Off-line advertising will include on-demand access to audiotapes, videotapes, and CDS. Healthcare providers will make promotional and educational information available through local libraries. Durable medical equipment companies will offer IVVR catalogs. Prosthesis manufacturers will let prospects try on their various prostheses via multimedia interactions. The healthcare marketing and selling opportunities are endless.

9. In time, the electronic or digital patient record will migrate toward IVVR, storing actual videos of tests, physicals, and surgical procedures for future reference, analysis, and litigation, making risk managers' jobs easier or more difficult depending on how you look at it. A provider's accountability will be on-the-line, on-line. The future IVVR birthing room is just around the network and will allow for the first time family members and relatives, from California to Maine, to watch the arrival of the blessed event in real-time.

10. How you market your physicians will take on challenging nuances as national consumer groups and regulating agencies openly report on a physician's education, credentials, board status, mortality rate, litigation record, malpractice profile, and fee structure. These open repositories will become the Better Physician Bureau for the community, a long overdue service. Doctors and other healthcare providers will no longer find sanctuary in the profession's unwritten code of silence. National databases will speak out on behalf of the consumer by tracking a physician's performance from graduation to retirement. The same holds true for all healthcare institutions and providers; the handwriting is on the wall, or more appropriately, the web page.

11. Though not new, interactive voice response (IVR) will develop into IVVR systems that provide users real-time access to both the information and a provider representative as needed. Telecommunications will enable self-caring to dominate the healthcare scene as demand management stakes its rightful claim as the number one healthcare cost reduction strategy.

12. Outsourcing one's marketing staff to reduce costs will also be an option to healthcare executives as telemarketing permits and simplifies IVVR conferencing. The best people, usually working out of their homes, will be available at the speed of light. Digitized ad hoc marketing (DAM) will see its presence grow as more healthcare providers embrace enabling technologies.

13. Healthcare providers will be watching your every move as satellite global navigational technology will be employed by implanting micro sensors in ID wristbands to monitor the whereabouts of patients within the hospital and long-term care facility, such as infants, children, and the physical and mentally challenged, especially Alzheimer patients. Are employees next?

This is not a short-lived fad or Star Wars hype; telecommunications technology will have strategy-altering implications on the way healthcare providers go about marketing their services. And in the event you do not have a firm understanding about these enabling and enhancing technologies and their marketing applications, your marketing bubble is about to burst. For good or for bad, telecommunications will permit consumer groups, managed care plans, and federal and state agencies to bare your facility's soul to the people and community you serve. This will in and of itself force providers to reevaluate their approach to marketing. You will also have to reevaluate your marketing strategies as heretofore difficult to gather data and information (yours) becomes readily available and strategically used by competitors, and visa versa. The future means quicker access, faster responses, and greater openness to useful patient, system, and educational information. Telecommunications will also provide marketeers a more powerful arsenal of statistical facts, mortality rates, outcome data, and competitive information for use in creating products, delivery systems, and business development strategies.

In the end, however, public domain healthcare provider information will change the way you market to the community and how the community perceives your quality of care and your right to exist. The time is rapidly approaching when marketeers will employ reverse-marketing to gain the various market shares required to achieve service area dominance. Reverse-marketing is defined as the ways and means to use critical competitive performance information to strengthen your own provider-of-choice position. Some see this new marketing approach taking on the trappings similar to the rampant negative campaign advertising permeating our airways today, but not so much mudslinging as fact-sharing in nature. Take a moment and reflect on the possibility of your competition having access to and the ability to distribute information about your facility, medical staff, and outcomes to support their claims of excellence (and denying your claims to fame) better than you can. So watch out for fiber optics and envision the changes, advantages, and opportunities telecommunications technologies offer the proactive healthcare provider and marketing team before the competition turns out the lights, your lights.

TELEPATIENT SURVEY

Telepatient satisfaction surveying is just a cable length away. In the not-so-far distant future, your patients will be completing all satisfaction surveys via a telephone, a television, or a computer, digitally. Everyone needing to know will have immediate access to your patient's thoughts on your caring, care, and service orientation. The future is fast becoming energizingly digitized, but Ultimate Patient Satisfaction will always be coming from the heart, though hearts are becoming digital; just ask the nearest person with a pacemaker.

Encouraging Verbal and Written Complaints

To find out if your service is sick, just listen to your patients . . .

BEYOND THE QUESTIONNAIRE

Patient feedback, especially verbal comments, is important to understanding the patient's overall satisfaction. However, focus groups and surveys are only one aspect of determining your overall patient satisfaction. You need to create a written policy and supporting instruments to actively collect, analyze, and respond to verbal and written complaints, and you need to conduct surveys. Most, if not all, accreditation programs, such as the Joint Commission of Health Care Organizations, the National Committee for Quality Assurance, and the Foundation for Accountability, require some form or another of the complaint handling processes. However, in early 1997, 42 California health maintenance organizations (HMOs) were fined by the state for not adequately publishing their complaint numbers. I guess it makes sense that patients have difficulty complaining if the process for complaining is not well publicized: no calls, no complaints. You and your organization need not stoop so low, stand up for your patients' right to complain. By taking the time for making sure you have carefully reviewed all accreditation requirements for handling verbal and written patient complaints before creating your program, you will be on the winning side, the patients' side. If more than one agency is accrediting your healthcare business or delivery system, you need to ensure that your complaint handling processes meet the requirements of each of the accrediting organizations.

THE POWER OF COMPLAINTS

Before dealing with verbal and written complaint dynamics, it is very important that you understand the power of complaints. This power comes from the fact that on average, 9 out of 10 people who perceive receiving inferior service will never register a formal complaint. If this is so, there is no reason to expect patients to behave otherwise, especially those who believe complaining patients are doomed to revengeful care from those they are complaining about. To truly benefit from the power of complaints, you have to begin taking complaints and complainants seriously. Keep in mind, there are many other patients and visitors probably feeling the same way, but for whatever the reason, they have passed on registering a formal concern. Put another way, if you received 100 complaints annually, statistics suggest that about another 900 people refrained from filing similar concerns and complaints. You need to start treating complaints as valuable clues for improvement. Similar to road markers, these improvement clues will keep you driving in the right direction on your journey toward Ultimate Patient Satisfaction. Each patient's complaint presents you and your organization with a golden opportunity to demonstrate the extent of your caring. A complaint is a warning sign, if read correctly, helping you in becoming more patient-friendly and providing the insight for improving future patient-staff encounters. Stop to think about it, you will surely agree that complaints do offer significant benefits to those who take grievances seriously. Your patients' complaints are, in essence, a wake-up call, letting you know you are dozing off. So wake up, you cannot afford to miss a single complaint. Consider taking a new approach and start treating your complainants as if they were from a service consultant. When was the last time you had free consulting services? By utilizing the service consultant approach, your mind-set will be more receptive and open to receiving complaints. You will also be experiencing less difficulty and objections in coming up with workable solutions that address everyone's needs. Tolerating and allowing people in your organization to take an adversarial and defensive attitude toward complaints and complainants is only making the situation worse, if impossible, to satisfactorily resolve. Remember, bad attitudes are always more costly in the end so wise up and kick the habit if you have it. The secret to dealing with and resolving patient complaints in your organization is to start holding everyone in your organization accountable for never having a dissatisfied patient.

System-Wide Complaining

You could probably guess and guess correctly that the larger the organization is, the greater the chances are for a customer's service incident complaint to fall through the ever-widening, so-what crack. An ancient Chinese proverb I made up goes like this, "The larger the organization, the more and greater will be the cracks for things to fall into." Did you know that cracks have an invisible life of their own? Dormant most of the time, lying in waiting, organization cracks start spreading to life to feed on the unwary, miscellaneous, and at the most critical of times, swallowing the most important of things. So stay on your toes because organizational cracks are more than they are cracked up to be, and an extreme danger in your quest for Ultimate Patient Satisfaction.

To ensure that cracktisity, defined by me as the innate ability for organizations, and the people within said organizations, for losing critical information or failing to execute a critical task at a most critical time within its area of responsibility and operating domain, does not bring down your patients' level of satisfaction. You need to start stamping out cracktisity in your organization by creating and using a system-wide service-incident complaint registration log and response policy, a SIC log for short, pronounced, "SICK." To see where your organization's service is hurting, check your SIC log. In many hospitals and healthcare facilities, formal and informal verbal and written complaints that are being made at the employee and department levels go unrecorded, and often unresolved. There are many reasons for using a system-wide service-incident complaint log. The following are just a few good reasons. A SIC log will help you in:

1. Establishing a unified approach for collecting, analyzing, and resolving service and incident complaints;
2. Organizing concerns, complaints, and grievances into similar categories for analytical purposes;

3. Comparing individuals, departments, facilities, and the organization's overall service performance;

4. Identifying system-wide service-incident complaint trends; and

5. Determining root reasons and circumstances that are contributing to poor patient-staff encounters.

Policy and Procedures

When creating your own verbal and written tracking and response system, consider the following three key areas:

1. Company policy and protocols;
2. Service-incident complaint logs; and
3. Service-incident complaint investigation form.

Company Policy and Protocols

Create a policy that states the company's position regarding service and incident complaints. Remember to check with accreditation organizations for any required protocols, format, and wordage. You are free to use or expand on the following example of a company policy:

It is the company's standing policy that all formally and informally expressed dissatisfaction by patients, visitors, and employees regarding our level of care and service will be immediately reported, recorded, promptly investigated, and action taken in good faith, to quickly resolve the dissatisfaction to the complainant's satisfaction. Furthermore, all employees who are directly or indirectly a witness to a registered or nonregistered adverse service situation, event, or issue will take it upon themselves to immediately report the witnessed incident to their immediate supervisor. All service and incident complaints will be posted at the appropriate organizational level, using approved methods and documentation, and communicated in writing to the officially designated quality control or performance improvement person. The company maintains a nonnegotiable position that all company personnel, contracted or otherwise, are accountable for their actions and for maintaining the highest level of patient satisfaction. Failure to conform to this standing policy and associated protocols is ground for immediate dismissal or termination of services.

Consider posting your company's service incident statement where employees, vendors, and contracted providers can see and read it on a daily basis. Now, for writing your protocols, you may want to consider the following 10 steps or simply modify as necessary to address your own needs. The 10-step process is as follows:

1. All verbal and written service and incident complaints will be posted in the provided SIC log books by the person receiving the complaint or witnessing an adverse patient-staff encounter using a SIC investigation form. The person taking the service or incident complaint will quickly notify the patient advocate or other designated person.
   a. The SIC investigation team is responsible for creating the service-incident complaint investigation form, SICI, and providing the SICI forms and log books to all departments.

2. All serious verbal service-incident complaints are required to be made in writing and registered as soon as possible by the complainant or their spokesperson. A serious service-incident complaint is one involving death, life-threatening, causing bodily harm, the potential to cause bodily harm, or requiring special intervention. (As these categories are suggestive in nature, you will have to determine your own classifications.)

3. A designated person is assigned to investigate the service-incident complaint and will:
   a. Notify the complainant that their complaint has been received, who will be investigating the complaint on their behalf, and how they will be notified regarding the investigative progress and the resolution. Official notification is usually in writing.
   b. Talk to all parties, including the complainant, and collect any additional information relevant to understanding, analyzing, and resolving the complaint.
   c. Maintain accurate records and SIC activity status using the SICI form, or other designated approach.

4. The SIC investigation team's designate is responsible for requesting and receiving written responses from all company employees, witnesses, and contracted or guest providers, such as therapists and physicians. All such documents will be assigned the original SICI number and be notarized if required.

5. All resulting service and incident complaints involving physician or medical intervention will be immediately presented to the organization's medical director, chief-of-medical staff, or other designated individual or group for reviewing, commenting on, and making professional recommendations on how to respond and resolve the incident.

   a. Risk management will also be immediately informed of the service-incident complaint and remain involved until its conclusion.

   b. A legal representative will also be notified, if warranted.

6. Upon the decided course of action in resolving the service or incident complaint, the SIC investigation team's representative will inform the complainant regarding the proposed resolution, followed up by the official written response, unless:

   a. A response is provided by the company's legal representative.

   b. The service-incident complaint was directed at a physician, in which case the physician needs to respond in appropriate fashion and time.

7. All service-incident complaints will be evaluated to determine if any company policies were violated, and as to whether all employees, vendors, or contracted or guest providers' performance was consistent with quality care and service, or inappropriate in nature, and for what reason(s). If conduct or performance was deemed inappropriate, corrective action will be pursued with the appropriate company authority, external governing body, or appropriate regulatory agency, including when necessary, actions against contracted providers and guest providers, such as physicians.

8. The SIC investigation team representative will review all service and incident complaints and the resolutions with designated managers and employees, and working with the same to create and distribute corrective preventive actions, policies, or other mechanisms necessary to eliminate a recurrence of any unacceptable behavior, adverse performance, and poor outcomes.

9. A designated quality or performance person will be responsible for collecting, tracking, and analyzing all service-incident complaints and resolutions using SICI data, to determine statistical trends, to conduct occurrence profiling, and to report on the same to designated administration, employees, vendors, and contracted and guest providers, including physicians.

10. Service and incident complaints will be key factors in determining employability, compensation, and ultimate patient satisfaction within the organization.

You cannot afford to waste any time in building your company's SICI team, and do not forget to empower the team to start creating, overseeing, and enforcing compliance to the policy.

SIC Investigational Form

The core of any complaint program is a document or instrument for registering and recording a complaint; usually, this is a complaint form. When a complaint is registered by a patient or their spokesperson, a complaint form is completed. I like the name, Service Incident Complaint Investigation Form, SICI for short (pronounced sickie). Many healthcare providers have already created their own complaint forms. To help you do the same or review your current complaint form, I have listed the more common types of information typically collected so you can pick and choose those that fit your specific data collection needs. So, depending on your healthcare provider status (that is, hospital, private practice, home healthcare) and the services you provide, you will want to consider including, requesting, and identifying, in some form or another, all or some of the following information:

SIC number;
Complainant's name(s);

Patient's name if different from the complainant;

Medical record number;

Relation to patient: referring doctor, family member, friend, employer, managed care plan (MCP), guardian;

Patient status: inpatient, discharged, outpatient, emergency;

Complaint type: (verbal) (written);

Incident type: death, bodily injury, life-threatening, safety concern, service-related, other;

Incident location;

Time of incident;

Date of incident;

Date of complaint;

Incident or complaint summary: attached;

Complainant's telephone number (home) (work);

Best day and time to contact;

Involved staff names;

Staff statements: (attached);

Physician(s) involved;

Physician statement: (attached);

Witness' name;

Witness' statements: (attached);

Relevant additional information: (attached);

Related corporate policy and procedures;

Complainant's position and disposition;

Complainant's requested resolution;

Date SIC investigation started;

Copy list: administrator, chief executive officer, president, board member, legal council, risk management, senior nurse, patient's physician, managed care plan, employer, quality manager, department head, involved staff, insurance agent, law enforcement agency or regulatory agency, person coordinating complaint process and their signature;

Recommended action to resolve;

Action taken to resolve;

Follow-up required;

Person authorizing resolution;
Date SIC investigation closed; and
Estimated financial impact.

Computerizing SICI

With the availability of enabling computer technologies, consider going digital. Creating a computerized SICI form, electronic log book, and reporting system is an easy task. A simple and inexpensive database approach can also be used to accomplish all of the above. Scanners enable you to input forms into your computer. Any of the top contact management software programs can also function as a basic SICI tool.

Encouraging Complaints

You cannot benefit from the power of complaints unless you start receiving complaints, so start encouraging your patients and visitors to complain. Now, do not go overboard. There is a limit to encouraging anything. Finding the right vehicle to solicit complaints is not too difficult a task, considering all the possibilities available to you and some are quite unique and revolutionary. The following is just a small sampling of possibilities:

1. The old suggestion box standby: several things to remember, the suggestion box must be visually inviting, easy to find, but strategically located for maintaining the suggester's confidentiality, out of the prying eyes of staff. A restroom, perhaps? Keep the suggestion box area well supplied with paper and writing instruments and a convenient writing surface. Try emptying the box on occasion since I have seen suggestion boxes that were taking on the appearance of trash disposal units and you can guess the message it sent to people passing by.

2. SIC Hotline: a SIC number that anyone can use to call in and leave a message, suggestion, complaint, or express a concern. The hotline can be answered by a live person (preferred) or an answering machine. The caller's message is passed on to the appropriate parties. As appropriate, any SIC is recorded in the SIC log book.

3. UPS Telephone: a *real-time*, system-wide network of strategically located UPS quick-response telephones throughout your facility(s) that auto-dial into the office of the administrator, chief exec-

utive officer (CEO), or president of the company. But you know most executives do not have enough time to get involved with patient satisfaction, that is, until it's too late. Ultimate Patient Satisfaction is a downhill battle, starting at the top. If the president does not have enough time to personally answer the UPS telephone, it only suggests patient satisfaction will always be placed on hold. Consider using colored telephones. I recommend a nice, robin's egg blue color, a most calming color under the circumstances. A sign above the UPS telephone reads:

Attention: This is a UPS Telephone

As a personal conveyance, this special auto-
dialing telephone has been installed so patients
and visitors to Johnny Bull Hospital can
quickly register any service issues and
concerns regarding our performance, caring,
and services directly to the President's office.

Ultimate Patient Satisfaction Starts at the Top

---

4. E-mail station: use a SIC e-mail address to receive a message, suggestion, complaint, or concern by intra or internet, follow up by having a designated employee responsible for bringing complaints to the appropriate party's attention, if a SIC, record it in the SIC log book.

5. Roving tell-me person: a specially trained patient advocate or volunteer identified as a SIC tell-me person who roams the corridors or is available at the information desk or a SIC center booth. Note: At minimum all patient advocates need to receive training in the following six areas:

Time management;
Negotiating;
Dealing with upset people;
Creative problem solving;
Effecting change; and
Coaching and team building.

6. SIC kiosks: Strategically located, patient-interactive, SIC kiosks or computer terminals to accomplish the above can be located in lobby or mall. If in a mall, include it as part of your referral development kiosk.

Patients Bill of Rights

Are healthcare providers so out of touch with their patients rights that the President of the United States of America has established a blue ribbon committee to write a national patient's right document to protect patients? Do not wait. You will discover that by informing people of their rights and responsibilities as a patient, upon their arrival, your organization will be in a better position to deliver healthcare. Providing patients a copy of their bill of rights and responsibilities beforehand greatly helps you in creating the right patient mind set from the beginning. Well-informed patients tend to do well. You may want to consider the following sample patient's bill of rights and responsibilities in creating or revising your own.

PATIENT'S BILL OF RIGHTS AND RESPONSIBILITIES

As a patient, you will find that the employees, healthcare professionals, and medical staff you encounter, in good faith and spirit, are wholly committed to your well-being, both physically and mentally, and will serve and care for you with the greatest respect in the words we speak, and in every deed we do, this we pledge to you, the patient. And to this end, we hereby adopt the following Patient Bill of Rights.

As a Patient, You Have the Right to:
1. Considerate and respectful care.
2. Treatment which is needed because of your condition, regardless of race, creed, sex, national origin, or source of payment for care.
3. Information concerning your diagnosis, treatment, and prognosis in terms easily understood.
4. Make informed decisions about your own care.
5. Refuse treatment to the extent permitted by law.

Continued

6. Give advance instructions to be executed as directed in the event of you being legally incompetent for medical reasons (Advance Directive) and to be informed of such by the hospital.
7. Privacy and confidentiality.
8. Review all records, documents, and diagnostic results pertaining to your medical care.
9. A safe, secure environment, and information regarding the use of protective measures, including the possibility of using bodily restraints.
10. Be informed if the hospital has business relationships with other agencies that may affect your care.
11. Expect that the hospital will give you health services to the best of its ability.
12. Know that a transfer is recommended, and if so, and prior to a transfer, you will be informed of the risks, benefits, and alternatives.
13. Consent or decline to take part in research.
14. Be informed about your self-care and continuing medical compliance throughout hospitalization and after discharge.
15. Be informed of hospital rules and regulations affecting your safety and care.
16. Review and receive a detailed explanation of your bill and charges.
17. Be informed of available resources for registering and resolving concerns, conflicts, or complaints.

As a Patient, You Are Responsible for:

1. Providing Requested Medical and Personal Information . . . about your condition including all symptoms, medications you are taking, previous illnesses, and other matters relating to your health. You should also report any changes in your symptoms or general condition to our healthcare team. A copy of your Advanced Directive should be provided upon admission.
2. Asking Questions . . . when you or your family does not understand what you have been told about your care or what is expected of you.
3. Knowing and Following Hospital Rules and Regulations . . . as discussed and outlined in the provided Patient Care and Guest Guide.

Concluded

4. Following Instructions . . . including your treatment plan developed by your doctor and our healthcare team and recognizing the effect adverse lifestyles are having on your personal health. You are also responsible for accepting the <u>consequences</u> of refusing treatment and not following instructions.
5. Showing Respect and Consideration . . . to other patients and hospital staff. This includes being considerate of other patients and hospital property.
6. Paying Hospital Charges . . . which includes providing the hospital with accurate and timely information concerning a reliable source of payment and ability to meet payment.

These rights and responsibilities can and should be exercised on the patient's behalf by a parent, guardian, designated surrogate, or proxy decision maker if the patient lacks decision-making capacity, is legally incompetent, or is a minor.

Visitor's Bill of Rights

Besides, a patient's bill of rights document, you may find that creating and posting a visitor bill of rights and responsibilities will be instrumental in reducing misunderstandings, communications, and complaints, and help you in achieving Ultimate Patient Satisfaction.

Hospital Patient Complaints

According to the Picker Institute, nearly a third of 24,000 patients polled said they felt they were released from the hospital before they were ready, 30% said they were not alerted upon discharge to danger signals to watch for, and 37% said they had no idea when they could resume normal activities. Picker Institute also found patients' complaining did not stop there, as follows:

Continuity and transition—29%;
Emotional support—27%;
Information and education—23%;
Involvement of family and friends—22%;
Coordination of care—23%; and
Respect for patients' preferences—22%.

21
CHAPTER

Dealing With
Upset Patients

If you can keep your head when all about you are losing theirs and blaming it on you . . . yours is the earth and everything that's on it!

Rudyard Kipling

For most healthcare professionals, one of the greatest joys comes from caring and helping our patients achieve maximum medical improvement and an improved and healthier life. Yet as strange as it may seem, we also find ourselves suffering some of our greatest frustrations, stress, and trying moments in dealing with patients and their family members. Delivering diagnostic, medical, and rehabilitation services would be so easy, if not ideal, if every patient were coherent, cooperative, and in compliance with your every word, request, and instructions. And what if every patient you saw, along with their family members, was pleasant, was very understanding, and was satisfied with your every action? Snap out of it! This is no time to daydream! Unfortunately, your world is a stressful world, revolving around giving and taking, caring and suffering, and sometimes, living and dying. A demanding world at best, where if you are truly committed and trying hard, you can expect to please most of your patients most of the time. The truth of the matter is that in such a world, you will not satisfy all of your patients all of the time, let alone their family members, though I like to believe you will die trying.

So regardless how well you think your organization is at satisfying its patients, there will be days and times when patients and visitors will put you to the supreme test of providing Ultimate Patient Satisfaction. You can expect over time to encounter patients who are upset or angry, maybe even difficult, and in some instances unrealistic for a variety of reasons, but the one thing they will all have in common is their desire and demand for better service. We often forget that the expected level of service is from the patient's perspective, not ours. Who knows better how you care for and treat a patient than the patients themselves? Keep in mind that providing Ultimate Patient Satisfaction means delivering second-to-none satisfaction to all people, no matter how demanding the person or stressful the circumstances. If you are not properly trained, this real and very essential part of your job can get to be downright stressful, get you down, wear you down, until you are down and out. In this chapter you will find the knowledge to prepare yourself for the inevitable, dealing with upset, difficult, and unrealistic patients and their family members. Sometimes delivering Ultimate Patient Satisfaction can be an earth-shattering experience or just plain out of this world. The patient was calm, but their spouse went ballistic. Houston, I think we have a problem.

HAPPINESS

Getting down to earth, a few words about happiness are in order before we explore the world of the upset. People's happiness is really and truly mind over matter, your mind over what really matters in life. Research tells us that people across the board are a lot happier than you might expect. And what is more important, people's happiness does not appear to depend significantly on external circumstances. Many scientists are now looking closer at and accepting suggestive research findings stressing that happiness stems almost entirely from nature rather than nurture. They believe our mood depends more on our genes than our loved ones, family members, friends, careers, or other circumstances. However, an international survey according to *Scientific America*, November 1996, indicates that cultural influences may also play a part in our happiness. Are you happy? Are you truly a really happy person? Here are just some of the more common traits happy people share and exhibit. You can decide for yourself how happy you really are by considering the following: happier people tend to like themselves, feel in control of their lives, are more optimistic about life itself, have a greater people orientation and interpersonal skills, and are more outgoing. And when compared to unhappy people, happy people tend to marry earlier in life, get better jobs, have more friends, and are healthier. While on the other side of the street, an unhappy person is less likely to like themselves as much as happy people, be less self-focused, be more hostile toward authority, become aggressive faster, be more abusive in nature, be withdrawn, and be more susceptible to disease.

If the above is true, take a few moments and reflectively and mentally digest the following statement: If an apple a day keeps the doctor away, then a joke a day helps keep disease at bay. Are we not talking an old, but renewed form of alternative medicine? Perhaps placing a joke book in every patient's room, a few in every visitor lounge, or heaven forbid, a waiting room, has medical merit. I am willing to wager that joke books in the patient room and atrium (waiting area) would reduce anxiety and enhance staff-patient encounters, sort of proactively setting a positive tone for things to come.

SUSCEPTIBILITY TO STRESS

Since the beginning of time, stress has been a condition of life itself. We all encounter stress to varying levels in our daily lives. However, for any given stressful situation, especially in our dealings with people, the level of stress is usually self-imposed due to many reasons. Why is it a certain task, an encounter, or a situation can generate significant stress in one person, and yet in another, not even the slightest emotional ripple is noticeable? The fact is that some of us are better at working in a stressful environment and handling stress than others. I believe that a person's whole being is responsible for creating, in varying individual degrees, an internal immunity, which acts as a defensive aura or mechanism against stress. This personal internal immunity is your biological, emotional, and environmental vaccination against stress and its side effects. And because of this internal immunity, when it comes to dealing with upset patients and their family members, those of us with a higher internal immunity to stress are better suited for this most demanding and often exasperating part of healthcare. You can discover your own suggestive susceptibility to stress by answering the following 10 questions using the 1 through 10 scale provided, where 10 is the highest rating possible. Tell the true and shame the devil. No one else will see your self-analysis, so be honest with yourself.

1. How well do you like who you are as a person?   1 2 3 4 5 6 7 8 9 10

2. How well do you like what you are as a person?   1 2 3 4 5 6 7 8 9 10

3. Do you feel in control of your life?   1 2 3 4 5 6 7 8 9 10

4. Are you very optimistic about life and things in general?   1 2 3 4 5 6 7 8 9 10

5. Do you consider yourself very outgoing?   1 2 3 4 5 6 7 8 9 10

6. Do you consider yourself to be very healthy?   1 2 3 4 5 6 7 8 9 10

7. How well do you handle frustration?   1 2 3 4 5 6 7 8 9 10

8. Do you consider yourself to be very organized?   1 2 3 4 5 6 7 8 9 10

9. Does it take a lot to upset or make you angry?   1 2 3 4 5 6 7 8 9 10

10. How well do you know your current job?   1 2 3 4 5 6 7 8 9 10

Once you have answered all 10 questions, add your individual responses together. The total sum is used as a gross indicator in determining your basic susceptibility to stress. Hence, the higher your total sum is, the greater is your internal (mental and physical) immunity to stress. Simply stated, the higher your number, the more it takes to stress you out. As an example, if your total sum is 85 or higher, it would suggest that under a given scenario you will be less susceptible to stress buildup compared to someone with a lower rating, say 35. And the opposite holds true for people with a low total score. If your total score is 55, you are more likely to be susceptible to stress under trying and challenging circumstances than a person with a higher total sum, say with a total sum of 90. How well each of us feels about ourselves and has control over our own lives greatly affects the buildup or magnitude of stress we succumb to eventually in our lives. Stress can often lead to overreaction and aggression. Stress management is training everyone needs in their life. Perhaps stress management needs to be taught early in life, perhaps in middle- or high-school, and made mandatory training in the workplace for new hires.

STOP COMPLAINING ABOUT PATIENT COMPLAINTS

Where there is smoke, there usually is fire. The same is true about patient complaints. So, if you do not want to be putting out fires all day, keep in mind that in an Ultimate Patient Satisfaction environment you want and should encourage your patients to complain! Here is why. First, according to many experts, 90% to 96% of dissatisfied customers will not complain directly to you, however they will complain to others. Typically, the dissatisfied patient or family member will tell anywhere from 10 to 20 people about their negative experience, including your referral source. Often their tale of woe is overly exaggerated. To make matters even worse, you are not there to tell your side of the incident. After all, there are three sides to every upset patient-employee encounter or incident: what the patient perceived, what the employee perceived, and what really transpired. Second, when their expectations are not met, most patients and their family members do not complain, they simply go elsewhere, especially when the choice is theirs. Knowing when your patients are upset is serious stuff. You need to start willingly accepting a complaint as an early wakeup call, or better yet, an indication that your patients feel comfortable complaining or expressing an opinion to you. You need to start treating each patient's complaint as a reality check and use it as an opportunity to show you really care by doing everything reasonable in your power to satisfy each and every dissatisfied patient. People usually complain because they want to continue doing business with an establishment. Your patients still want to use your services when medical intervention is necessary, that is mostly why they complain.

DEALING WITH UPSET PATIENTS

One of the secrets to providing Ultimate Patient Satisfaction is understanding and meeting your patients' three basic requirements: their need for personal attention, appropriate care, and their psychological demands. How most healthcare organizations and staff get themselves in trouble is by losing focus on the basics. While in the process of providing personal attention and delivering good quality care, your employees are often distracted or just simply forgetful about the patient and their family members' psychological needs. In the quest for Ultimate Patient Satisfaction and minimizing the occurrence of upset patients, you must be willing and able to address the patient's relevant emotional state and psychological needs 100% of the time. Remember, when dealing with an upset, irate, or unrealistic patient or family member, before you attempt to defuse the situation and resolve their concerns, you must first provide for their psychological needs. In most instances, understanding and addressing your patients' psychological needs, starting from the initial patient-organization contact, sets the satisfaction stage and increases your chances for a great performance in the eyes of your patient.

The first rule in dealing with upset patients is not to upset them in the first place. Here is where a little preventive thought and effort on the part of you and your employees will go a long way in helping minimize the number of upset, angry, and difficult patients you have to deal with on any given day. But before you can effectively start creating an environment and building an employee base that are contributing to minimizing patient complaints, you need to know the patients and their family members' most common reasons for complaining, criticizing, griping, protesting, and whining. To this end, and to help you in better preparing your organization for delivering Ultimate Patient Satisfaction, 15 of the most common reasons why patients and their family members complain are as follow:

1. The patient didn't get what they expected.
2. Someone was rude to them.
3. No one went out of their way to provide service.
4. The patient experienced indifference from staff, no one took them seriously.
5. No one listened to their question or concern.

6. No one answered their question or addressed their concern to their satisfaction.

7. The patient encountered an employee with what they perceived as a negative attitude.

8. The facility or their room was dirty.

9. Someone embarrassed them.

10. The patient is tired, under stress, or frustrated.

11. The patient feels an employee is not properly trained.

12. The patient feels the lack of service is because you are prejudiced.

13. The patient's medical bill appeared outrageously high for the perceived services.

14. The patient received a bodily injury while in your care and charge.

15. The patient died while in your care and charge.

As you can see from the previous list of common reasons for complaining, you can expect to experience three basic categories or types of complaints: service expectations, personal injury, and a patient's death. As you can see, service expectations account for the highest upset patient incident frequency, and the least (we hope) are related to a patient's death. You can expect any high-volume hospital or facility to have its daily share of encounters with upset patients. However, a common thread that can unravel the best healthcare provider's intentions while delivering quality care is medical malpractice. Be on your guard against questionable medical care, or lack thereof, by your staff members and attending physicians. Any and all care that is deemed inappropriate by the patient or a family member will surely generate unnecessary problems. Speak up and break the code of silence that permeates the medical and healthcare profession. After all, is it not in the best interests of your patients for you to speak up? Remember that Ultimate Patient Satisfaction requires you to proactively guard your patients from all forms of harm and that means physical, mental, and financial. A point in passing regarding financial harm. Healthcare fraud places an unseen but heavy burden on all Americans, especially patients in the form of increased costs and financial abuse. According to a 1993 survey by the Health Insurance Association of America (HIAA) of private insurers' healthcare fraud investigations, overall healthcare fraud activity broke down as follows:

Fraudulent diagnosis—43%;
Billing for services not rendered—34%;
Waiver of patient deductible and copayment—21%; and
Other—2%.

Healthcare fraud in 1996 is estimated to exceed $100 billion. I am upset, are you? For more insight in healthcare fraud contact the National Healthcare Anti-Fraud Association by calling 202-659-5955.

After reviewing the reasons that patients and family members complain, you may want to consider creating a training program designed to inform and instruct your employees about the same and how to avoid or minimize being the cause of a patient's complaint. You may also want to consider providing each employee the opportunity to take an upset patient encounter self-analysis.

UPSET PATIENT ENCOUNTER SELF-ANALYSIS

Encountering an upset patient is no bed of roses, though it can be sticky at times. Adverse or stressing patient encounters can bring the worst out in the best of us on occasion. To get an idea how well you might be in reacting and responding with upset patients and their family members in stressful encounters and pressure situations, take the following quick and simple self-analysis. Start by answering the 23 questions provided using the response scale provided, where one means never, and five indicates always. Keep in mind that no one else will see your self-analysis, so be honest with yourself. Tell the truth and shame the devil.

1 = Never   2 = Rarely   3 = Sometimes   4 = Usually   5 = Always

When confronted with an upset patient or family member, I:

1. Do not get angry, but stay calm;   1 2 3 4 5
2. Do not interrupt the person speaking;   1 2 3 4 5
3. Focus on listening;   1 2 3 4 5
4. Remain focused on learning the reason for   1 2 3 4 5
   their concern;
5. Do not become defensive to personal   1 2 3 4 5
   accusations;

6. Assume a tentative and positive body language;   1 2 3 4 5

7. Exhibit caring and attentive facial expressions;   1 2 3 4 5

8. Maintain caring and attentive eye contact;   1 2 3 4 5

9. Show empathy toward the person and their situation;   1 2 3 4 5

10. Use a reassuring and confident tone of voice;   1 2 3 4 5

11. Use words that are not argumentative in nature;   1 2 3 4 5

12. Demonstrate a willingness to help;   1 2 3 4 5

13. Do not put the blame on others for causing the problem;   1 2 3 4 5

14. Do not blame the organization for causing the problem;   1 2 3 4 5

15. Take notes and collect pertinent information as necessary;   1 2 3 4 5

16. Stay focused on quickly resolving their concern;   1 2 3 4 5

17. Know when to call my supervisor for assistance; and   1 2 3 4 5

18. Try to solve the problem to everyone's satisfaction.   1 2 3 4 5

The next five questions deal with your well-being after a dissatisfied patient encounter. After a dissatisfied patient encounter, I:

19. Am in control of my emotions;   1 2 3 4 5

20. Analyze how I handled the situation;   1 2 3 4 5

21. Take corrective action to ensure non recurrence;   1 2 3 4 5

22. Do not dwell on reliving the encounter; and   1 2 3 4 5

23. Feel confident I can calm most upset persons.   1 2 3 4 5

Determine your total score by summing the individual responses. Your total score: _____

Rate yourself using the following rating ranges by finding the numerical range your total score falls into. Once that is done, read your suggested ability to deal with upset patients and their family members.

Range Rating

115-92 = **Excellent,** you are a patient satisfaction encounter guru, so start sharing your knowledge and skills with others. However, work on any factor that you rated as a four or less.

91-69 = **Good,** start working on improving those factors you rated below a four, ask your supervisor for suggestions and help.

68-46 = **Not so good,** you need additional training in dealing with upset people. Ask your supervisor for suggestions and help. You will find role playing a very helpful tool in improving your dealing with upset patient skills.

45-23 = **Concerned,** you need basic training in dealing with upset people. Ask your supervisor for suggestions and help. You will find role playing a very helpful tool in improving your dealing with upset patient skills.

22-0 = **Seriously concerned,** you need extensive training in dealing with upset people. Ask your supervisor for suggestions and help. You will find role playing a very helpful tool in improving your dealing with upset patient skills. Also, you may want to seek a position where there is no customer contact.

Staying calm when dealing with upset patients is not easy for most of us, but having a systematic approach will help you. Furthermore, there is no one single approach that works in every upset patient and family member encounter. However, there are things that you can do to perform well in such situations. One key point in dealing with upset patients is to always remember that the right solution to every upset patient's problem comes from the spirit of caring and cooperation. Quite often, untrained or uncaring employees exhibit a defensive "us against them mentality." Put another way, you have to care about the patient before you can care for the patient.

F I G U R E   2 1 – 1

UPS Approach to Dealing with Upset Patient Face-to-Face

Action	Skill	Result
1. **Remain calm**	Do not take comments personally, refrain from becoming emotional or defensive	Has calming effect, sign of strength
2. **Do not interrupt**	Listen to what is being said, read between the lines	Let the patient tell it in their own words, way, and to vent their frustrations
3. **Respond in a controlled voice and manner**	Sound confident and competent, not annoyed, use appropriate body language	Patient senses your interest and caring, reflects a professional attitude and demeanor, you remain objective
4. **Calm the situation**	Show respect, empathy, and desire to resolve the concern	Lets the patient recoup emotionally, to regain their composure, settle down
5. **Do not get distracted**	Avoid distractions, such as phones, people, and routines	Shows you are focused on their concern, you take them and their concern seriously
6. **Gather critical information, facts, and feelings**	Ask probing and fact-finding questions, get to the root of the problem, read the feelings exhibited	Shows interest and concern to understand the situation and resolve the root problem or cause

UPS FACE-TO-FACE APPROACH

The face-to-face Ultimate Patient Satisfaction (UPS) approach to dealing with an upset patient and their family member is a 13-step process. Each step is designed to calm and reassure the patient that you care about them and want to quickly address their concern. Whenever you are dealing with an upset patient or person, they want to be reassured that you are taking their concern seriously. Failing to quickly and effectively communicate your undivided attention and your grasp of

F I G U R E 2 1 – 1

UPS Approach to Dealing with Upset Patient Face-to-Face—Cont'd.

Action	Skill	Result
7. Repeat understanding	Paraphrase your understanding of the situation or problem	Patient knows you know their concern and how they feel
8. Take responsibility	Keep from blaming others or the organization for the problem, the buck stops with you	Patient senses the "buck" stops here, they are talking to the right person
9. Avoid giving orders	Keep from aggravating the situation further by being too forceful and domineering	Patient feels in control, less threatened, and more cooperative in nature
10. Take corrective action	Quickly responding to resolve the complaint, take action	Patient senses the urgency on your part to address their concern
11. Seek solution accord by gaining agreement	Establish a win-win situation for all concerned parties. Do not make it difficult, offer options	Patient and you are in agreement, satisfied, and the relationship can continue
12. Report incident	Analyze the situation, how resolved, and resulting patient satisfaction level	Next patient will not experience the same
13. Follow-up	Ensure that all time, action, and financial commitments are kept	Opportunity to build rapport, reactivate the relationship

the seriousness of their concern will only generate greater frustration for all concerned, especially for the dissatisfied patient, thus fueling, not defusing, a potential volatile situation. So remember, you communicate the seriousness of the situation by your words, your body language, and your actions or lack thereof. Take all complaints seriously and your patients will see you are serious about meeting their needs. To get good at dealing with upset patients, you need to spend the necessary time to learn and execute the 13-step process to the point where it becomes instinctive or second nature. The steps for dealing with upset patients are listed in Figure 21–1, UPS Approach to Dealing with Upset Patient Face-to-Face Table.

Now that you have familiarized yourself with the 13-step process, you need a little practice. How would you respond to the following 10 patient complaints? The upset patient complained:

1. I had difficulty finding a parking space.
2. The hospital food is horrible, it is making me ill.
3. Ouch, you are hurting me again.
4. Why did you not answer my call button faster?
5. That employee was very rude to me just now.
6. Someone took my wallet from the nightstand.
7. I demand to see my doctor, now!
8. I want another room, I do not like my roommate.
9. Look over there, why is this hospital so dirty?
10. This bill is outrageous and I am not going to pay it.

Remember to analyze your approach using each of the 13 steps outlined earlier. You may also want to consider having another individual, a group of employees, or even physicians participate in a role-playing exercise. Record their interactions using a videotape recorder and analyze their words, body language, and actions using the playback feature. To help bring consistency to how your employees handle upset patients, you may find it worthwhile creating and posting guidelines for dealing with upset patients at all work stations.

Taking the Heat

Another basic, but often used approach in dealing with upset patients is called H.E.A.T., which is an acronym for:

Hear them out,
Emphathize,
Apologize, and
Take responsibility for action.

HELP

One of my own helpful acronyms is H.E.L.P., which takes HEAT a few steps further and stands for:

HEAT,

Evaluate encounter,

Learn root reason for dissatisfaction, and

Protect patients from reoccurrences.

HEAT and HELP, two little acronyms with a big impact on helping you achieve Ultimate Patient Satisfaction.

TELEPHONE TANGLES

Dealing with upset patients and their family members over the telephone is slightly different, especially since the individual is not standing in front of you, or in your face as it were. The following 15-step process in Figure 21–2, UPS Telephone Approach for Dealing with Upset Patients Ear-to-Ear Table, for dealing with upset people over the telephone will make you all ears.

By practicing, you increase the chances that your performance will be perfect. Role playing telephone encounters with various upset patient scenarios is a very constructive and effective method of honing your skills. As with the face-to-face role playing, employ an audio or videotape recorder to analyze encounters. With all things said and done, a few words on listening may be worth reading. You may also want to record actual upset people's telephone conversations for analyzing at a later date. Check for any legal requirements in recording telephone conversations.

LISTENING SKILLS

Listening is an art, not a science, and difficult to do for most of us, including me, or so Cathy, my wife, would testify. Depending on what part of the country you grew up in, when any person is talking to you, expect to hear words pushed or flung at you between 85 and 165 words a minute. However, that wonderful marvel, your brain, can comprehend about 600 words per minute. Simply put, at any given time that someone is talking to you, you are only using about one fourth to one third of your brain's capacity to process audio sounds. Hence, about three fourths to two thirds of your brain has gone into a search mode, that is, looking for something else to fill the mental void. We sometimes call this gray matter exercising, daydreaming. The resulting

FIGURE 21–2

UPS Telephone Approach for Dealing With Upset Patients Ear-to-Ear

Action	Comments
1. **Initial contact:** inviting greeting and identification	Establishes a friendly yet business rapport and identifies with whom the patient is talking
2. **Presentation:** smile, tone of voice, and projected attitude	Conveys an optimistic feeling and establishes a positive note to the conversation and actions to follow with the patient
3. **Listen:** identify the patient's concern or problem	If you are ready to respond before the patient stops talking, you have stopped listening; concentrate on what the patient is saying
4. **Verbally:** cushion the concern	Lets you calm the patient, use the feel, felt, and find technique: we sure do not want you to *continue feeling* that way, though I can understand why you *felt* that way, but I am sure we can *find* a solution to your concern
5. **Apologize:** for any inconvenience or situation	Lets the patients know you are really sorry, your tone of voice should convey sincerity
6. **Indicate:** you want to help or resolve the situation to everyone's satisfaction	Lets the patients know you want to quickly address their concern
7. **Seek:** additional information and feelings	Determine their needs, get the facts, read the patient's tone of voice to help determine their true feelings

mental wandering causes you to lose your focus. Listening is difficult at best. You are hearing. You heard. However, you have stopped listening. Some research on the subject from the University of Oregon suggests that people hear with their ears, but listen with their eyes. When a person is talking to you, your eyes are busy darting in and around their mouth, observing communicative lip formations and tongue gyrations. Well, that is not too strange a revelation to swallow, since we often think with our hearts, taste with our noses, and vote with our feet. But regardless of the many difficulties associated with becoming an effective listener, there are many things you can do to start improving your listening skills. I have listed 17 skills in Figure 21–3, Listening Action Skills Enhancement Table, that will help you in becoming a better listener, but again, like any new skill, it takes practice to master.

FIGURE 21-2

UPS Telephone Approach for Dealing With Upset Patients Ear-to-Ear—Cont'd.

Action	Comments
8. **Repeat:** your understanding of the concern or situation	Lets the patients know you understand their concern or situation
9. **State:** you value their patronage	Lets the patients know you are concerned, and want their future business, you want to be their healthcare provider of choice
10. **Explain:** proposed resolution options	Establish a clear understanding with the patient, ask for their option preference
11. **Summarize:** all actions to be taken and establish mutual agreement	Lets you get agreement to the resolution and the actions to be taken and by when by all parties
12. **Take:** appropriate notes	Keep accurate records of events and promises
13. **Disconnect:** concluding dialog	Leave the patient with a feeling of accomplishment, and reassurance that you will keep your end of the agreement, let the patient hang up first
14. **Report:** incident	Analyze the patient telephone encounter, evaluate appropriateness of solution and the patient's after the fact satisfaction, and any corrective actions taken or needed
15. **Follow up:** with the patient	Call back when you said you would, keep your promises, use this contact to build rapport

The preceding face-to-face and ear-to-ear UPS approaches for dealing with upset patients and family members can be used when you are confronting upset people other than the patient, such as coworkers, physicians, your own family, and significant others. With a few extra steps you can convert or modify the upset patient approach to handling the really upset patient, the angry patient, the irate patient, or the in-your-face person.

DEALING WITH ANGRY PATIENTS

The time will come when you will be confronted by an angry or irate patient. Do not panic, you have already learned how to handle and deal with an upset patient face-to-face and ear-to-ear. For all practical

FIGURE 21-3

Listening Action Skills Enhancement

Action Skill	Comments
Asking	Using open-ended questions to explore and uncover details and close-ended questions to confirm
Clarify	Defining all imprecise words and phrases used to describe a state of dissatisfaction or problem
Communicating	Employing verbal and visual signs to communicate that you are listening, head nodding and uh-huhs
Confirming	Repeating or paraphrasing their message frequently
Controlling	Becoming overly emotional can greatly distract you from your ability to focus on listening
Expressing	Periodically, express your interest and exhibit a sense of importance to the events at hand
Focusing	Clearing your mind, avoiding the urges to daydream or tune out, stay focused
Identifying	Identify the key concern, central idea, or concept being communicated, the message within the message
Ignoring	Do not let distractions or uncomfortable surroundings diminish your ability to remain attentive
Interrupting	Abstain from interrupting verbally and otherwise
Latching	Avoid latching to key words and missing the message
Maintaining	Making and keeping eye contact is very important in face-to-face encounters
Reading	Learning how to read beyond the spoken word, the tone of voice, and body language
Responding	Keep your responses short, avoid becoming verbally involved early on
Talking	Start talking less, zipper-up and let them open-up, it is that simple
Visualizing	Try to see the concern, problem, or situation from the other person's perspective
Writing	Get in the habit of taking pertinent notes and keeping good mind-jogging ticklers

purposes, an angry patient is an upset patient, but only more emotionally elevated. Your job is to let angry patients down without letting them down. Defusing the situation and saving a potentially explosive relationship. Dealing with angry patients requires employing five additional steps.

1. **Be Prepared:** You need to prepare yourself physically and mentally for the encounter. Get yourself ready by taking several deep breaths of air, assume a confident stance or position, adjust your attire and posture, radiate a smile, check your body language for negative signals, clear your mind, and demonstrate a positive attitude. Remember, you are a professional, communicate that message to the angry patient.

2. **Be Ready:** Remember HEAT, the letter "H" stands for hearing them out. Let the angry patient vent their frustration and anger, get it off their chest, spit it out, or go ballistic, do not interrupt. It is their complaint, so listen attentively to the very end.

3. **Be Exact:** Repeat the patient's complaint in their <u>own</u> words, establish your understanding of their problem or concern, and get agreement that your understanding is correct. It is important to get the angry patient to agree with you as quickly as possible. Once an initial agreement is reached with the patient, the process for psychologically defusing the situation starts to occur.

4. **Be Open:** Ask the angry patient what they want done to resolve the problem. If their wants are reasonable, grant them on the spot if you can. If the solution is more complex or mutual agreement is necessary, involve the patient in the solution. Develop patient ownership of the solution. To enhance your ability of effecting ownership, ensure you make provisions for allowing several realistic options for the patient to choose from.

5. **Be Relaxed:** Do not take the patient's vented anger personally, let it go. After the angry patient encounter, take the time and appropriate actions to defuse your own emotional state and relax. Take a break, a short walk, or just spend a few quiet moments alone, take a couple of deep breaths and call upon your favorite stress management techniques. Just take it easy, regain your composure, your calmness, and your charming attitude. Relax and get ready for your next angry patient encounter. It is just down the hall, around the corner, or through the doorway of time.

In actuality, however, sometimes one or more of the dealing with angry patients steps will become verbally blurred with one of the previously outlined upset patient steps. That is all right, just make sure you know when to inject one or more of the additional five steps when dealing with angry patients. The last category is those patients and family members who are unrealistic in their wants.

UNREALISTIC DEMANDS

Just when you thought you had the situation well in hand, you realize the patient's expectation or demand is unrealistic. The patient has placed conditions upon solving their problem and you quickly realize the patient is jockeying for position, making forceful demands, and you also detect a hint of Negotiating 101 emerging. Stay calm. You may or may not be able to meet the patient's unrealistic demands, but that is no reason to lose your cool or your patience. Again, you revert to using the guidelines set forth for dealing with an upset patient. To those guidelines you have the following four additional steps to consider:

1. **Determining:** You need to determine the realistic or unrealistic nature of the patient's demands. If they are realistic, resolve them as quickly as possible to the patient's satisfaction. If unrealistic, such as,

   Patient: I demand to see the doctor now. My appointment was 30 minutes ago. And at this rate I will miss a very important client meeting this afternoon.

   Move on to step 2.

2. **Establishing:** You need to identify your solution options and authority to fulfill those demands, seeking additional authority as warranted,

   Staff: Dr. Russell has informed me that she is available to see you now. I am sorry for the delay and any inconvenience.

   If you cannot or will not meet the demand, move to step 3.

3. **Acknowledging:** You need to acknowledge the patient's dissatisfaction using an empathic statement, such as:

   Staff: I understand why you are angry because you have been waiting more than 30 minutes to see the doctor and you might miss your important afternoon meeting.

Then proceed to step 4.

4. **Explaining:** The impact of their demands on all concerned parties, such as:

Staff: Dr. Russell is with another patient who went into cardiac arrest, and if she stopped attending the patient so she could see her other patients at their scheduled appointments, the chances are very likely that the patient she is with and needing emergency care will suffer irreversible damage or even die.

Remember, the extra four steps to use when confronted with an unrealistic request or demand are used in conjunction with the steps for dealing with an upset patient. You will find that the convenient comparison in Figure 21–4, UPS Approaches in Dealing With Upset Patients Comparison Table, will help you in putting it all together and selecting the best sequence of steps to follow in dealing with upset, angry, or unrealistic demands face-to-face and ear-to-ear. As with any system or process, it takes getting used to. You and your employees need to be spending adequate time practicing and role playing to master the skills necessary for dealing with upset patients and visitors.

WALKING TIME BOMBS

Upset, angry, and irate patients and visitors, if not defused quickly, become walking time bombs, ready to go off at any time, around anybody, but they usually give off telltale signs of approaching critical mass. You and your employees need to recognize those warning (warring) signals, such as out of control and forceful body language, rapid stride, strained speech, elevated tone of voice, flushing skin, increasing perspiration, heavy breathing, contorted facial expressions, and a rapid series of complaints. Learn to anticipate an exploding patient-employee encounter and defuse the situation rapidly.

WHEN IN DOUBT, ALWAYS, BUT NEVER

Regardless of the approach you are using in dealing with upset, angry, irate, and unrealistic patients and visitors, if you are interested in

FIGURE 21-4

UPS Approaches in Dealing With Upset Patients Comparison Table

Face-to-Face	Ear-to-Ear	Angry	Unrealistic
Encounter	Initial contact		
Remain calm		Be prepared	
	Presentation		
Do not interrupt	Listen	Be ready	
Respond in a controlled voice and manner			
Calm the situation	Verbally		
Do not get distracted			
	Apologize		
	Indicate		
Gather critical information, facts, and feelings	Seek		Determining
Establish authority	Authority		Establishing
Repeat understanding	Repeat	Be exact	Acknowledging
Take responsibility			Explaining
	State		
Avoid giving orders			
Take corrective action			
	Explain		
Seek solution accord by gaining agreement	Summarize	Be open	
	Take		
	Disconnect		
Report incident	Report		
Follow-up	Follow-up		
		Be relaxed	

making the whole process less stressful, more productive, and positive for all concerned parties, you need to adhere to the following 31 important Ultimate Patient Satisfaction guidelines.

Always:

Always listen and hear the patient out;

Always be proactively looking for things that upset people;

Always respect their point of view;

Always change your behavior to avoid upsetting people;

Always show a positive attitude in everything you say and do;

Always search for a win-win solution;

Always keep your promise;

Always exhibit confidence;

Always keep your cool; and

Always be flexible.

Never:

Never let a patient lose face;

Never get into an argument with a patient;

Never stop being courteous to a patient;

Never physically or otherwise threaten a patient;

Never call a patient names;

Never verbally attack a patient;

Never question a patient's integrity or honesty;

Never be rude, indifferent, discourteous, or unpleasant to a patient; and

Never be sarcastic to a patient.

Your Image:

Your body language is reassuring and radiates confidence;

Your hair is clean, brushed or combed, and well kept;

Your makeup is applied neatly, moderately, and appropriately;

Your clothing is clean, neat, pressed, shoes are clean, and all are in good condition;

Your personal hygiene is not offensive, such as bad breath or body odors;

Your hands and fingernails are clean, no chipped fingernail polish;

Your face is shaved, facial hair well groomed;

Your jewelry and fragrance are worn in moderation and not overpowering; and

Your demeanor is calm under stress.

FIGURE 21-5

The Anatomy of Ultimate Patient Satisfaction

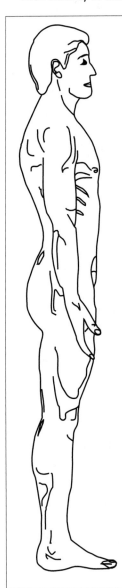

THE BODY . . . always maintain a professional demeanor

BRAIN . . . think like a patient

EYES . . . constantly look for ways to improve service

EARS . . . listen to patients and their family members

NOSE . . . stick it in someone's else's business to help a patient

MOUTH . . . maintain patient confidentiality

NECK . . . empower yourself on the spot to solve a problem

SHOULDERS . . . lend them when needed

CHEST . . . take pride in what you do

HEART . . . show empathy toward patients' concerns and needs

RIBS . . . give without expecting something in return

ARMS . . . openly reach out to help patients, embrace change

SPINE . . . stand up for patient rights

STOMACH . . . do not turn away from upset patient issues

INTESTINES . . . rely on gut feelings, display fortitude, take charge

BLADDER . . . respect patients privacy and dignity

BUTTOCKS . . . get up off it, helping out without being asked

HANDS . . . always be ready to give a helping hand

FINGERS . . . be accountable, do not point to blame others

LEGS . . . respond quickly, move fast

KNEES . . . do not buckle under upset patient pressures, stay calm

FEET . . . do not jump to conclusions and become defensive

TOES . . . stay on them, anticipate patient's needs

HEELS . . . be flexible, do not dig in from giving in

THE SOUL . . . demonstrate a caring love for what you do and whom you care for

Copyright © 1995 Strategic Visions, Inc.

Your Options:

Know when to advance the upset patient to your supervisor;
Know your authority to commit resources and forgive debt; and
Know when you are in over your head and need assistance if
not downright help.

As a daily reminder and Ultimate Patient Satisfaction review, consider starting your day looking into a mirror and checking yourself out, from top to bottom, and using your body as an anatomical road map to Ultimate Patient Satisfaction. You can use Figure 21–5, Anatomy of Ultimate Patient Satisfaction Chart, as a quick reminder and reference. A color, 17 × 11 inch copy of the Anatomy of Ultimate Patient Satisfaction Chart can be ordered from Strategic Visions Inc., 205-995-8495.

22

CHAPTER

Patient
Crisis Management

Oops, now what? . . .

Crises happen, and happen for a wide variety of reasons. Crises appear as the expected and the unexpected. Crises come and go in people's and organizations' lives, and have the power to enhance or destroy those lives. Crises are designated major or minor. A crisis' designation is totally dependent on the severity of the consequences. Crises come in two flavors, managed and non-managed. A well-managed crisis is always the less destructive and most palatable of the two. This chapter deals with managing patient crises in an Ultimate Patient Satisfaction environment. And for our purposes, an Ultimate Patient Satisfaction crisis is defined as any employee-patient encounter or event, and the resulting consequence that causes a patient's death or bodily injury or subjects a patient to undue mental stress. Keep in mind that a non-managed patient crisis is a crisis on a self-destruction course, spinning out of control, easily turning into any healthcare provider's worst nightmare. Some crises are all-consuming in nature, devouring management time, resources, and disrupting that healthcare provider's or entity's ability to carry on its function or daily business as usual. Not managing a crisis is, in and of itself, yet another crisis.

290

ROOT REASONS

You will find in healthcare that the root reason patient crises, or any crisis for that matter, develop can usually be traced to one or more of the following 10 occurrences:

1. Human errors;
2. Equipment failures;
3. Technology failure;
4. Technology availability;
5. Technological rate of change;
6. Insufficient staff training;
7. Organizational status quo contentment;
8. Lacks appropriate knowledge;
9. Disregard for safety regulations; or
10. Compromising speed and greed.

LEVELS OF SEVERITY AND CHALLENGE

As a healthcare professional, you can expect to be confronted with many anticipated and unforeseen crises that will surely challenge your interpersonal and managerial skills. You and your staff need to know how to recognize and manage a crisis. Though noninclusive, take a moment for reviewing the following list of patient crises a healthcare provider can expect to encounter:

1. Missed patient appointment;
2. Patient noncompliance;
3. Equipment down and unavailable;
4. Supplies or product shortages;
5. Patient medical record lost;
6. Computer data lost;
7. Patient property missing;
8. Skilled staff shortages;
9. Adverse reaction to medication;
10. Patient injury;
11. Surgical mishap;
12. Medical malpractice;

13. Patient missing; or

14. Patient death.

Reviewing the patient crises list, you immediately realize the broad spectrum of patient crises expected or unexpected in nature. Take death as an example, depending on the circumstances, a patient's demise can be expected or unexpected, such as caused by a terminal disease or medical malpractice. Also evident to you is the fact that some crises are of a more serious nature than others, that is, missing an appointment is not as serious as a patient dying. However, missing an appointment could have serious effects on the patient's treatment and medical outcome. As you might expect, each possible crisis situation demands and challenges your skills at anticipating, planning, and managing such happenings and events. Your first step in patient crisis management is conducting a crisis assessment audit.

PATIENT CRISIS ASSESSMENT AUDIT

In the event of a patient crisis, the first assessment rule is to remain calm. The more serious the crisis, the calmer you must stay, at least on the outside. You will quickly discover that stress management is a personal asset in managing a serious crisis. If you have not already done so, consider learning how to deal with stress. However, remaining calm is easier if you have a crisis action plan to fall back on and follow. You will be learning that aspect of crisis management shortly.

The second assessment rule is to determine the patient crisis category confronting you. Is the patient crisis expected or unexpected? Using Figure 22–1, Crisis Category Assessment Table, you can quickly determine the patient crisis category by analyzing three deciding factors: influence, effect, and action.

FIGURE 22-1

Crisis Category Assessment

Crisis	Influence	Effect	Action
Expected	Temporary	Minor 10%–30%	Tactical
Unexpected	Extended	Major >50%	Strategic

Ask yourself these three questions:

1. Is the crisis influence temporary or extended? As an example, a patient losing their false teeth is a temporary crisis, however, a medical malpractice claim can go on for an extended period of time.

2. What effect is the crisis having on consuming management time, corporate resources, and disrupting your organization's ability to carry on its function or daily business as usual? A patient missing their false teeth is a minor crisis having little effect on the organization, but on the other hand, a major medical malpractice claim is costly, and very often ends up keeping patients from your doors, especially if publicly debated and tried.

3. What action or response is needed to satisfactorily end the crisis? The patient missing their false teeth is reunited after a diligent canvassing of the laundry room, or a new set or plate is purchased, a front-line tactical decision, minimal organizational disturbance. Now consider the medical malpractice claim. You may be forced to establish new procedures and revise current protocols, to make expensive facility and equipment repair, to pay a costly attorney and award, and to engage in an aggressive and costly image-building public relations campaign, all senior management strategic decisions, potential effect on business operations is significant. Your assessment of the two crisis scenarios should have concluded that the missing false teeth are expected. The medical malpractice was unexpected, especially if you have a benchmark quality control program in place.

The third assessment rule is to determine the severity of the patient crisis and the rate at which the event and resulting consequence are disrupting or destroying your ability to carry on with your function or daily business. In determining a patient crisis severity level, you need to consider two key areas, the urgency of the crisis, and whether the crisis is internal or external. Figure 22–2, Patient Crisis Severity Assessment Table, provides a few examples of severity assessments.

Using Figure 22–2, a higher severity priority is attributed to patient crises outside your organization's self-imposed control, than to

FIGURE 22-2

Patient Crisis Severity Assessment

Urgency		Severity Level		
Strategic (high)	3	Patient not responding Low patient satisfaction Electrical power failure	4	Patient injured Patient death Medical malpractice lawsuit
Tactical (low)	1	Key employee leaves Lost patient lab results Patient property missing	2	Patient failing to keep appointment Patient out of medical compliance Product shortages
		Internal **(Entity)** **External**		

an internal patient crisis where you have the empowerment to address and better manage the total patient crisis on the spot. As you would expect, level four severity crises typically bring in third-party entities, such as family members, inspectors, law enforcement officials, regulators, attorneys, and news reporters. Your self-imposed control over the patient crisis has been deposed to people outside your organization, outside your immediate control, and outside looking in wondering why, and each outsider having a different personal agenda. Looking at Figure 22-2, you can see how a level three can quickly become a level four. You will find that critical to crises management is speed, quick response time, a mind-set for action, not diversionary and spin tactics.

Crisis assessment rule four is to determine the effect on your healthcare delivery system and its supporting network partners' dynamics. You need to identify which network's common values and relationships may be adversely affected, damaged, or destroyed by the patient crisis. Acting as a bonding agent, common value between you and your supporting network partners has the power to hold you both together during a crisis. You need to realize that your various healthcare partners will usually have different common values. An example is detailed in Figure 22-3, Patient Crisis Network Assessment Table. The table presents the supporting network partners (participants) comprising a typical hospital's delivery system. As you know, a patient's death resulting from gross medical malpractice can have a devastating effect on your established network relationships. Using

Figure 22–3 as a reference, theorize about the possible adverse effects, a second patient's death, caused by gross medical malpractice, within 15 days of the first death, might have on the following network participants. How would a similar patient crisis affect your hospital, practice, or business?

PATIENT CRISIS CONTROL

Once you have finished assessing the patient crisis, your next step in crisis management is to quickly understand the control you and your organization have over the current circumstances, the follow-up action plan, and the ensuing consequences. Using Figure 22–4, Crisis Control Analysis Table, you can quickly see that there are three primary control states: direct, indirect, and none, and two secondary control elements: expected and unexpected. Start using Figure 22–4 for determining your direct and indirect control. You must master the art of customer, public, and supplier relations and the art of effectively influencing others, when your crisis control is indirect. However, not having any control is no reason not to manage the patient crisis. You can still present a controlled reaction and appearance as detailed in Figure 22–4. When it comes to managing a patient crisis, though, anticipating the expected is a proactive approach to avoiding a patient crisis and best enables you to effect control. But on the other side of the crisis coin, you will find yourself reacting when the unexpected happens. Expecting the unexpected is expected of every senior executive and risk manager, but not knowing unexpected's who, what, where, when, and how makes it only speculative at best. However, knowing your state of control and having a core crisis action plan in place, and that is quickly and aggressively executed in managing a patient crisis, especially a serious incident, is a very stabilizing force for everyone concerned and the organization itself, as you would expect.

"Actions speak louder than words in any crisis situation"

PATIENT CRISIS ACTION GUIDELINES

You need to keep in mind that it is impractical and impossible to prepare a contingency plan for every possible patient crisis. However, knowing what to do, who will do what, and when is key to your success in managing a patient crisis. To help you create your own patient

FIGURE 22-3

Patient Crisis Network Assessment

Network Participants	Common Values	Established Relationship
Referral sources	Need quick access, cost-effective, and proven medical services, care, and quality outcomes	Quality services, satisfied patients, and minimal practice disruptions (side effects)
Staff physicians	Respect, fairness in treatment, competitive compensation, and professional opportunities	Medical proficiency, honest day's work, and contributing to overall profitability and success
Managed care plans	Need for cost and outcome-effective continuum of medical intervention and care	Pricing concessions, quality services, satisfied patients, and continuum of care availability
Retailers-suppliers	Provide access to consumer products and services, timely delivery and payment	Quality products, price sensitivity, availability, and responsive service
Employees	Respect, fairness in treatment, competitive compensation, and personal growth opportunities	Low maintenance, honest day's work, and contribution to overall profitability
Patient (end user)	Need for safe, effective medical care, open communications	Quality care, service, and price sensitivity, positive outcomes and minimal adverse side effects

crisis program and action plans, consider the following 17 guidelines in designing your own patient crisis action plan (CAP). Like capping an oil well, by CAPping a patient crisis, you keep it from getting out of control. The suggested 17-step approach to creating your own CAP is as follows:

1. Identifying, anticipating, and planning for expected patient crises and acting accordingly;
2. Being flexible in your planning, clearly explaining the plan, and responsive actions;
3. Involving and informing people at all levels within your organization, seeking input from many sources;

FIGURE 22-3

Patient Crisis Network Assessment—Cont'd.

Network Participants	Common Values	Established Relationship
Family members (the patient's)	Need for safe, effective medical care, open communications	Quality care, service, and price sensitivity, positive outcomes and minimal adverse side effects
Community	Stewardship for community medical care, patient safety, and environmental responsibility	Positive community-oriented values, safety-oriented, accountability, and high ethics
Employers	Needs to reduce employee healthcare costs without compromising employees' medical care	Safe and cost-effective medical intervention, satisfied employee-patients, open information exchange
Media	Openness with media, the right for people to know the facts	Fair treatment in exchange for factual information and honesty
Regulators	Accurate medical and surgical information, records, and compliance	Fair, non intrusive regulations, easy to interpret, and cost-effective to administer
Financial institutions	Provide access to financial products and services	Favorable long- and short-term financing, banking, and investment services

4. Timing is everything, the more severe the patient crisis, the quicker the decision-making process and responsive actions need to be;

5. Do not always search for human error, instead start focusing on, and correcting the root problem for the patient crisis;

6. Creating new business strategies for addressing your current patient crisis situation needs and ensuring the avoidance of a similar crisis in the future;

7. Assigning a lead-person empowered to oversee the crisis management effort, best, a person who is not directly involved with the initial patient crisis, a neutral party;

FIGURE 22-4

Crisis Control Analysis

Control	Expected-Action	Unexpected-Action
Direct	Administrative and medical policies, procedures, and delivery system protocols, employees, suppliers, and staff physicians	Organizational and employee competencies, safety policies, and procedures
Indirect	Influencing through political, regulatory, religious, media, industry, associations, and community leaders	Influence through common values that political, regulatory, religious, media, industry, associations, and community leaders will respect and respond to
None	Stay calm, control your reactions, responsiveness, and tactical direction to resolve the crisis	Stay calm, revise your position, core strategies, products, and services to prevent any recurrence, admit faults

8. Choosing substance over spin, adhere to your values at all costs, do not become a spin doctor, prescribing creative cover-up spin methodologies, the side effects will usually kill you, besides spinning is a political art form best left to the government;

9. Worrying about your employees first, but know when and how to cut your losses and people;

10. Evaluating, revising, and eliminating people, policies, and procedures as necessary to avoid a similar patient crisis in the future;

11. Remembering that your responsive efforts in trying to resolve a patient crisis are more important than the results obtained in trying, stay focused at all costs;

12. Establishing a serious patient crisis "notification tree" that identifies internal and external people and agencies that need to know past events, present actions, and future safeguards;

13. Practicing your crisis action plan and revising the same for any inadequacies;

14. Identifying areas of responsibilities and level of authority, especially yours;
15. Hiring an experienced public relations firm when dealing with a level four patient crises;
16. Collecting unbiased and accurate incident information and supportive documentation for analyzing, making decisions, taking corrective action, reporting purposes, and tracking resolution progress pertaining to the patient crisis; and
17. Staying calm sets the tone for all others to emulate.

PATIENT CRISES AT THEIR BEST

You will benefit the greatest by never approaching a patient crisis with an adversarial mind-set and temperament, though a serious patient crisis can have sobering consequences and shake the foundation and tarnish the image of the most prestigious healthcare provider or institution. You must remain open-minded and not close-mouthed concerning all patient crises. Every patient crisis, no matter how serious, offers an opportunity for seeking and administering self-improvement. I believe in the principle that every patient crisis has a silver lining. In essence, the looming darkening patient crisis cloud has a silver lining, that is, if you are looking at it with the right perspective. Though it may not seem that way at first, a crisis' silver lining has the potential for making you and other healthcare entities better providers in the not so dismal future. And as you weather the storm, you will discover that by keeping an open mind, by following proven patient crisis management techniques as outlined in this chapter, and by depending on the patient crisis type and severity, valuable lessons and revealing insights are at hand, revealing important information and windows of opportunities to be exploited, and it is all yours for the taking. As an example, yours or someone else's patient crisis may present you with one or more of the following 12 strategic opportunities for:

1. Redefining and refocusing on your core competency;
2. Increasing market share opportunities;
3. Introducing quick change;
4. Embracing austerities, returning to the basics, keeping it simple;

5. Identifying internal and external weaknesses;

6. Terminating inefficient relationships and employees;

7. Launching a new product or service;

8. Challenging an existing federal or state healthcare regulation;

9. Acquiring new technology;

10. Acquiring a competitor;

11. Dominating an industry; and

12. Building industry solidarity.

CRISIS MANAGEMENT'S GOLDEN RULE

Simply put, by properly controlling and maintaining your healthcare delivery environment, you stand a better chance of not having patient crises. Even though obtaining Ultimate Patient Satisfaction lessens your chances for a patient crisis, the inevitable happens, and after the smoke clears and the potshots taper off, you will sustain less damage if you remembered and executed my golden rule of crisis management, which is, "To quickly analyze the situation, make ethical and value-based decisions, communicate openly, and focus on rectifying the root cause of the crisis." It's really that simple!

23

Ultimate Patient Satisfaction

It's not an incident, but a way of life . . .

Ultimate Patient Satisfaction (UPS), that is what it is all about, delivering the best patient satisfaction. By the time you get to reading this chapter, you have been exposed to numerous ideas, concepts, and philosophies regarding patient satisfaction. However, in and of themselves, those ideas, concepts, and philosophies are useless without the proper UPS mind-set. I believe that there is a direct and strong correlation between a person's UPS mind-set and their outlook on life, on people, and on the things around them. I further believe that UPS is not an incident, but a way of life. UPS is not just an organizational, hospital, or departmental thing but a personal thing. UPS is a quest, a special way of living your life to its fullest, driven internally by an inner divine force or philosophy that makes you feel good about yourself, about others, and about the world around you. Are you UP to it? This chapter will provide you specific information, approaches, and promotional materials for creating, introducing, and executing a dynamic and effective program designed to deliver Ultimate Patient Satisfaction. But before you emerge yourself in the UPS program, we need to test your UPS-ability. Are you ready?

UPS-ABILITY

To determine your UPS-ability rating, carefully read each of the following 50 UPS self-analysis statements and score yourself using the UPS value.

$$6 = \text{Always} \quad 5 = \text{Most of the time} \quad 4 = \text{Usually}$$
$$3 = \text{Sometimes} \quad 2 = \text{Seldom} \quad 1 = \text{Never}$$

You will only benefit from this self-analysis if you answer all 50 UPS statements and answer each truthfully. Be honest with yourself. And remember, only you will know how best you are about providing Ultimate Patient Satisfaction. The UPS-ability test will also reveal what areas you need to work on for improving your UPS mind-set.

   1. I am genuinely pleasant to all our patients. _____
   2. I am genuinely pleasant to our patients' family members. _____
   3. I am genuinely pleasant to our patients' guests. _____
   4. I tend to our patients' needs first, putting the patients' needs before my own work. _____
   5. I immediately interrupt what I am doing when a patient stands before me or needs help. _____
   6. I am willing to spend extra time with our patients to address their needs. _____
   7. I often do something out of the ordinary for our patients. _____
   8. I am patient with our patients, especially those who appear insecure, unsure, or confused. _____
   9. I do not humiliate or talk down to our patients. _____
   10. I do not humiliate or talk down to our patients' family members and guests. _____
   11. I am genuinely concerned about maintaining our patients' dignity. _____
   12. I am genuinely concerned about our patient outcomes and well-being. _____
   13. I make every effort to make patients feel comfortable and reduce any anxiety. _____

14. I make every effort in my actions to make our patients feel special and important. _____

15. I make every effort in my actions to make our patients feel wanted. _____

16. I treat all our patients courteously regardless of their sex, color, religion, language, and nationality. _____

17. I never get angry with a patient. _____

18. I never vent my own frustrations on patients. _____

19. I never get angry with our patients' family members and guests. _____

20. I never vent my own frustrations on our patients' family members and guests. _____

21. I let patients vent their anger and feelings without getting defensive or angry at them. _____

22. I let patients' family members and guests vent their anger and feelings without getting defensive or angry with them. _____

23. I never talk about our patients in an unfavorable way to physicians and fellow employees. _____

24. I never talk about our patients' family members and guests in an unfavorable way to physicians and fellow employees. _____

25. I am always soliciting patient feedback to their satisfaction. _____

26. I am always soliciting patients' family members and guests for feedback regarding the patient and their own satisfaction. _____

27. I always greet our patients, their family members, and guests in a friendly manner. _____

28. I genuinely smile more than wear a frown. _____

29. I do not argue with our patients. _____

30. I do not argue with our patients' family members and guests. _____

31. I do not use profanity or obscene gestures during work _____

32. I wake up excited about my job. _____

33. I enjoy my job and responsibilities. _____
34. I enjoy my working environment. _____
35. I believe my supervisor is genuinely concerned about my well-being. _____
36. I enjoy working with my fellow employees. _____
37. I enjoy working at _____ . _____
38. I have many friends at _____ . _____
39. I go out of my way to help other departments and staff.

    _____

40. I do not spread unfavorable gossip about my fellow employees. _____
41. I take responsibility for the continuum of communications between departments. _____
42. I take accountability for my actions. _____
43. I genuinely take pride in my work. _____
44. I work well with our medical staff physicians. _____
45. I try to set a good example for other employees to learn from and follow. _____
46. I often stop in the corridors to provide assistance to patients in need. _____
47. I genuinely feel good when one of our patients has a positive outcome. _____
48. I often go outside my official job description to help our patients. _____
49. I am good at anticipating our patient needs. _____
50. I am good at anticipating our patients' family members' and guests' needs. _____

Add your UPS-ability self analysis statement scores together to calculate your UPS-ability rating. My total UPS-ability score is _____ .

UPS-ABILITY STATUS

Check your total UPS-ability score to determine how *UP* you are to providing Ultimate Patient Satisfaction.

Score	Suggests:
300-270	**UPS-ability at its best.** Congratulations. You are an UPS-ability guru. You have the right mind-set, habits, and interpersonal skills needed to provide Ultimate Patient Satisfaction. Now start influencing others to emulate your example. You are the light at the end of the tunnel, shine bright so others do not give up hope on the journey to Ultimate Patient Satisfaction.
269-240	**UPS-ability is within your grasp.** A little more self-discipline and effort on your part will push you up and over the barriers keeping you from becoming an UPS-ability guru. Review each UPS statements that you scored a four or below on, and start creating an UPS action plan for changing fours into fives or better. You are *UP* to it, your high score says so.
239-225	**UPS-ability is up for grabs.** Increase your focus on UPS issues by reviewing all UPS statements you have an individual score of four or less on, and start creating an UPS action plan for changing fours into fives or better. You are on the right road, but without a continuous and prioritized focus you will get lost and detoured from UPS, your final destination.
224 or less	**UPS-ability appears to be an uphill battle.** However, do not give up. You may have lost a battle, but you can still win the war by raising your expectations. Start making UPS-ability your number one priority at work. Quest for the best by reviewing each UPS statement that you scored a four or below on, and start creating an UPS action plan for changing fours into fives or better. You become better by questing the best. Just by taking the UPS-ability self-analysis you are now pointed in the right direction. The rest is *UP* to you. Go for it.

Note—There is a direct correlation between your UPS-ability rating and your outlook on life and the people and things around you. UPS is a way of life. UPS is not just a healthcare thing, but a personal thing. UPS is a way of living your life that makes you feel good about yourself, others, and the world around you. Give it a try. Get up and start living your days one at a time. You can kick the bad habits the UPS way.

ATTITUDE CHECK TOWARD YOUR JOB AND WORK

As a special bonus, a mini self-analysis about your attitude toward your job and work is available at no additional charge or effort. To check your job and work attitude, you just add up your statement scores for UPS statements 32 through 45. Your total UPS special group score is

_____ .

Score	Suggests:
85-76	Congratulations. You are very happy and excited about your job, responsibilities, and working environment. You feel good about yourself and others. Life is an adventure.
75-67	You tend to be satisfied more with your job, responsibilities, and working environment. You like what you do, working and helping with others.
66-59	You appear to be satisfied with your job, responsibilities, and working environment. You might want to consider reviewing the special group UPS statements that you scored a four or below on and develop a UPS action plan to change that habit into a five or better.
58 or less	A rating less than 59 suggests you may not be fully satisfied with your job, responsibilities, and working environment. Unhappy employees tend not to reach their fullest potential. You may want to discuss your score with your supervisor to determine what can be done to raise your satisfaction level with your job, responsibilities, and working environment. A career move may also be something worth thinking about, and if desirable, exploring.

THE UPS WAY

One reason that I strongly believe many healthcare providers do not achieve Ultimate Patient Satisfaction is the lack of a written position or philosophy declaration defining their beliefs, intentions, and conduct as they relate to patient satisfaction. I suggest that your UPS philosophy declaration consist of the following three distinct and related elements:

1. Vision statement;
2. Mission statement; and
3. Value statement.

Such a fundamental and important document will enable everyone, internal and external to your organization, to know your commitment, to the patient, to quality, and to service. You will find the following sample philosophy declaration includes the three key element statements and provides a good springboard for documenting your organization's own commitment.

1. Vision Statement—The vision statement describes the future.
   To become the healthcare provider of choice in the communities and markets we serve for people in need of healthcare and/or seeking medical intervention, by creating and maintaining a benchmark patient-friendly, quality healthcare delivery system, and environment that exceed our patients' expectations.
2. Mission Statement—The mission statement describes the reason for your existence.
   We pledge to Establish a healthcare delivery system and environment that encourage excellence in all we execute, Exceeding our patients' expectations whenever financially and medically practical, Excelling at quality, for eventually quality wins out over everything else, Empowering our employees to excel at delivering excellence in care and service, Eclipsing our competition in patient satisfaction, and Expecting and earning a fair return for our efforts.
3. Value Statement—The value statement describes your code of conduct.

> We believe that satisfied patients equal profits, our growth,
> and prosperity; that patient care is delivered one-patient-
> at-a-time; that every patient is a very important person and
> will be treated as such; that we must anticipate and seek
> out patient encounters and interactions to ensure positive
> experiences; that we must inform our patients what to
> expect and exceed those expectations whenever possible; that
> patients are not the source of our stress, frustrations, and
> failures, but the purpose for our being and our primary
> source of revenue; that when a patient is dissatisfied, it is
> usually because of a disparity between the patient's
> expectations and reality, hence, their expectations must
> become our reality; and that we must never be satisfied with
> our patients' satisfaction, that is never!

The preceding UPS philosophy declaration is provided as a reference you can use, or create your own. Remember that the UPS philosophy declaration should augment your corporate mission statement, maybe replace it if I dare to be so bold, but for the patient's
sake, I am, so I did.

THE QUEST

In your quest for Ultimate Patient Satisfaction, there are five specific
areas you need to focus on. Each has a major effect on a patient's overall perception of quality and satisfaction as follows:

> Quality (benchmark);
> Utilization (cost-effective care and control);
> Employees (empathy and empowerment);
> Service (orientation); and
> Timeliness (response and proactiveness).

UPS FORMULA

There is a simple formula that describes the relationship among the
three major ingredients necessary to achieve Ultimate Patient
Satisfaction. The UPS formula is $P_1 \times P_2 \times P_3 = P_t$. In the UPS formula, P_1 represents having the right person, in the right job, with the

right training, with the right management support, with the right attitude, and with the right resources; P_2 refers to your patients having great expectations; P_3 reflects the extent employees' performance consistently exceeds your patients' expectations; and P_t equals organizational prosperity. Your prosperity will be self-generating in the form of increasing revenues and decreasing costs resulting from provider-of-choice loyalty, repeat patient business, patient-influenced referrals, and earning a fair profit for your services. Basically, the formula indicates that by increasing P_1, P_2, or P_3, the greater your prosperity will be. Of the three P's, increasing P_3 causes the greatest prosperity.

UPS GOLDEN RULES

To help your organization in delivering its services better than the competition, you can start living the 15 golden UPS rules on a daily basis, and watch your P_3 increase. To ensure you are gaining the maximum benefit from living by the 15 golden UPS rules, you must be proactive in nature. So remember, when it comes to your patients, their family members, and fellow coworkers, thou will proactively:

1. Look up and speak to people, be cheerful, warm, and inviting;
2. Spend more time smiling on the outside, a smile energizes an encounter and reduces anxiety;
3. Call people by name, a person finds pleasure in hearing their name;
4. Do not compromise a person's dignity by your thoughts and actions;
5. Be friendly, speak and act graciously toward others;
6. Radiate a genuine pleasure in caring about and for others;
7. Display the greatest interest and confidence in your responsibilities;
8. Show empathy toward others by being considerate of their feelings and situation;
9. Seek out every occasion to help without being asked;
10. Show patience with your patients and others;
11. Offer positive reinforcement, not criticism;
12. Exhibit a good sense of humor;

13. Generously praise others providing UPS;

14. Make a positive difference in the world around you; and

15. Never be satisfied with your customer's satisfaction.

"Proactively do unto your patients as you would want done
unto you, if you were a patient"

John F. O'Malley

GETTING CAUGHT

In the process of following the 15 golden rules, it is also critical for
you to be caught demonstrating your commitment to UPS. Managers
especially must make a special effort to get caught carrying out the
UPS philosophy statements. Organizational executives, leaders, and
trend setters must actively pursue setting an example for others to emulate. So place yourself in a position to get caught by patients, their
family members, friends, and visitors to your facilities, such as the
clergy, vendors, and high-profile community leaders. Remember, you
are only encouraging and reinforcing negative patient-employee encounters by failing to demonstrate the following with consistency:

Caring for the patient;

Empathy for their concern and situation;

Understanding the root reason for their dissatisfaction;

Willingness to satisfactorily resolve their dissatisfaction;

Quickness to act in resolving their dissatisfaction;

Respect for the patient during the process; and

Professionalism throughout the process.

THE UPS PROCESS

UPS is fragile. It only takes one person who falters in demonstrating
the organization's UPS philosophy on a daily basis to inadvertently reinforce a negative patient-employee interaction. Hence, an employee's
action, or lack thereof, resulting in an initial, negative patient interaction, which otherwise could have been quickly converted into a positive encounter, instead exploded into a crisis situation! Because UPS is
a downhill battle, everyone within an organization, top to bottom,

must be dedicated to demonstrating their way toward Ultimate Patient Satisfaction. Achieving UPS is a marathon, not a sprint. The UPS process flow diagrams created and used by Strategic Visions Inc. is shown in Figures 23–1 a & b, UPS Program, and presents all the major participants and processes required for creating, using, and managing an UPS program. You can use the same flow diagram for creating your own approach to Ultimate Patient Satisfaction.

UPS IS UP TO EVERYONE

Since Ultimate Patient Satisfaction is up to everyone, and that means you, get up, get going, and start living your day the UPS way. And because achieving Ultimate Patient Satisfaction is up to everyone within your organization, you need to be setting the example for others to follow. You start by demonstrating the desire and ability to consistently:

Ante UP and make a serious contribution and commitment to patient satisfaction;

Back UP your fellow employees without being asked or told;

Break UP your day with a little laughter;

Call UP customers to keep informed of their wants, desires, and needs;

Catch UP with those around you delivering better service;

Check UP on your progress, leave nothing to chance;

Cheer UP and radiate a positive attitude, be the light at the end of the tunnel;

Clam UP and do not spread gossip;

Clean UP your own work space, break area, and department;

Climb UP on the patient satisfaction bandwagon;

Close UP the gap between talking-the-talk and walking-the-walk;

Come UP with ideas to improve patient, physician, and employee interactions;

Cover UP your mistakes and you are doomed to detection and failure, seek help;

Dress UP to look your best and present yourself as a professional at all times;

FIGURE 23-1

UPS Program

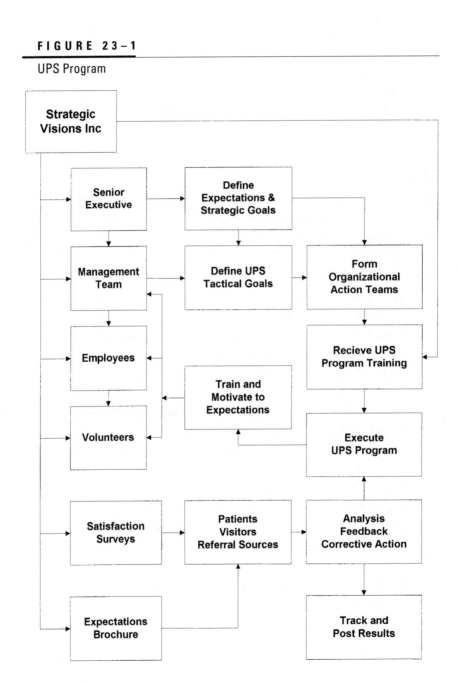

Finish UP what you start, never give up;

Fix UP internal and personal differences for the betterment of the organization;

Follow UP and resolve patient complaints quickly;

Gear UP and prepare yourself and others for changing times;

Get UP and contribute to the effort in a positive way without being asked or told;

Give UP on patient satisfaction and your patients will give up on you;

Hang UP the old ways and your bad habits;

Heads UP seek opportunities to serve customers, improve care, and save resources;

Hook UP with the right people for the right reasons;

Hurry UP and do not procrastinate when it comes to providing great service;

Jump UP energized to help a patient or fellow worker without being asked or told;

Light UP a patient's life;

Lighten UP your workload by learning and using time management techniques;

Line UP behind your leader and give he or she your total support;

Listen UP to your patient's wants, desires, and needs;

Look UP and find a mentor who provides the best at what you do;

Loosen UP and stop taking everything so seriously, relax;

Make UP with your enemies, perceived or otherwise;

Move UP to the next level of patient satisfaction;

Open UP your lines of communications with patients and fellow workers;

Pick UP trash inside and outside the facility as a matter of habit;

Put UP with the right attitudes and terminate the wrong attitudes;

Rise UP every morning with a positive attitude, energized for the day's adventures;

Read UP on how to be a better person, parent, a friend, and
caregiver;

Round UP and surround yourself with all the beautiful things
in life;

Screw UP once in a while, take a chance and learn from your
mistakes;

Set UP your coworkers to succeed;

Shake UP your biased assumptions about people, work, and
reality;

Shape UP and start an exercise program to improve your
overall well-being;

Shore UP your interpersonal, professional, and technical skills;

Show UP for work and meetings on time;

Shut UP about the past, it is gone forever, your future is now;

Sign UP to deliver the highest level of patient service possible;

Sit UP and take notice, the old ways are quickly disappearing,
change is inevitable;

Smarten UP and never stop learning about your job and
mastering new skills;

Snuggle UP to a good book and broaden your horizon;

Speak UP to force change, to praise another, help someone in
need, or to succeed;

Spruce UP your work area, department, and facility;

Stand UP and be accountable for your actions and what you
believe in;

Stay UP-to-date on patients' and visitors' expectations;

Step UP your efforts to be proactive and service-oriented;

Stir UP the caring emotions inside yourself and force a
difference;

Straighten UP and act professional in all you do;

Take UP the cause and become the champion of patient
satisfaction;

Thumbs UP to others for a job well done;

Tighten UP and reduce your operating costs without being told;

Turn UP the heat on those dragging their feet when it comes
to needed change;

Use UP supplies before ordering replacements;

Wake UP and smell the roses, you can make a difference in patient satisfaction;

Walk UP the stairs, freeing elevators for patients and their guests;

Wise UP and understand that Ultimate Patient Satisfaction means increased revenues;

Work UP solutions to pressing problems without being asked or told;

Write UP suggestions to improve service and patient satisfaction; and

Zip UP those lips when it comes to patient confidentiality.

Can you come up with additional UP things to do? Consider holding an UPS contest, awarding those who come up with the most appropriate UPS. Keep adding to the UPS list provided. Once UPS-ups become habitual, Ultimate Patient Satisfaction is not far behind. To instill the UPS philosophy in every physician, manager, and employee requires an aggressive commitment to training, monitoring and modifying behavior, positive reinforcement, and feedback. Patient satisfaction is simple but Ultimate Patient Satisfaction is not easy.

> Focus on creating a partnership with your patients that makes "*your* business, *their* business" by encouraging and making it easy for your patients to tell you how you can be better meeting their needs and service expectations.
>
> *John F. O'Malley*

BEHAVIORAL MODIFICATION REINFORCEMENT AIDS

To assist you with the ongoing task of teaching, reminding, and reinforcing the UPS way of life concepts, consider using any and all of the special tests, acronyms, quotes, poems, tables, forms, and call-to-action collateral distributed throughout the pages of this book. Permission to use the material contained in this book is only intended for your immediate facility, your physical place of employment, nowhere else, without the expressed written permission from Strategic Visions Inc., Birmingham, Alabama. You will find that the following UPS collateral is especially useful in helping you to get the message out. The UPS collateral contained in this book can be used in paycheck

envelopes, newsletters, handouts, overheads, slides, positioning statements, posters, role-playing exercises, and discussions. The material
can also be converted to mouse pads, screen-savers, buttons, tee-shirts,
cups, and anything else that can take graphics. Your creativity is the
only limiting factor. Consider creating your own teaching, reminding,
and reinforcing aids employing teams, departments, or contests.

C.A.R.E., patients' self-determine the level of caring received
by the way we communicate to them, our attitude toward them in trying times, our responsiveness to their needs, and the empathy we
show for their situation. You must never get tired of caring, for caring is a critical part of your fiduciary responsibilities as a healthcare
professional and provider. When patients can sense your caring using
all their senses, patient satisfaction is ensured.

> ### C · A · R · E
> Communications
> Attitude
> Responsiveness
> Empathy

G.E.T., to get your patients to come back, remember to be
greeting them with open arms on arrival, enhancing their experience
during their stay, and giving them a genuine thank-you when they
leave.

> ### G · E · T
> Greet
> Enhanced encounter
> Thank you

K.E.E.P., a patient forms their opinion about your caring, performance, and service based on previous knowledge, personal expectations, their encounter experience, and positive communications. If you
want your patients to leave satisfied and K.E.E.P. coming back, make
sure that you address these four key patient satisfaction influencers in
everything you are saying and doing of concern to patients.

> **K · E · E · P**
>
> Knowledge
> Expectations
> Experience
> Positive communications

One Step At a Time, patient satisfaction is delivered one person, one patient, and one interaction at a time. Patient satisfaction is like building a brick house, one brick (interaction) at a time until you reach the zenith, the last top brick. Each UPS day you start building another house. As you can see, UPS is not a sprint, but a marathon of interactions, each building one on top of another.

> **ONE-ON-ONE**
>
> One person
> One patient
> One interaction
> One step at a time

E.A.R.S., when it comes to great patient satisfaction you must keep your ears to the ground and know what is coming and respond appropriately. Explain things to patients, anticipate patients' needs based on your experience, respond quickly to their needs, and satisfy patient needs as often as possible. Remember, be all ears regarding your patients.

> **E · A · R · S**
>
> Explain
> Anticipate
> Respond
> Satisfy

Gap Jumper, every staff member must become a gap jumper, a person who turns patients' expectations into reality whenever physically, clinically, and financially feasible. The patient's expectations must become your reality. Reality is really a balance between great patient expectations and good healthcare and business practices. Gap jumpers are high-impact employees!

```
┌─────────────────────────────────────────┐
│  G A P    J U M P E R                     │
│  Expectations → (Gap) ← Reality           │
│                                           │
│  Your patient's expectations . . .        │
│     must become your reality!             │
└─────────────────────────────────────────┘
```

D.E.E.D.S., we all do them, some better than others, and some we would rather not talk about. Ultimate Patient Satisfaction requires you and your organization to be excelling at everything you both do. In UPS terms this means doing unto others as you would want them doing unto you, but do yours better and first.

```
┌─────────────────────────────────────────┐
│  D · E · E · D · S                        │
│  Demonstrating caring                     │
│  Energized executions                     │
│  Exceeding expectations                   │
│  Delivering benchmark quality             │
│  Smile sincerely                          │
└─────────────────────────────────────────┘
```

SMILE CURVE

Research shows that at any given moment, one third of all people are frowning, one third of all people display a neutral facial expression, and only one third of all people wear a smile. You may be smiling within, but people who encounter you think otherwise because that genuine inner-smile is not radiating through your outer smile. One has to get in the habit of smiling. To enhance patient satisfaction, you have to be on the upper part of the smile curve (Figure 23–2). You smile with your cheek muscles, not your lips. It takes approximately 43 muscles to frown, and only 16 to smile, so why wear yourself out frowning? If you want to exercise the UPS way, start ripping those smiles, a cheek-activated smile burns about 10 calories. In dealing with patients, a smile, not backed with competence, is only a shallow grin!

FIGURE 23-2

Smile Curve

Smile Curve

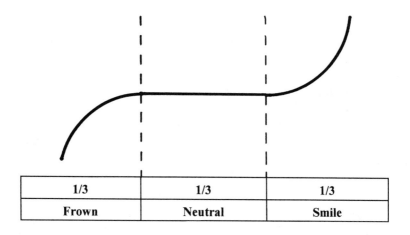

1/3	1/3	1/3
Frown	**Neutral**	**Smile**

BE CAREFUL

We are creatures of habit and as such, if we think or say something over, and over, and over, it eventually becomes a mental reality, a physical habit. So be careful what you think about your patients. Here is another, so-called poem, it is called, "Be Careful" and I believe it will help you and others stay focused on the UPS way of life.

Be Careful
John F. O'Malley

Be careful of what you think,
For you become what you think.
Be careful of your thoughts about your patient,
For your thoughts become your words.
Be careful of your words,
For your words become your actions.
Be careful of your actions toward your patient,

For your actions become your habits.
Be careful of your habits,
For your habits become your character.
Be careful of your character,
For your character defines our patients' satisfaction.

DO NOT SURROUND YOURSELF WITH UGLINESS

At 17 years of age, I ran away from home and joined the Marines (that is another book) and my life has been an adventure ever since. But I want to share with you an experience and the words of wisdom that took me some 20 years of denseness to finally understand. It all started while sitting in the Shamrock Bar in old San Juan, Puerto Rico, passing a few hours of liberty boredom, having a beer with Gunnery Sergeant Thomas, a Marine who earned his salt. The Gunny, recovering from a distant stare, said "Boot (a name given to any Marine your junior), never surround yourself with ugliness." Well here I am, 19 years old, confused, with a light buzz, sitting with a marine's Marine, drinking warm beer, trying to decipher what the gunny just grunted to me. I got it, do not hang out with ugly women, surely that is what the gunny was telling me. That must be right because Eleanor Roosevelt once referred to marines as oversexed killers. Visually reconnoitering the shady, musty room for the proximity of ugly women, I was confident my interpretation was correct. I grunted back, yeah, I know what you mean. Gunny Thomas glared at me and grunted back, "Do you really, Boot?" slurping down his remaining beer, and grunting, let's move out, in a disappointing tone. Marines do a lot of grunting and outsiders swear it is our gene pool. Anyway, some 20 years after leaving the corps, I was fishing in northern Wisconsin on Lake Gilmore, better known as Pete's Lake. Waiting for the big strike, I drifted away from fishing, Marine's never had a long attention span, and relived that night in old San Juan with Gunny Thomas. He was more than a Marine, he was my mentor in many ways and I missed him. Do not surround yourself with ugliness, do not surround yourself with ugliness, was echoing and pinballing around in my idle brain housing. Suddenly, a stuttering smile of enlightenment crept over my face. I felt that smile. You know, the kind of smile that forces you to look side-to-side with a growing internal satisfaction. Finally, after all those years, I finally understood. The gunny was not making a sexist comment that night, even though my hormone-saturated brain thought otherwise. He was paraphrasing an eternal philosophy in one statement. Do not surround yourself with ugliness. To him, it really means you should not be surrounding yourself with people who act ugly (men or women), do not use ugly language or words, do not think ugly things, do not read ugly books, do not think ugly thoughts about people, and do not go to ugly places. Do you not get it? Don't. Just do not do it. I felt really good the rest of that day, thinking about Gunny Thomas and his words of wisdom that I had not the wisdom to comprehend at the time, how better my life if only I had. In his own way, the gunny was Gung Ho on the UPS way of life. So what, who cares about ugliness, you say? It is simple, we all have to care. We have to shed our ugly baggage and weed out ugliness within our organization, facility, and coworkers. It is an ugly job, but someone has to do it. So remember, be very careful what you think and how you act because your patients can sense how you feel about them and will return in kind, or not so kind.

IMPEDING PERSONAL BAGGAGE

We all carry ugly baggage around with us, no matter where we go, and no matter how smartly we pack our inner thoughts. How we deal with people is greatly affected by the amount of ugly baggage we drag along with us. Your ugly baggage will not only drag you down, but causes you to put others down. How much baggage are you carrying today? Just as I thought, too much. You may find that my ugly-baggage checklist is beneficial in helping you in unpacking for a better journey through life.

> **B**ad blood, usually spilled years ago;
> **A**llegations, usually false;
> **G**ossip, usually negative;
> **G**reed, usually for the wrong things;
> **A**ssumptions, usually unfair;
> **G**loom and doom, usually your own; and
> **E**xpectations, usually too high.

Start dumping your excessive and ugly baggage and you will feel better traveling lighter.

WHO IS THERE?

Do you care? Show me! Often in our busy world of telephone calls (personal and otherwise), paperwork, and social affairs with fellow coworkers, we forget who is there. To proactively improve your ability to deliver UPS, you need to actively seek out patient encounters and interactions. Look, it is simple, to get started, all you have to do is be:

Looking alert (for encounter opportunities);

Looking up (for patients in need);

Looking around (for ways to help);

Looking interested (in your job);

Looking professional (in demeanor and grooming);

Looking confident (in what you do and say); and

Looking forward (to patient encounters).

Who is there? Just me . . . your patient . . . do you care?

RAYS

RAYS, radiate a positive attitude and you will succeed in life! At some point in our lives, most of us have looked for a safe harbor in times of trouble, during upsetting change, and confusing uncertainties. Patients are no different. UPS forces you to radiate a positive attitude about life, giving spirit, comfort, and support to your patients, their family members, and coworkers.

"In times of darkness, be the **light** at the end of the tunnel!"

John F. O'Malley

ZAP

Start ZAPping employees who do not exhibit the interpersonal skills and behavior necessary to achieve and maintain Ultimate Patient Satisfaction. You owe it to your patients. Establish a mentality and policy for . . . zero tolerance for attitude-deficient people!

YESTERDAY

Start asking yourself and fellow coworkers the following 16 questions to challenge and change both of your behaviors. Each of us is responsible for the success of our organization and its ability to deliver UPS. So ask all employees, did you do anything yesterday:

To assist a patient?

To assist a patient's family member?

To enhance physician relations?

To reduce operating costs?

To acquire new business?

To enhance our image?

To help a fellow employee?

To solve a problem?

To cause a problem?

To increase your employability?

To assume new responsibilities?

Outside your job description?

That you could have done better?

That made someone feel better?

So you would not have to do anything?

That kept someone else from doing their job?

Consider creating a colorful, UPS "Did you do anything yesterday?" poster and post the same in areas where employees and physicians gather, take breaks, or eat. Get your people to start thinking about their responsibility and supportive actions or lack thereof. We have to start doing the right things in a timely fashion without being asked.

BODY LANGUAGE

Are you and your people speaking the right body language? Research shows that 60% to 80% of what you communicate to others with whom you are speaking is via your body language. That is right, your body language. As strange as it may seem, you hear with your ears but subconsciously listen with your eyes. The person you are speaking to is subconsciously analyzing your telltale body language gestures, lip movement, and tongue placement. Your facial expression, eye movement, stance, tone of voice, hand and arm positions, and personal grooming and dress all contribute to the message. Your body language is a living billboard for all to read, conveying the true meaning of your message to the listener. However, over time many of us have become very fluent in negative body language. Without realizing it, you know more than 25 ways to say "Leave me alone;" more than 20 ways to say "Can't you see that I am busy;" more than 15 ways to say "I am nodding yes, but really mean, yeah, right, are you for real;" more than 10 ways to say "I know that you know that I am only pretending to care about your problem;" and more than five ways to say "I am having a bad day, so you better watch out." One of the secrets to having great interpersonal skills is to become proficient at using and conveying positive body signals. Each of us needs to consciously and subconsciously radiate to our patients that we are here and do what we do because we really care. So the next time you interact with a patient or fellow employee, speak up and shut up. Begin using your body language to send the right message, a positive "I do care" message. By going the extra smile, your life and the lives of those around you will start looking up and no worse for the journey.

UPS Body Language

Make and keep eye contact when speaking to people;
Stand and sit up straight, do not slouch;
Firm handshakes. No dead fish or finger grips please;
Exhibit a radiating smile, kill the frown, save the encounter; and
Groom and dress to convey a positive and professional image.

When You Speak to Others

Use a positive tone of voice;
Speak with confidence; and
Choose your words wisely, avoid using slang, negative, and offensive words.

UPS TAG LINES

The following tag lines can be used for kicking off training programs, statement buttons, posters, and the like:

TABLE 23-1

Body Language Signals

No.	Body Language Signal	Positive	Negative
1.	Frequent eye contact	✔	
2.	Arms folded across chest		✔
3.	Leaning back in a chair to listen	✔	
4.	Blank expression		✔
5.	Frequent head nods	✔	
6.	Stroking the chin	✔	
7.	Little or averted eye contact		✔
8.	Fiddling with an object on desk		✔
9.	No smile		✔
10.	Head tilted slightly to one side	✔	
11.	Open arms and hands	✔	
12.	Swiveling in chair		✔
13.	Reading or shuffling papers		✔
14.	Downward and away glances		✔
15.	Reluctance to shake your hand		✔
16.	Leaning forward, especially to speak	✔	
17.	Uncrossed legs	✔	
18.	Eager acceptance of literature	✔	✔
19.	Frequent hand movement to face area		✔
20.	Increased blink rate		✔
21.	Dilated pupils	✔	
22.	Shoulder shrug gesture		✔
23.	Head and chin are down		✔
24.	Picking imaginary pieces of lint off clothes		✔
25.	Chin cradled in hand position	✔	✔

What's UPS Doc?
Ask me what I am UPS to!
Guess what I am UPS to!
Get the lowdown on being UPS!
We are UPS to something worthwhile!
We are UPS to our necks helping you!
Try creating your own UPS lines.

WHAT IS IT ALL ABOUT ALFIE?

Ultimate Patient Satisfaction is all about people, those being served, those doing the serving, those who care, and those who do not. If you do not get it, get out, and give someone else a chance for delivering Ultimate Patient Satisfaction. UPS is also about intentions. The patient's intention to return, the physician's intention to keep referring, the payor's intention to reimburse, and your intentions to care, address grievances, and focus on quality service, outcomes, and people. It is that simple.

A P P E N D I X :
R E F E R E N C E
S O U R C E S

This resource reference list is provided as a convenience. It lists additional books, material, software, services, and suppliers offering various products and services that you will find informative and helpful as you journey toward achieving Ultimate Patient Satisfaction. So, please make every effort to contact all listed sources to request product information and samples (as appropriate) to evaluate on your own. When available a toll-free number is provided. Knowledge is power.

ON-HOLD MESSAGES

The Message On Hold Network—800-776-3486

RESEARCH DATA AND INFORMATION

Acute Low Back Problems in Adults—800-358-9295
AHCPR InstantFAX—301-594-2800
American Demographics Magazine—800-828-1133
Case Management Resource Guide—800-627-2244
Chamber of Commerce (local)
Competitive Healthcare Market Reporter—800-516-4343
Congressional Research Service Reports—contact your
   congressional representative
Corel Corporation—800-772-6735
Encyclopedia of Associations—313-961-2242
Health Care Consumers in the 90's—800-828-1133
Health, United States—202-512-1800
Joint Commission on Accreditation of Healthcare
   Organizations—708-916-5800
Journal of Direct Marketing—212-850-6645

Libraries designated as repositories of federal publications
Mac Ray Blue Book—212-673-4700
Marketing Tools—800-828-1133
Medicare Cost Reports
Mental Health, United States—202-512-1800
Modern Healthcare's Daily FAX—800-678-9595
National Center for Health Statistics—301-436-8500
People's Medical Society—800-624-8773
Public Citizen—202-588-1000
Psychology & Marketing—212-850-6645
R. L. Polk City Directory—313-393-0880
State Medical and Professional Associations
State Insurance Commission
State Hospital Association
State Health Planning & Regulatory Agencies
State Self-insured Association

MANAGED CARE BOOKS, NEWSLETTERS, AND INFORMATION

Business & Health, Solutions in Managed Care—
   800-432-4570
Capital Publications Inc.—800-655-5597
Group Health Association of America—202-778-3247
Health Insurance Associates of America—800-848-0773
Healthcare Managed Care Marketing Manual—800-627-2244
HMO/PPO Directory—800-222-3045
HMO Industry Profile—202-778-3247
Managed Care Outlook—800-327-7203
Managed Care Desk Reference, Terminology Guide—
   214-748-9408
Managed Care Strategies, 1996—800-535-8403
Managed Care Week—800-521-4323
National Committee for Quality Assurance—800-839-6487
The PPO Letter—800-655-5597

The Managed Care Year Book—800-516-4343
The Managed Care Information Base—800-516-4343
The Executive Report on Managed Care—800-516-4343
Thompson Publishing Group—800-516-4343

STOCK PHOTOGRAPHY AND CLIPART

Corel Corporation (Photos & Clipart)—800-772-6735
Electronic Word (Logo)—800-228-8561
PhotoDiscs—800-528-3472
Picture Agency Council of America—800-457-7222

NEWSLETTER ASSISTANCE

Dartnell—800-865-0588

DIRECT MAIL

Answers Direct Mail LTD. (Lists)—800-257-5242
Center for Consumer Healthcare (Lists)—800-627-2244
Direct Mail Made Easy (Software)—800-865-0588
Medical Marketing Services (Lists)—800-633-5478

FAX MARKETING

Delrina Communications Services—408-363-2345
FAX This Book (Cover Sheets), Coldwell, Workman
    Publishing

MAPPING SOFTWARE

MapLink—800-370-8967

DIGITAL CAMERA

Olympus D200/D300 Series—800-622-6372

ON-LINE COMPUTER SERVICES

America Online—800-827-6364
Compuserve—800-848-8199
Dialog—800-334-2564
Mindspring—800-719-4664
Nexis—800-346-9759
Prodigy—800-776-3449

WEB SITE DEVELOPMENT

C&C Associates—205-991-8679
KF Consulting—918-493-3664

SPEED BROCHURE MATERIAL

Beaver Prints & Software—800-923-2837
Corel Draw 6.0—800-772-6735
MyBrochures Software—800-325-3508
Paper Direct & Software—800-272-7377

BOOKS

HEALTHCARE

A Short History of Medicine, Ackerknecht, John Hopkins
Health Care Consumers in the 1990s, Thomas, American
   Demographic Books
The State of Healthcare in America, Business & Health Magazine,
   Med. Economics Publishing
The Crisis in Healthcare, Coddington, Keen, Moore, & Clark,
   Jossey-Bass, Inc.
Statistical Abstract of the United States, U.S. Department of
   Commerce
The Best Medicine, Robert Arnot, M.D., Addison-Wesley
   Publishing

The Great White Lie, Bogdanich, Simon & Schuster
Medicine on Trial, Inlander, Levin & Weiner, Prentice-Hall Press
Medical Sociology, Cockerham, Prentice-Hall Press
The Health Care Book of Lists, Thomas, Paul M. Deutsch Press
Working Together, Allcorn, Probus Publishing
Not What the Doctor Ordered, Bauer, Probus Publishing
Healthcare Publications Catalog, Sage Publications
Silent Violence, Silent Death, Harvey Rosenfield, Essential Books

MANAGED CARE

Source Book of Health Insurance Data, Health Insurance
   Association of America
Consumers Guide to Health Plans—800-529-9615
HMO-PPO Digest—800-529-9615
NCQA Accreditation Status List—800-839-6487

USING THE TELEPHONE

Cold Calling Techniques, by Stephan Schiffman, Bob Adams, Inc.
Powerful Telephone Skills, Career Press—800-227-3371
Telephone Power, George Walters—800-843-8353

BODY LANGUAGE

Body Language, Julius Fast, MJF Books
Body Language, Gordon Wainwright, Teach Yourself Books
Body Language in the Workplace, Julius Fast, Penguin Books
Signals, by Allan Pease, Bantam Books

MARKETING

Market Mapping, Baker & Baker, McGraw-Hill
Marketing Research, Dodge, Fullerton & Rink, Charles E.
   Merrill Publishing Company

Marketing For Healthcare Organizations, Kotler, Clarke, Prentice Hall

Information Please Business Almanac-Source Book, Houghton Mifflin Co.

The New Competitor Intelligence, Fuld, John Wiley & Sons

Guerrilla P.R., Michael Levine, HarperBusiness

Healthcare Marketing In Transition, Rynne, Irwin Professional Publishing

CUSTOMER SERVICE

AMA Handbook on Customer Satisfaction, Alan Dutka, NTC Business Books

Kaizen, Imai, McGraw-Hill

The Customer Connection, Guaspari, AMACOM

How To Win Customers and Keep Them for Life, LeBoeuf, Berkley Books

Measuring and Managing Patient Satisfaction, Steiber & Krowinski, American Hospital Publishing

Take This Book to the Hospital With You, Inlander & Weiner, People's Medical Society

The Survey Kit, Sage Publications, American Demographics

Consumers for Quality Care, 10951 W. Pico Blvd., Third Floor, Los Angeles, CA 90064

Safe Medicine for Consumers, P.O. Box 878, San Andreas, CA 95249

The National Center for Patients' Rights, 666 Broadway, Suite 410, New York, NY 10012

The Coalition for Consumer Rights, 225 West Ohio Street, Suite 250, Chicago, IL 60610

PERSONAL IMPROVEMENT

Eat Smart-Think Smart, Robert Hass, Harper Collins

Jumping The Curve, Imparato & Harari, Jossey-Bass

Mentally Tough, by Dr. James Loehr, M. Evans and Company, Inc.

The Memory Book, Lorayne & Lucas, Stein & Day

OTHER HEALTHCARE BOOKS BY JOHN O'MALLEY

Manage Care Referral, How to develop a system approach for building your referral business in today's healthcare environment, 358 pages, Irwin Professional Publishing, 800-634-3966

94 Strategies for Referral Development, A guide to growing your diagnostic imaging business, 85 pages, Diagnostic Imaging, Miller Freeman Inc., 415-905-2235

JOIN ONE OR MORE OF THE NATIONAL HEALTHCARE MARKETING ASSOCIATIONS

The Alliance for Healthcare Strategy and Marketing— 312-704-9700

The American Marketing Association, Healthcare Division— 800-262-1150

The Society for Healthcare Strategy and Market Development—312-422-3738

BIBLIOGRAPHY

94 Strategies for Referral Development, John F. O'Malley, Diagnostic Imaging, Miller Freeman, Inc.

A Short History of Medicine, Ackerknecht, John Hopkins

After Marketing, Terry G. Vavra, Irwin Professional Publishing

AMA Handbook on Customer Satisfaction, Alan Dutka, NTC Business Books

Attitude, Elwood N. Chapman, Crisp Publications, Inc.

Beyond Reengineering, Michael Hammer, HarperCollins Publishing

Beyond the Wall of Resistance, Rick Maurer, Bard Publishing

Body Language, Gordon Wainwright, Teach Yourself Books

Body Language, Julius Fast, MJF Books

Body Language in the Workplace, Julius Fast, Penguin Books

Bottom Line Year Book 1996, 1997, Boardroom, Inc.

Bring Out The Best in People, Aubrey C. Daniels, McGraw-Hill, Inc.

Calming Upset Customers, Rebecca L. Morgan, Crisp Publications, Inc.

Competition in the 21st Century, Kirk W. M. Tyson, St. Lucie Press

Conflicts of Interest in Clinical Practice and Research, Roy G. Spece, Jr.; David S. Shimm; Allen E. Buchanan, Oxford University Press

Consumers for Quality Care, Los Angeles, California

Consumers' Guide to Health Plans, Center for the Study of Services

Customer Service Skills, Karen Eberhardt, Help Desk Institute

Discipline Without Punishment, Dick Grote, AMACOM Publishing

Eat Smart-Think Smart, Robert Hass, Harper Collins

Effective Telephone Communication Skills, Mia Schiffman Melanson, Help Desk Institute

Effective Information Gathering Techniques, Randall S. Pearson, Help Desk Institute

Exploring the USA's Language Gap, Special Report, USA Today, February 28, 1997

Fraud in Managed Healthcare Delivery and Payment, National Healthcare Anti-Fraud Association, December, 1994

From the Barracks to the Boardroom, Robert Carey, Performance Strategies, March, 1996

Getting a Project Done on Time, Paul B. Williams, AMACOM Publishing

Getting Employees to Fall in Love with Your Company, Jim Harris, Ph. D, AMACOM Publishing

Guerrilla P.R., Michael Levine, HarperBusiness

Health Care Consumers in the 1990s, Thomas, American Demographic Books

Health Against Wealth: HMOs and the Breakdown of Medical Trust, George Anders, Boston, Houghton, Mifflin Publishing

Healthcare Market Research, Eric N. Berkowitz, Louis G. Pol, Richard K. Thomas, Irwin Professional Publishing

Healthcare: An Industry in Search of a Brand, Ian P. Murphy, Marketing News, February 3, 1997

Healthcare Marketing In Transition, Rynne, Irwin Professional Publishing

How to Design and Write Effective Customer Satisfaction Surveys, Patrick Bultema, Help Desk Institute

How to Argue and Win Every Time, Gerry Spence, St. Martin's Press

How To Win Customers and Keep Them for Life, LeBoeuf, Berkley Books

How to Handle Difficult Customers, Gary Case, Patrice Rhoades-Baum, Help Desk Institute

How To Be a Great Communicator, Nido R. Qubein, John Wiley & Sons

Human Resource Professional Must Deliver, Not Just Talk, Dave Ulrich, Harvard Business School Press

Information Please Business Almanac-Source Book, Houghton, Mifflin Co.
Inspiring Commitment, Authony Mendes, Ph. D, Irwin Professional Publishing
Jumping The Curve, Imparato & Harari, Jossey-Bass
Kaizen, Imai, McGraw-Hill
Keeping the Team Going, Deborah Harrington-Macklin, AMACOM Publishing
Language Barriers in Medicine in the United States, Steven Woloshin, MD; Nina A.
    Bickell, MD, MPH; Lisa M. Schwartz, MD; Francesca Gany, MD; H. Gilbert
    Welsh, MD, MPH; JAMA, March 1, 1995-Vol 273, No. 9
Leadership Skills for the Nurse Manager, Kathleen O'Sullivan Mott, Irwin Professional
    Publishing
Leading Change, John P. Kotter, Harvard Business School Press
Leading Outlound, Terry Pearce, Jossey-Bass, Inc.
Leading Change, James O'Toole, Jossey-Bass, Inc.
Liberating the Human Spirit in the Workplace, William Bickham, Irwin Professional
    Publishing
License to Steal: Why Fraud Plagues American's Healthcare System, Malcolm K. Sparrow,
    Westview Press
Managed Care Referral, John F. O'Malley, Irwin Professional Publishing
Managerial Excellence, edited by Rajat Gupta, Harvard Business School Press
Managing Unresolved Service Requests, Gary Case, Help Desk Institute
Managing People is Like Herding Cats, Warren Bennis, Executive Excellence Publishing
Managing Non-Profit Organizations, Peter Drucker, HarperCollins Publishing
Market Mapping, Baker & Baker, McGraw-Hill
Marketing For Healthcare Organizations, Kotler, Clarke, Prentice Hall
Marketing Research, Dodge, Fullerton & Rink, Charles E. Merrill Publishing
    Company
Maximizing the Value of Customer Feedback, John Goodman; David DePalma; Scott
    Broetzmann; Quality Progress, December 1996
Mean Business, Albert J. Dunlap with Bob Andelman, Times Business
Measuring and Managing Patient Satisfaction, Steiber & Krowinski, American Hospital
    Publishing
Measuring Customer Satisfaction, Bob E. Hayes, ASQC Quality Press
Medical Sociology, Cockerham, Prentice-Hall Press
Medicine on Trial, Inlander, Levin & Weiner, Prentice-Hall Press
Mentally Tough, Dr. James Loehr, M. Evans and Company, Inc.
Mission Possible, Ken Blachard; Terry Waghorn, McGraw-Hill Companies
Motivating People, Kurt Hanks, Crisp Publications, Inc.
Navigating Through Change, Harry Woodward, Irwin Professional Publishing
New England Medical Journal
Not What the Doctor Ordered, Bauer, Probus Publishing
Now Hiring, Steve Lauer; B. Jack Gebhardt, AMACOM Publishing
Organizing Genius, Warren Bennis; Patrica Ward Biederman, Addison Wesley, Inc.
Overcoming Resistance, Jerald M. Jellison, Simon & Schuster, Inc.
Overdrive, Managing in Crisis-filled Times, Michael Silva, Terry McGann, John Wiley
    & Sons, Inc.
Post-Capitalist Society, Peter F. Drucker, Harper Business
Real Change Leaders, Jon R. Katzenbach, Times Business
Relentless, Johny K. Johansson; Ikujiro Nonaka, HarperBusiness
Rethinking the Future, edited by Rowan Gibson, Nicholas Brealey Publishing
Safe Medicine for Consumers, P.O. Box 878, San Andreas, CA 95249
Seven Survival Skills for a Reengineered World, William N. Yeomans, Penguin Books

Shaping Healthcare: Developing a Program Evaluation Questionnaire, Dan Noonan, Journal for Healthcare Quality, Vol. 19, No. 1
Signals, by Allan Pease, Bantam Books
Silent Violence, Silent Death, Harvey Rosenfield, Essential Books
Simplicity Wins, G. Rommel; J. Kluge; Rolf-Dieter Kempis; R. Diederichs; F. Bruck, McKinsey & Company
Start Up, William J. Stolze, Career Press
Statistical Abstract of the United States, U.S. Department of Commerce
Stop Managing, Start Coaching, Jerry W. Gilley, Nathaniel W. Boughton, Irwin Professional Publishing
Super-Motivation, Dean R. Spitzer, AMACOM Publishing
Take This Book to the Hospital With You, Inlander & Weiner, People's Medical Society
Team Reconstruction, Price Pritchett & Ron Pound, Pritchett Publishing Company
Team Building, Robert B. Maddux, Crisp Publications, Inc.
Teamthink, Ava S. Butler, McGraw-Hill
Telephone Skills From A to Z, Nancy J. Friedman, Crisp Publications, Inc.
The Business of Learning, Diane Bone, Crisp Publications, Inc.
The Survey Kit Series, Sage Publications
The Customer-Drive Company, William E. Eureka, Nancy E. Ryan, ASI Press
The State of Healthcare in America, Business & Health Magazine, Med. Economics Publishing
The Health Care Book of Lists, Thomas, Paul M. Deutsch Press
The Power of Patient Perception, A conversation with Dr. Eugene Nelson
The Corporate Communicator's Quick Reference, Peter Lichtgarn, Business One Irwin
The Crisis in Healthcare, Coddington, Keen, Moore, & Clark, Jossey-Bass, Inc.
The World on Time, James C. Wetherbe, Knowledge Exchange
The Great Game of Business, Jack Stack, Bantam, Doubleday, and Dell Publishing Group
The First-Time Trainer, Tom W. Goad, AMACOM Publishing
The New Competitor Intelligence, Fuld, John Wiley & Sons
The Best Medicine, Robert Arnot, M.D., Addison-Wesley Publishing
The Leader in You, Dale Caregie, Simon & Schuster, Inc.
The Art of Communicating, Bert Decker, Crisp Publications, Inc.
The Leader of the Future, edited by Frances Hesselbein, Marshall Goldsmith, Richard Beckhard, Jossey-Bass Inc.
The Customer Connection, Guaspari, AMACOM
The Total Service Medical Practice, Vicky Bradford, Ph.D, Irwin Professional Publishing
The Quality of Mercy, Shannon Brownlee; Joannie M. Schrof; U.S. News & World Report, March 17, 1997
The Great White Lie, Bogdanich, Simon & Schuster
The Loyalty Effect, Frederick F. Reichheld, Harvard Business School Press
The Complete Guide to Performance Appraisal, Dick Grote, AMACOM Publishing
The National Center for Patients' Rights, 666 Broadway, Suite 410, New York, NY 10012
The Coalition for Consumer Rights, 225 West Ohio Street, Suite 250, Chicago, IL 60610
The Seven Universal Laws of Customer Value, Stephen C. Broydrick, Irwin Professional Publishing
The Marine Officers Guide, Kenneth W. Estes, Naval Institute Press
The Deming Management Method, Mary Walton, Perigee Books
The Memory Book, Lorayne & Lucas, Stein & Day
The Discipline of Market Leaders, Michael Treacy, Fred Wiersema, Addison-Wesley Publishing

The Art of War (Sun Tzu) for Executives, Donald G. Krause, Perigee Books

Total Quality Service, Sheila Kessler, ASQC Quality Press

Transforming the Bottomline, Tony Hope; Jeremy Hope, Harvard Business School Press

Trends 2000, Gerald Celente, Warner Books, Inc.

Understanding Customer Competence Levels, George Spalding, Help Desk Institute

Value Migration, Adrian J. Slywotzky, Harvard Business School Press

Working Together, Allcorn, Probus Publishing

ABOUT THE AUTHOR

Mr. O'Malley is gaining a growing national following of healthcare professionals, executives, and providers who have attended his seminars and read his books and articles and in the process, have become inspired by his visionary and insightful views of the industry. The love of teaching and helping others help themselves, he says, lead him into the consulting and training field after many successful and adventurous years in the healthcare trenches. He is the first to tell you he is often politically incorrect communicating strategic issues in an effort to perk up the status quo. He believes that where there is contentment, there is no progress, and all great things are born of progress. Mr. O'Malley also strongly believes that Ultimate Patient Satisfaction is just such a politically incorrect book because it is intended not only to help the healthcare industry, but shake it up. Care-ism before capitalism is his message, if not battle-cry, to healthcare providers everywhere. When not consulting, training, and writing, Mr. O'Malley searches for quality time to spend with Cathy, his wife, Ross, his son, and the family's two dachshunds, Petie and Shaka, in the pursuit of internal happiness.

INDEX

transpose, 115–116
types of, 118
Third-party influences, 218–219
Thomas, Gunny, 320
Time
analysis log, 83
management, 77–89
Total customer satisfaction (TCS), 14–16
Total expected compensation (TEC), 176
Total quality management (TQM), 176–177
Tours, promotional, 203–204
TQM. *See* Total quality management

Ugliness, 320–321
Ultimate Patient Satisfaction (UPS). *See also*
Patient satisfaction
ability status score, 304–306
anatomy of, 288
commitment to, 310
delivering the best, 301–326
determining ability rating, 302–304
employee satisfaction and, 127
era of, 3–5
evaluation elements, 168–170
face-to-face approach, 276–278
formula for achieving, 308–309
golden rules of, 309–310
literature on, 334–337
participation in, 311–315
philosophy declaration, 307–308
process, 310–311
program, 312
pronunciation, 4
rewarding system, 170
teams, 99–111
termination protocol guide, 137
written position on, 307–308

VAE. *See* Value-added employee
Value statement, 307–308
Value-added employee (VAE), 146–148
Vision statement, 307

Visitor satisfaction program (VSP), 198
Visitors, 10–11
bill of rights, 265
enhancing visit from, 198
parking for, 198–199
as potential customers, 195–204
waiting areas for, 201
Visual switching, 115
Volunteers
ambassador rating, 183–184
appearance, 181–182
assignment allocation, 181
attire, 181–182
benefits packages, 189–190
buddy mentor, 192
conduct of, 182–183
directory of, 192–193
encounter assessment, 187
identification of, 184
importance, 178–179
incentives, 189–190
infection control and, 182
mission statement for, 180
patient advocacy and, 193–194
pool cleaning, 190
recognition system, 184–186
recruiting, 187–190
services, 180–181
tracking service, 186
training program, 190–192
VIVA program, 179–180, 186–187
VSP. *See* Visitor satisfaction program

Waiting areas, visitors, 201
Wall Street, 6
Web site, 242–252
resources, 330
"Why Teams Fail," USA Today, 105

ZAPping employees, 322
Ziglar, Zig, 72–74